7-26-72

TWELVE WORKS
OF
NAÏVE GENIUS

TWELVE WORKS
OF
NAÏVE GENIUS

●

EDITED

BY

WALTER TELLER

●

HBJ

HARCOURT BRACE JOVANOVICH, INC.

NEW YORK

CONTENTS C793520

ILLUSTRATIONS

———•———

Literature is the effort of man to indemnify himself for the wrongs of his condition.

—Emerson

NOTE

———•———

Except for cutting, and correcting obvious typographical errors, I made no changes in these works. I left things as I found them—spelling, punctuation, capitalization, etc.

W. T.

INTRODUCTION

———•———

Twelve Works of Naïve Genius is a collection of first-hand accounts of life experience told simply and convincingly by persons who were not professional writers. I found them a great discovery. Transmitting a sense of their time and place, they open a view of the past from within. I feel these works, though rough-edged and unpolished, have a slot in American literature.

There is no telling how many works of naïve genius exist, but the number could be large. Some have been published by state and local historical societies, by small regional publishers, and by university presses. In selecting my twelve I set up certain criteria. I chose only works that appealed to me strongly. In addition, the work had to be American, out of print, and not easily available, or one that is little known and has not received its due. Above all, it had to show native talent. The writer's credentials must be evident in his writing.

What do I mean by a naïve genius? An exceptionally well-endowed person who has had little schooling and in general is unaware of the conventions and traditions of literature and art. Uncovering the world for himself is characteristic of naïve genius; nothing is given him on a silver spoon. Self-taught, fresh and unjaded, ingenuous, homespun, and vernacular, he is an original, a natural. He is outside the influence of wealth and fashion. Feeling a deep need to express himself, he turns unself-consciously to recording and describing what he knows and lives with. He seldom thinks of himself as making a contribution to literature, but even when he has literary aims his writing remains incidental to his occupation or situation. Locked in his own experience, he is usually a one-shot writer.

In his physical make-up the naïve genius is a person out of the ordinary. He has energy and marked ability to resist fatigue. Seth Hubbell must have been a veritable Samson. Joshua Slocum showed notable agility. Samuel Thomson, lame from birth, worked tirelessly as doctor and nurse, exposed to all manner of illness. Linda Brent survived seven years of imprisonment in a tiny attic. Nancy Luce departed from the norm physically and mentally, though not in a happy way. Having said this much, I hasten to add that naïve genius is a casual phrase and is best understood instinctively. It cannot be tightly defined.

There is an excitement in these works written by men and women who struggled for survival, who did not accept life passively but strived against its injustices, obstacles, and difficulties. Diverse and various as persons, they shared a common theme—the potentialities inherent in the individual. Brave, audacious, practical, or imaginative, each in his own way told a story of victory and triumph.

The works are arranged chronologically by the authors' date of birth; the writers include a pioneer settler; two physicians, one botanic, the other osteopathic; three painters, one of whom was also a minister and mechanic; a runaway slave; a freedman; a subsistence farmer who called herself a "doctor of hens"; a housewife; a seagoing wife; a master mariner in sail. Eight were men, four were women; two of the twelve were black. The earliest was born in 1759, the last died in 1933.

The twelve came from backwoods, village, farm, plantation, or seafaring environments. Not surprisingly, half of them had their origins in New England. Edward Hicks was born in Pennsylvania, Jacob Stroyer in South Carolina. Andrew Taylor Still grew up on the Kansas-Missouri frontier. Only one, the latest born, Albert Pinkham Ryder, went to live and work in a large city.

Since they had limited access to books, these writers drew only lightly on others. They were not affected by what had already been thought and said. They were not imitative; their approaches were wholly their own. No doubt some of them received editorial help, either more or less. Chester Harding's *My Egotistigraphy* was gone over by his daughter. The name of Linda Brent's editor appeared on the title page of *Incidents in the Life of a Slave Girl*. Editing can refine a work but cannot create it; the writer's distinctive gift must be there first. "I do not think I was born . . . a 'book writer,' " Andrew Taylor Still wrote, "but it is perhaps better that I leave a small legacy than none at all. . . . The style may be harsh and crude; if so, I will offer only this as an apology; it is spoken after my manner and custom of speech."

One of these works appeared in 1905, one in 1908, and the rest in the nineteenth century. Nineteenth-century America was the golden age of naïve literature. Conditions were favorable—the individual had relative isolation, few diversions, and a slower pace of daily existence. The ideals of democracy encouraged self-development in men and women of every degree. The advent of widespread public education and the growth of literacy meant that self-expression was no longer the exclusive province of an upper class. Anyone who chose to might engage in writing. And also in publishing what he wrote; self-publication was common, accepted practice. Most of the works included here were published by the writers themselves. They range in length from a good-sized book to a slender pamphlet, even a brief article.

With the coming of the twentieth century, technology roared ahead. Fast transportation and communications spread the prevailing culture throughout the land, intensifying the pressures toward standardized and conforming modes of living. These changes made it practically impossible for anyone to remain untouched and uninfluenced. Inevitably, the naïve tradition vanished.

Today, when everyone is reached by countless persons and things, saturated by endless voices and pictures, it becomes increasingly hard to be one's self and make one's separate assessment. Never has it been so easy for the individual to lose his individuality. Dated though they are, these works of naïve genius speak to this predicament. They reaffirm the personal values. Life, they seem to be saying, is a salvaging operation; every man must seek his own way to go from worse to better.

TWELVE WORKS
OF
NAÏVE GENIUS

SETH HUBBELL

(1759–1832)

A Narrative of the Sufferings of Seth Hubbell & Family in his Beginning a Settlement in the Town of Wolcott, in the State of Vermont. E. & W. Eaton, Printers, Danville, Vt., 1829. 24 pp.

This is Seth Hubbell's story of his bitter struggle pioneering in northern Vermont. He was sixty-five when he wrote it, poor, and living by permission of relatives on land that was no longer his. But *Sufferings* is no apologia. On the contrary, it is self-vindication. Pioneer life was disappearing so rapidly that unless Hubbell told what his life had been like, his descendants, who may have looked on him as a failure, would never know what he had endured and in fact accomplished.

Almost nothing is known about him beyond what he himself tells. Wolcott, where he settled, halfway between Montpelier and the Canadian border, was in his time an almost roadless area. Though apparently no one bearing the name Hubbell is living in Wolcott today, Seth Hubbell's line may not have vanished. Most of his children were daughters.

Sufferings was printed by Ebenezer Eaton, publisher of *The North Star,* a well-known newspaper in Vermont in those days. It was a beautiful job—on durable rag paper, with pages four and three-fourths inches wide and varying in length from seven to eight and one-half inches. Since Hubbell's narrative occupied only seventeen of its twenty-four pages, the remaining leaves were filled out with verse: "Joy and Trouble," "Dull Cares," and "Auld Lang Syne."

Did this little book find its way outside the family circle? The one thing certain now is that it is very scarce. The only copy I know of is in the Rare Book Division of The New York Public Library.

NARRATIVE, &c.

————•————

This narrative was written for the private use and gratification of the sufferer, with no intention of its ever appearing before the public, but certain reasons connected with his present circumstances have induced him (by the advice of his friends) to commit it to the press. It is a simple narration of real facts, the most of which many living witnesses can now attest to. The learned reader will excuse the many imperfections in this little work: the writer not being bred to literary knowledge, is sensible of his inability to entertain the curious: but if his plain and simple dress can reach the sympathy of the feeling heart, it may be gratifying to some. It may also serve to still the murmurings of those who are commencing settlements in the neighborhood of plenty, and teach them to be reconciled to their better fate, and duly appreciate the privileges they enjoy, resulting from the toils of the suffering few who broke the way into the wilderness.

In the latter part of February, 1789, I set out from the town of Norwalk, in Connecticut, on my journey for Wolcott, to commence a settlement and make that my residence; family consisting of my wife and five children, they all being girls, the eldest nine or ten years old. My team was a yoke of oxen and a horse. After I had proceeded on my journey to within about one hundred miles of Wolcott, one of my oxen failed; but I however kept him yoked with the other till about noon each day; then turned him before, and took his end of the yoke myself, and proceeded on in that manner with my load to about fourteen miles of my journey's end, when I could get the sick ox no further, and was forced to leave him with Thomas W. Connel, in Johnson; but he had neither hay nor grain for him. I then proceeded on with some help to Esq. McDaniel's in Hydepark: this brought me to about eight miles of Wolcott, and to the end of the road. It was now about the 20th of March;

the snow not far from four feet deep; no hay to be had for my team, and no way for them to subsist but by browse. As my sick ox at Connel's could not be kept on browse, I interceded with a man in Cambridge for a little hay to keep him alive, which I backed, a bundle at a time, five miles, for about ten days, when the ox died. On the 9th of April I set out from Esq. McDaniel's, his being the last house, for my intended residence in Wolcott, with my wife and two eldest children. We had eight miles to travel on snow-shoes, by marked trees—no road being cut: my wife had to try this new mode of travelling, and she performed the journey remarkably well. The path had been so trodden by snow-shoes as to bear up the children. Esq. Taylor, with his wife and two small children, who moved on with me, had gone on the day before. We were the first families in Wolcott: in Hydepark there had two families wintered the year before. To the east of us it was eighteen miles to inhabitants, and no road but marked trees: to the south about twenty, where there was infant settlements, but no communication with us; and to the north, it was almost indefinite, or to the regions of Canada.

I had now got to the end of my journey, and I may say almost to the end of my property, for I had not a mouthful of meat or kernel of grain for my family, nor had I a cent of money to buy with, or property that I could apply to that purpose. I however had the good luck to catch a saple. The skin I carried fifty miles, and exchanged for half a bushel of wheat, and backed it home. We had now lived three weeks without bread; though in the time I had bought a moose of an Indian, which I paid for by selling the shirt off my back, and backed the meat five miles, which answered to subsist upon. I would here remark that it was my fate to move on my family at that memorable time called the "scarce season," which was generally felt through the state, especially in the northern parts in the infant settlements: no grain or provision of any kind, of consequence, was to be had on the river Lamoille. I had to go into New-Hampshire, sixty miles, for the little I had for my family, till harvest, and this was so scanty a pittance that we were under the painful necessity of allowancing the children till we had a supply. The three remaining children that I left in

Hydepark, I brought one at a time on my back on snow-shoes, as also the whole of my goods.

I moved from Connecticut with the expectation of having fifty acres of land given me when I came on, but this I was disappointed of, and was under the necessity soon after I came on of selling a yoke of oxen and a horse to buy the land I now live on, which reduced my stock to but one cow; and this I had the misfortune to lose the next winter. That left me wholly destitute of a single hoof of a creature: of course the second summer I had to support my family without a cow. I would here notice that I spent the summer before I moved, in Wolcott, in making preparation for a settlement, which, however, was of no avail to me, and I lost the summer; and to forward my intended preparation, I brought on a yoke of oxen, and left them, when I returned in the fall, with a man in Johnson, to keep through the winter, on certain conditions; but when I came on in the spring, one of them was dead, and this yoke of oxen that I put off for my land was made of the two surviving ones. But to proceed, in the fall I had the good fortune to purchase another cow; but my misfortunes still continued, for in the June following she was killed by a singular accident. Again I was left without a cow, and here I was again frustrated in my calculations: this last cow left a fine heifer calf that in the next fall I lost by being choaked. Soon after I arrived, I took two cows to double in four years. I had one of my own besides, which died in calving. In June following, one of those taken to double, was killed while fighting; the other was found dead in the yard; both of which I had to replace. In the same spring, one of my neighbour's oxen hooked a bull of two years old, which caused his death soon after. Here I was left destitute—no money to buy, or article to traffic for one; but there was a door opened. I was informed that a merchant in Haverhill was buying snakeroot and sicily. This was a new kind of traffic that I had no great faith in; but I thought to improve every means or semblance of means in my power. Accordingly, with the help of my two oldest girls, I dug and dried a horse-load, and carried this new commodity to the merchant; but this was like most hearsay reports of fine markets; always a little way a-head, for he knew nothing about this strange article, and would not even venture to make an offer; but after a long conference I importuned with the good merchant to give me a three year old heifer for my roots, on certain conditions too tedious to mention. I drove her home, and with joy she was welcomed to my habitation, and it has been my good fortune to have a cow ever since. Though my faith was weak, yet being vigilant and persevering, I obtained the object, and the wilderness produced me a cow.

When I came into Wolcott my farming tools consisted of one axe and an old hoe. The first year I cleared about two acres, wholly without any team, and being short of provision was obliged to work the chief of the time till harvest with scarce a sufficiency to support nature. My work was chiefly by the river. When too faint to labor, for want of food, I used to take a fish from the river, broil it on the coals, and eat it without bread or salt, and then to my work again. This was my common practice the first year till harvest. I could not get a single potatoe to plant the first season, so scarce was this article. I then thought if I could but get enough of this valuable production to eat I would never complain. I rarely see this article cooked, but the thought strikes my mind; in fact to this day I have a great veneration for this precious root. I planted that which I cleared in season with corn; and an early frost ruined the crop, so that I raised nothing the first year: had again to buy my provision. My seed corn, about eight quarts, cost me two and a half yards of whitened linen, yard wide, and this I had to go twenty miles after. Though this may be called extortion, it was a solitary instance of the kind; all were friendly and ready to assist me in my known distress, as far as they had ability. An uncommon degree of sympathy pervaded all the new settlers, and I believe this man heartily repented the act, for he was by no means indigent, and was many times reminded of it by way of reproof.

My scanty supply of bread-corn made it necessary to improve the first fruits of harvest at Lake Champlain, to alleviate our distress, it being earlier than with us. Accordingly, on the last days of July or first of August, I took my sickle, and set out for the Lake, a distance of better than forty miles. When I had got there, I found their grain was not ripe enough to begin upon; but was informed that on the Grand-Isle they had began their harvest. I was determined to go on, but had nothing to pay my passage. I finally hired a man to carry me over from Georgia for the small compensation of a case and two lances that I happened to have with me; but when I had got on to the Island, I found I was still too early. There was no grain ripe here, but I found the most forward I could, plead my necessity, and stayed by the owner till I got one and a half bushel of wheat, and worked for him to pay for it: it was quite green; I dried it and set out for home; but my haste to get back prevented my drying it sufficiently. I found a boat bound for Mansfield's mills, on the river Lamoille, and got my grain on board, and had it bro't there free from expense. I got it ground or rather mashed, for it was too damp to make meal. I here hired my meal carried on to Cambridge borough for my sickle, and there got it ground the second time, but it was still far from good meal. From the Borough I was so fortunate as to get it home on a horse. I was a fortnight on this tour. My wife was fearful some accident had happened, and sent a man in pursuit of me, who met me on my way home. I left my family without bread or meal, and was welcomed home with tears: my wife baked a cake, and my children again tasted bread.

I had the good fortune to buy on trust, the winter after I lost my corn, of a man in Cambridge, twenty-four miles from home, twelve bushels of corn, and one of wheat. This, by the assistance of some kind friends, I got to Esq. McDaniel's. I also procured by digging on shares in Hydepark, twelve or thirteen bushels of potatoes. This grain and potatoes I carried eight miles on my back. My common practice was one half bushel of meal, and one half bushel of potatoes at a load.

The singular incidents that took place in getting this grain on, though tedious to mention, may be worthy of notice. Soon after I set out from home, sometime in the month of March; it began to rain, and was a very rainy day and night. The Lamoille was raised—the ice became rotten and dangerous crossing—many of the small streams were broken up. The man of whom I purchased the grain was so good as to take his team and carry it to the mill. The owner of the mill asked me how I expected to get my meal home. I answered him as the case really was, that I knew not. The feeling man then offered me his oxen and sled to carry it to the Park, and I thankfully accepted his kind offer. He then turned to the miller, and directed him to grind my grist toll free. While at the mill a man requested me to bring a half hogshead tub on my sled up to Johnson. By permission of the owner of the oxen, he put the tub on the sled, and it was a Providential circumstance; for when I came to Brewster's branch, a wild stream, I found it broken up, run rapid and deep. At first I was perplexed what to do. To go across with my bags on the sled would ruin my meal; I soon thought of the tub; this held about half of my bags; the other half I left on the shore, and proceeded into the branch and crossed with safety. Though I was wet nearly to my middle, I unloaded the tub and returned into the branch, holding the tub on the sled, but the stream was so rapid, the tub being empty, that in spite of all my exertions I was washed off the sled and carried down the stream, holding on to the tub, for this I knew was my only alternative to get across my load. At length I succeeded in getting the tub to the shore, though I was washed down the stream more than twenty rods, sometimes up to my armpits in the water, and how I kept the tub from filling in this hasty struggle, I know not, but so it was. The oxen, though turned towards home, happily for me, when they had got across the stream, stopt in the path, till I came up with the tub. I then put in the other half of my load, and succeeded in getting the whole across the branch, and travelled on about three miles and put up for the night. Wet as I was, and at that season of the year, it is easy to conceive my uncomfortable situation, for the thaw was over, and it was chilly and cold. In the morning I proceeded for home—came to the river: not being sensible how weak the ice was, I attempted to cross, but here a scene ensued that I can never forget. When about half across the river, I perceived the ice settling under my oxen. I jumped on to the tongue of my sled, and hastened to the oxen's heads, and pulled out the pin that held the yoke. By this time the oxen were sunk to their knees in water. I then sprang to the sled, and drawed it back to the shore, without the least difficulty, notwithstanding the load, and returned to my oxen. By this time they had broken a considerable path in the ice, and were struggling to get out. I could do nothing but stand and see them swim round

—sometimes they would be nearly out of sight, nothing scarcely but their horns to be seen; they would then rise and struggle to extricate themselves from their perilous situation. I called for help in vain; & to fly for assistance would have been imprudent and fatal. Notwithstanding my unhappy situation, and the manner by which I came by the oxen, &c. I was not terrified in the least—I felt calm and composed—at length the oxen swam up to where I stood and laid their heads on the ice at my feet. I immediately took the yoke from off their necks; they lay still till the act was performed, and then returned to swimming as before. By this time they had made an opening in the ice as much as two rods across. One of them finally swam to the down stream side, and in an instant, as if lifted out of the water, he was on his side on the ice, and got up and walked off; the other swam to the same place and was out in the same way. I stood on the opposite side of the opening, and saw with astonishment every movement. I then thought, and the impression is still on my mind, that they were helped out by supernatural means; most certainly no natural cause could produce an effect like this: that a heavy ox six and a half feet in girth, can of his own natural strength heave himself out of the water on his side on the ice, is too extraordinary to reconcile to a natural cause; —that in the course of Divine Providence events do take place out of the common course of nature, that our strongest reasoning cannot comprehend, is impious to deny: though we acknowledge the many chimeras of superstition, ignorance and barbarism in the world; and when we are eye witnesses to such events, it is not for us to doubt, but to believe and tremble. Others have a right to doubt my testimony; but in this instance, for me to doubt would be perjury to my own conscience, and I may add ingratitude to my Divine Benefactor. In fact a signal Providence seemed to direct the path for me to pursue to procure this grain. Though I was doomed to encounter perils, to suffer fatigue and toil, there was a way provided for me to obtain the object in view. In the first onset I accidentally fell in with the man of whom I purchased at the Park. I found he had grain to sell. I requested of him this small supply on trust: we were strangers to each other—a peculiar friend of mine, happening to be by, volunteered his word for the pay. I knew not where nor how to get the money, but necessity drove me to make the purchase, and in the course of the winter I was so fortunate as to catch saple enough to pay the debt by the time it was due. Though I hazarded my word, it was in a good cause— it was for the relief of my family, and so it terminated. But to return.

I had now gone to the extent of my abilities for bread corn, but was destitute of meat; and beef and pork were scarcer in those times. Accordingly I had to have recourse to wild meat for a substitute, and had the good luck to purchase a moose of a hunter; and the meat of two more I brought in on shares—had the one for bringing in the other. These two were uncommonly large—were judged to weigh seven hundred weight each. The meat of these three moose I brought in on my back, together with the large bones and heads. I backed them five or six miles over rough land, cut up by sharp ridges and deep hollows, and interspersed with underbrush and windfalls, which made it impracticable to pass with a hand sled, which, could I have used, would much eased my labor. A more laborious task was this than that of bringing my meal, &c. from the Park.

My practice was to carry my loads in a bag, to tie the ends of the bag so nigh that I could but comfortably get my head through, so that the weight of my load would rest on my shoulders. I often had to encounter this hardship in the time of a thaw, which made the task more severe, especially in the latter part of winter and fore part of the spring, when the snow became coarse and harsh, and will not so readily support the snowshoe. My hold would often fail without any previous notice to guard against it—perhaps slide under a log or catch in a bush and pitch me into the snow with my load about my neck. I have repeatedly had to struggle in this situation for some time to extricate myself from my load, it being impossible to get up with my load on. Those who are acquainted with this kind of burden may form an idea of what I had to encounter—the great difficulty of carrying a load on snow-shoes in the time of a thaw, is one of those kinds of fatigue that it is hard to describe, nor can be conceived but by experience. It is wearisome at such times to travel without a load; but with one, especially at this late season, it is intolerable: but thaw or freeze my necessities obliged me to be at my task, and still to keep up my burthen. I had to draw my firewood through the winter on a hand sled: in fact, my snow-shoes were constantly hung to my feet.

Being destitute of team for four or five years, and without farming tools, I had to labor under great embarrassments: my grain I hoed in the three first years. After I raised a sufficiency for my family, I had to carry it twelve miles to mill on my back, for the three first years: this I had constantly to do once a week. My common load was one bushel, and generally carried it eight miles before I stopped to rest. My wife at one time sold her shirt to purchase a moose hide which I was obliged to carry thirty miles on my back, and sold it for a bushel of corn, and bro't the corn home in the same way.

For a specimen of the hardships those have often to encounter who move into the wilderness, I will give the following, that took place the winter after I came on: We had a remarkable snow, the first of consequence, that fell; it was full two feet deep. Our communication was with the inhabitants of Hyde-park, and it was necessary for us to keep the road, or rather path, so that we could travel; we were apprehensive of danger, if we did not immediately tread a path through this snow. I was about out of meal, and had previously left a bushel at a deserted house about five miles on the way. I agreed with Esq. Taylor, he being the only inhabitant with me, to start the next day on the proposed tour. We accordingly started before sunrise; the snow was light, and we sunk deep into it. By the middle of the day it give some, which made it still worse; our snow-shoes loaded at every step; we had to use nearly our whole strength to extricate the loaded shoe from its hold. It seemed that our hip joints would be drawn from their sockets. We were soon worried—could go but a few steps without stopping: our fatigue and toil become almost insupportable—were obliged often to sit down and rest, and were several times on the point of giving up the pursuit, and stop for the night, but this must have been fatal, as we had no axe to cut wood for a fire; our blood was heated, and we must have chilled. We finally, at about dusk, reached the deserted house, but was in effect exhausted. It seemed we could not have reached this house had it been twenty rods further: so terrible is the toil to travel through deep snow, that no one can have a sense of it till taught by experience. This day's journey is often on my mind; in my many hard struggles it was one of the severest. We struck up a fire and gathered some fuel that lay about the house, and after we had recovered strength, I baked a cake of my meal. We then lay down on some hewn planks, and slept sound till morning. It froze at night; the track we had made rendered it quite feasible travelling. The next day I returned home with my bushel of meal.

Another perilous tour I will mention, that occurred this winter. It was time to bring on another load of meal from Esq. McDaniels. I proposed in my mind to go early the next morning. There had been a thaw, and in the time of the thaw a man had driven a yoke of oxen from Cabot, and went down on my path, and trod it up. The night was clear—the moon shone bright, and it was remarkably cold. I awoke, supposing it nearly day, and sat out, not being sensible of the cold, and being thinly clad I soon found I was in danger of freezing, and began to run, jump, and thrash my hands, &c. The path being full of holes, and a light snow had just fallen that filled them up, I often fell, and was in danger of breaking my limbs, &c. The cold seemed to increase, and I was forced to exert my utmost strength to keep from freezing: my limbs became numb before I got through, though I ran about every step of the eight miles, and when I got to McDaniel's the cocks crowed for day. I was surprised upon coming to the fire to find that the bottoms of my mockasins and stockings were cut and worn through, the bottoms of my feet being entirely bare, having cut them by the holes in the path, but not withstanding the severity of the frost, I was preserved, not being frozen in any part. Had I broken a limb, or but slightly spraint a joint, which I was in imminent danger of doing, I must have perished on the way, as a few minutes of respite must have been fatal.

In the early part of my residence in Wolcott, by some means I obtained knowledge of their being beaver on a small stream in Hardwick; and desirous to improve every means in my power for the support of my family, and to retrieve my circumstances, I determined on a tour to try my fortune at beaver hunting.

Accordingly, late in the fall, I set out in company with my neighbor Taylor on the intended enterprise. We took what was called the Coos road, which was nothing more than marked trees: in about seven miles we reached the stream, and proceeded up it about three miles farther, and searched for beaver, but were soon convinced that they had left the ground. We, however, set a few traps. Soon after we started it began to rain, and before night the rain turned into a moist snow that melted on us as fast as it fell. Before we reached the hunting ground, we were wet to our skins; night soon came on—we found it necessary to camp (as the hunters use the term); with difficulty we struck up a fire, but our fuel was poor, chiefly green timber—the storm increased—the snow continued moist; our bad accommodations grew worse and worse; our fire was not sufficient to warm us and much less to dry us; we dared not attempt to lay down, but continued on our feet through the night, feeding our fire and endeavoring to warm our shivering limbs. This is a memorable night to me; the most distressing I ever experienced; we anxiously looked for day. At length the dawn appeared, but it was a dismal and a dreary scene. The moist snow had adhered to every thing in its way; the trees and underwood were remarkably loaded, were completely hid from sight—nothing to be seen but snow, and nothing to be heard but the cracking of the bended boughs under the enormous weight, we could scarcely see a rod at noon day. When light enough to travel, we set out for home, and finding it not safe to leave the stream for fear of getting bewildered and lost, we followed it back; it was lined the chief of the way with beaver meadow, covered with a thick growth of alders; we had no way to get through them but for one to go forward and beat off the snow with a heavy stick. We thus proceeded, though very slowly, down the stream to the Coos road, and worried through the ten miles home at the dusk of the evening, nearly exhausted by fatigue, wet and cold, for it began to freeze in the morning; our clothes were frozen stiff on our backs; when I pulled off my great coat it was so stiff as to stand up on the floor. In order to save our traps we had to make another trip, and one solitary muskrat made up our compensation for this hunting tour.

A painful circumstance respecting my family I must here

mention. In the year 1806, we were visited with sickness that was uncommonly distressing, five being taken down at the same time, and several dangerously ill. In this sickness I lost my wife, the partner of my darkest days, who bore her share of our misfortunes with becoming fortitude. I also lost a daughter at the same time, and another was bedrid about six months, and unable to perform the least labour for more than a year. This grievous calamity involved me in debts that terminated in the loss of my farm, my little all; but by the indulgence of feeling relatives I am still permitted to stay on it. Though I have been doomed to hard fortune I have been blest with a numerous off-spring; have had by my two wives seventeen children, thirteen of them daughters; have had fifty-one grand-children, and six great grand-children, making my posterity seventy-four souls.

I have here given but a sketch of my most important suffer-ings. The experienced farmer will readily discover, that under the many embarrassments I had to encounter, I must make but slow progress in clearing land; no soul to help me, no funds to go to: raw and inexperienced in this kind of labor, though fu-ture wants pressed the necessity of constant application to this business, a great portion of my time was unavoidably taken up in pursuit of sustenance for my family; however reluctant to leave my labor, the support of nature must be attended to, the calls of hunger cannot be dispensed with. I have now to remark, that at this present time, my almost three score years and ten, I feel the want of those forced exertions of bodily strength that were spent in those perils and fatigues, and have worn down my constitution, to support my decaying nature.

When I reflect on those past events, the fatigue and toil I had to encounter, the dark scenes I had to pass through, I am struck with wonder and astonishment at the fortitude and presence of mind that I then had to bear me up under them. Not once was I discouraged or disheartened: I exercised all my powers of body and mind to do the best I could, and left the effect for future events to decide, without embarrassing my mind with imagi-nary evils. I could lay down at night, forgetting my troubles, and sleep composed and calm as a child; I did in reality experi-ence the just proverb of the wise man, that "the sleep of the laboring man is sweet, whether he eat little or much." Nor can I close my tale of sufferings without rendering my feeble tribute of thanks and praise to my benign Benefactor, who supplies the wants of the needy and relieves the distressed, that in his wise Providence has assisted my natural strength both of body and of mind to endure those scenes of distress and toil.

———

County of Orleans, *Nov'r.* 1824.

The undersigned, having read in manuscript the foregoing narrative, and having lived in habits of intimacy with, and in the neighborhood of Seth Hubbell at the time of his sufferings, we are free to inform the public, that we have no doubt but his statements are, in substance, correct. Many of the circumstances therein narrated we were at the time personally knowing to, and are sensible more might be added without exaggeration, in many instances wherein he suffered.

THOMAS TAYLOR, *Justice of Peace.*
DARIUS FITCH, *J. of Peace.*
JOHN McDANIEL, *J. P.*
JESSE WHITNEY, *J. P.*

SAMUEL THOMSON

(1769-1843)

New Guide to Health; or Botanic Family Physician . . . to which is prefixed, A Narrative of the Life and Medical Discoveries of the Author. By Samuel Thomson. Printed for the Author, and sold by his General Agent, at the Office of the Boston Investigator, J. Q. Adams, Printer, Boston, 1835. Two volumes in one. 228 pp. and 168 pp.

Samuel Thomson was a botanic physician who developed his own way of treating disease. The Thomsonian System, as it was called, consisted chiefly of emesis, vapor baths, and vegetable remedies. Unlike the regular school of physicians, Thomson used organic rather than mineral or chemical materials. He found his remedies in the native plants of the countryside.

Thomson's doctoring proved in many cases to be beneficial; at worst, not harmful. His contribution to mankind and medical science lay in the influence he exerted against the prevailing damaging medical practices of his day. He "discarded utterly the methods in common use,—the lancet, leech, cupping glass and Spanish fly, together with the various mineral drugs and poisonous vegetable productions which constituted the fashionable physician's armament," wrote Alexander Wilder, M.D., in his *History of Medicine . . . in the Nineteenth Century.*

Thomson obtained his first medical patent in 1813. He then asked Benjamin Rush and Benjamin Smith Barton, professors of medicine at the University of Pennsylvania, and foremost among the medical men of the time, to back his system; they did not. Barton, however, "acknowledged there was no art or science so uncultivated as that of medicine." Thomson wrote, "I stated to him pretty fully my opinion of the absurdity of bleeding to cure disease; and pointed out its inconsistency, inasmuch as the same method was made use of to cure a sick man as to kill a well beast. He laughed and said it was strange logic enough."

17

In 1823 Thomson received a second patent. He then trained people and sold them rights to practice his system. But the trouble with selling rights was that it attracted persons who saw an easy way to the title of doctor. Virtually all Thomson's licensees turned out to be dishonest and caused him continual embarrassment. He spent his last years practicing in Boston.

Thomson published his first book in 1821. Only thirty-six pages, it bore a long title—*A Brief Sketch of the Causes and Treatment of Disease; addressed to the people of the United States; pointing out to them the pernicious consequences of using poisons as medicine, such as mercury, arsenic, nitre, antimony, and opium . . . Designed as an introduction to a full explanation to be published hereafter, of the system of practise discovered by the author.* It was printed for the author, in Boston, by E. G. House. In 1822 came *A Narrative of the Life and Medical Discoveries . . .* and also *New Guide to Health. . . .* About 1834 Thomson wrote and published a verse satire, *Learned Quackery Exposed.*

Before Thomsonian medicine ran its course—it petered out in the early 1850's—several editions of *Life and Medical Discoveries* and *New Guide to Health* were called for. All have become rare. A neat, pocket-size, three-by-five-inch "tenth edition" of the *Life and Medical Discoveries*, 256 pages, "Printed and Published by Jarvis Pike & Co., General Agents," Columbus, Ohio, appeared in 1833. Some editions combined the *Life* and *New Guide* in one volume.

The selections that follow make up about one fourth of *A Narrative of the Life and Medical Discoveries* and adhere to the pattern of the whole: one long take, without chapter or other division.

NARRATIVE

OF THE

LIFE, &c. OF SAMUEL THOMSON.

————•————

There is nothing, perhaps, more unpleasant than to write one's own life; for in doing it we are obliged to pass over again, as it were, many scenes, which we might wish to have forgotten, and relate many particulars, which, though they may seem very important to ourselves, yet would be very uninteresting to the reader. It is not my intention to attempt to write a history of my life, nor would it be in my power to do it if I had such a wish; but as I have been the greater part of my life engaged in one of the most important pursuits, and which is of more consequence to the great human family, than any other that could be undertaken by man; that of alleviating human misery, by curing all cases of disease by the most simple, safe, and certain method of practice, I think the public will be interested to know something of me, and the reason of my having taken upon myself so important a calling, without being regularly educated to the profession, which is thought by the world to be indispensably necessary; but I shall take the liberty to disagree a little with them in this particular; for, although learning may be a great advantage in acquiring a profession, yet that alone will never make a great man, where there is no natural gift. . . .

I was born February 9, 1769, in the town of Alstead, county of Cheshire, and State of New Hampshire. My father, John Thomson, was born in Northbridge, county of Worcester, and State of Massachusetts; he was twenty-five years old when I was born. My mother's name was Hannah Cobb; she was born in Medway, Mass., and was four years older than my father. I had one sister older than myself, and three brothers and one sister younger, who are all living except my second brother, who died in his fourteenth year. . . .

That country was a wilderness when I was born; my father had began there about a year before, at which time there was no house within three miles one way, and about one the other; there were no roads, and they had to go by marked trees. The snow was very deep when they moved there, and my mother had to travel over a mile on snow shoes through the woods to get to their habitation. My parents were poor, having nothing to begin the world with; but had to depend upon their labor for support. My father had bought a piece of wild land on credit, and had to pay for it by his labor in what he could make off the land, which caused us great hardships and deprivations for a long time.

As soon as I began to form any correct ideas of things, my mind was much irritated by the impressions made on it by my parents, who, no doubt with very good intentions, filled my young head with all kinds of hob-goblin and witch-stories, which made a very deep impression on my mind, and which were not entirely eradicated for many years. I mention this as a caution to parents, not to tell their children any thing but the truth; for young children naturally believe whatever their parents tell them, and when they frighten them with such stories, for the purpose of making them behave well, it will most generally have a very bad effect; for when they arrive at years of discretion, and find that all those stories are falsehoods, they will naturally form very unfavorable opinions of their parents, whose duty it is to set them better examples.

My father and mother were of the Baptist persuasion, and were very strict in their religious duties. They attended meeting every Sabbath, and my father prayed night and morning in his family. One day they went to meeting, and left me and my sister at home alone, and told us that if we were wicked they should send the bear or the knocker to carry us off. While they were absent I was at play, when we heard a hard knocking on the outside of the house, which frightened us very much, and when they came home I told them what had happened; but instead of letting us know what it was, they told us it was the knocker they had told us of, and that or the bear would always come, if we were wicked, and did not mind and do as they told us. It was several years after that my reason taught me that this knocker, as they called it, was a wood-pecker that came on the end of the house. Parents ought to be careful to impress on the minds of young children, correct ideas of things, and not mislead their understandings by telling them falsehoods; for it will be of the greatest importance as respects their future conduct and pursuits in life.

When I was between three and four years old, my father took me out with him to work. The first business I was set to do was to drive the cows to pasture, and watch the geese, with other small chores, which occupation kept me all day in the fields. I was very curious to know the names of all the herbs which I saw growing, and what they were good for; and, to satisfy my curiosity was constantly making inquiries of the persons I happened to be with, for that purpose. All the information I thus obtained, or by my own observation, I carefully laid up in my memory, and never forgot. There was an old lady by the name of Benton lived near us, who used to attend our family when there was any sickness. At that time there was no such thing as a Doctor known among us, there not being any within ten miles. The whole of her practice was with roots and herbs, applied to the patient, or given in hot drinks, to produce sweating; which always answered the purpose. When one thing did not produce the desired effect, she would try something else, till they were relieved. By her attention to the family, and the benefits they received from her skill, we became very much attached to her; and when she used to go out to collect roots and herbs, she would take me with her, and learn me their names, with what they were good for; and I used to be very curious in my inquiries, and in tasting every thing that I found. The information I thus obtained at this early age, was afterwards of great use to me.

Sometime in the summer, after I was four years old, being out in the fields in search of the cows, I discovered a plant which had a singular branch and pods, that I had never before seen, and I had the curiosity to pick some of the pods and chew them; the taste and operation produced was so remarkable, that I never forgot it. I afterwards used to induce other boys to chew it, merely by way of sport, to see them vomit. I tried this herb in this way for nearly twenty years, without knowing any thing

of its medical virtues. This plant is what I have called the
Emetic Herb, and is the most important article I make use of in
my practice. . . .

At five years of age my father put me to hard work, and was
very strict, using the greatest severity towards me. I used to
suffer very much from pains in my hips and back, being lame
from my birth, and the hard work made me so stiff, that in the
morning it was with difficulty I could walk. My father's severity
towards me made me very unhappy; for I was constantly in
fear lest he should call and I should not hear him, in which
case, he used to punish me very severely. I continued in this
situation till I was eight years old, when my brothers began to
be some help, which took part of the burthen off from me. We
suffered great hardships and lived very poorly; but we always
had something to eat, and were contented, for we knew of nothing better; a dish of bean-porridge and some potatoes, were our
constant fare, and this was better than many others had. The
greatest part of this winter we had to live in the barn. In July
my father had got a part of the roof of a new house covered,
and we moved into it; which was more comfortable than the
barn. About this time my mother was taken sick, and was carried to Mrs. Benton's for her to take care of, where she remained for several weeks, during which time, by using such
means as this old lady prescribed, she recovered. At this time I
had never been to school, or had any chance whatever to learn
to read. My father kept me constantly at work, all week days,
and on Sunday I had to go a considerable distance on foot to
meeting, and the rest of the day was kept on my feet in hearing
him read the catechism, creed and prayers, so that I had little
time to rest on that day.

The winter I was eight years old, I was very sick with the
canker-rash; but was attended by the widow Benton, who cured
me by making use of such medicine as our country afforded,
and I was in a short time able to be about. After I had got well,
my mind was more attentive to the use of roots and herbs as
medicine, than ever. I had at that time a very good knowledge
of the principal roots and herbs to be found in that part of the
country, with their names and medical uses; and the neighbors
were in the habit of getting me to go with them to show them

such roots and herbs as the doctors ordered to be made use of in sickness, for syrups, &c. and by way of sport they used to call me doctor. While in the field at work I used often to find the herb, which I tasted when four years old, and gave it to those who worked with me, to see them spit and often vomit; but I never observed any bad effect produced by it, which simple experiments eventually led me to observe the value of it in disease.

When I was about ten years old, there was a school a little more than a mile from my father's, where I had the opportunity of attending for one month. The weather was cold and the going bad, which caused me to make very slow progress in my learning; but the chance we considered a great privilege, for the country was new and people poor, and the opportunity for children to get learning very small. I took a great dislike to working on a farm, and never could be reconciled to it; for nothing could strike me with greater dread than to hear the name of a plough, or any other thing used on a farm mentioned. This I have always attributed to the hardships I underwent, and the severity which my father used constantly to exercise towards me from the time I was five to ten years old. At that time, I used to think that if ever I had any land I would not plough it; and if my father's treatment of me was the effect of his religion, I never wished to have any. This was when he was under the strongest influence of the Baptist persuasion, and used to be very zealous in his religious duties, praying night and morning, and sometimes three times a day. He was a man of violent and quick temper, and when in his fits of passion, my mother used frequently to remind him of certain parts of his prayer; such as this, which I never forgot: "May we live soberly, righteously, and godly, in the present evil world." She was a woman much respected in the town where we lived.

About the time I was fourteen years old, my father left the Baptist persuasion and embraced that of universal salvation; By grace are ye saved, through faith not of yourselves, it is the gift of God. If he ever experienced a change of heart for the better, it was at this time; his love to God and man was great, and I had great reason to rejoice, for he was like another man in his house. He continued to enjoy the same belief, with much comfort to the time of his death, which took place in August, 1820, aged 76. My mother remained many years in the full belief of the salvation of all men, and continued so till her death.

Sometime during the year that I was sixteen years old, I heard my parents say, that as my mind was so much taken up with roots and herbs, they thought it best to send me to live with a Doctor Fuller, of Westmoreland, who was called a root doctor. This pleased me very much, and in some measure raised my ambition; but I was soon after disappointed in my hopes, for they said I had not learning enough, and they did not know how to spare me from my work, which depressed my spirits, and was very discouraging to me. I now gave up all hopes of going to any other business, and tried to reconcile myself to spend my days in working on a farm, which made me very unhappy. I had little learning, and was awkward and ignorant of the world, as my father had never given me any chance to go into company, to learn how to behave, which caused me great uneasiness.

In the year 1788, when I was in my nineteenth year, my father purchased a piece of land on Onion river, in the state of Vermont, and on the 12th day of October, he started from Alstead, and took me with him, to go to work on the land and clear up some of it to build a house on, as it was all covered with wood. In about four days after our arrival, we were enabled to clear a small spot and to build us a camp to live in; we had to do our own cooking and washing; our fare was poor, and we had to work very hard; but we got along tolerably well till the 2d of December, when I had the misfortune to cut my ancle very badly, which accident prevented me from doing any labor for a long time, and almost deprived me of life. The wound was a very bad one, as it split the joint and laid the bone entirely bare, so as to lose the juices of my ancle joint to such a degree as to reduce my strength very much. My father sent for a Doctor Cole, of Jericho, who ordered sweet apple-tree bark to be boiled, and the wound to be washed with it, which caused great pain, and made it much worse, so that in eight days my strength was almost exhausted; the flesh on my leg and thigh was mostly gone, and my life was despaired of; the doctor said he could do no more for me; my father was greatly alarmed

about me, and said that if Dr. Kitteridge, of Walpole, could be
sent for, he thought he might help me; but I told him it would
be in vain to send for him, for I could not live so long as it
would take to go after him, without some immediate assistance.
He said he did not know what to do; I told him that there was
one thing I had thought of which I wished to have tried, if it
could be obtained, that I thought would help me. He anxiously
inquired what it was, and I told him if he could find some com-
frey root, I would try a plaster made of that and turpentine. He
immediately went to an old place that was settled before the
war, and had the good luck to find some; a plaster was prepared by my directions and applied to my ancle, the side opposite to the wound, and had the desired effect; the juices stopped
running in about six hours, and I was very much relieved;
though the pain continued to be very severe and the inflamma-
tion was great; the juices settled between the skin and bone,
and caused a suppuration, which broke in about three weeks;
during which time I did not have three nights sleep, nor did I
eat any thing. This accidental remedy was found through necessity, and was the first time the mother of invention held
forth her hand to me. The success which attended this experiment, and the natural turn of my mind to those things, I think
was a principal cause of my continuing to practise the healing
art to this time.

Our stock of provisions being now exhausted, and my wound
somewhat better, my father was very anxious to return to Alstead. He asked me if I thought I could bear the journey, if he
should place me on a bed laid in a sled. I answered that I was
willing to try. He immediately went to work and fixed a sled,
and put me in it on a straw bed; and on the first day of January, 1789, we began our journey. There was very little snow,
and the road rough, which caused the sled to jolt very much,
and my sufferings were great. It was very doubtful with my
father, and likewise with me, whether I should live to perform
the journey; but we proceeded on, however, without any thing
important happening, except wearing out the runners of our
sled, and having to make new ones, and accomplished twenty
miles the first day. . . .

At a place where we stopped on the third night, a circumstance had occurred which, from its novelty, I think worth mentioning. A young woman who lived in the family had discovered a strong inclination to sleep more than what is common; and had expressed a wish that they would let her sleep enough once. She went to bed on Sunday night, and did not wake again till Tuesday morning, having slept thirty-six hours. On awaking, she had no idea of having slept more than one night; but began to make preparation for washing, as was the custom on Mondays, till she was informed that they had washed the day before. Her health was good and she never after that required more sleep than other persons.

When we got on to the high land there was considerable snow, and we got along much more comfortably. I had to be carried in on the bed and laid by the fire, every night during the journey. The people generally, where we stopped, treated me with kindness, and showed much pity for me in my distressed situation; but they all thought that I should not live to get through the journey. The doctors had advised to have my leg cut off, as the only means of saving my life, and all those who saw me during our journey, expressed the same opinion; and I think it would have been done had I given my consent; but I positively refused to agree to it, so the plan was given up. I preferred to take my chance with my leg on, to having it taken off; which resolution I have never repented of, to this day.

On arriving in Walpole, my father proceeded immediately to the house of the famous Dr. Kitteridge, to have him dress my wound, and get his opinion of my situation; he not being at home, and it being nearly dark, we concluded to put up for the night, and I was carried in on my bed and laid by the fire. The doctor soon came home, and on entering the room where I was, cried out in a very rough manner, Who have you here? His wife answered, a sick man. The devil, replied he, I want no sick man here. I was much terrified by his coarse manner of speaking, and thought if he was so rough in his conversation, what will he be when he comes to dress my wound; but I was happily disappointed, for he took off the dressing with great care, and handled me very tenderly. On seeing the strings that were in the wound, he exclaimed, what the devil are these halters here for? My father told him they were put in to keep the sore open. He said he thought the sore open enough now, for it is all rotten. Being anxious to know his opinion of me, my father asked him what he thought of my situation. What do I think? said he, why I think he will die; and then looking very pleasantly at me, said, though I think young man, you will get well first. In the morning he dressed my ancle again, and gave me some salve to use in future; and my father asked him for his bill, which was, I think, for our keeping and his attending me, about fifty cents. A great contrast between this and what is charged at the present time by our regular physicians; for they will hardly look at a person without making them pay two or three dollars. I have been more particular in describing this interview with Dr. Kitteridge, on account of his extraordinary skill in surgery, and the great name he acquired, and justly deserved, among the people throughout the country. His system of practice was peculiarly his own, and all the medicines he used were prepared by himself, from the roots and herbs of our own country. He was a very eccentric character, and uncouth in his manners; but he possessed a good heart, and a benevolent disposition. He was governed in his practice by that great plan which is dictated by nature; and the uncommon success he met with is evidence enough to satisfy any reasonable mind, of the superiority of it over what is the practice of those who become doctors by reading only, with their poisons and their instruments of torture.

We left Walpole, and arrived at our home about noon, and my mother, brothers and sisters, were much rejoiced to see me, though grieved at my distressed situation; and never was any one more in need of the tender care of friends than I was at this time. My mother proved to me the old saying, that a friend in need is a friend indeed. My case was considered doubtful for some time. I was from the first of December to the first of March unable to walk; but by good nursing and constant care, I was enabled in the spring to attend to the business at home, so that my father left me in charge of the farm, and went with my brother to Onion river, again to work on his land.

On the 9th of February, 1790, I was twenty-one years of age, and my father gave me a deed of one half of his farm in Alstead, consisting of one hundred and twenty-five acres; and I carried it on for three years, and he had the liberty to take such stock as he pleased. He then made preparations and removed to Onion river, and left my mother and sister in my care. Soon after I took a bad cold, which threw me into a slow fever. In the month of March we all had the meazles, and my mother had what the doctors called the black kind, and was so bad that her life was despaired of. The disease turned in and seated on her lungs, and she never recovered her health. Several doctors attended her without doing her any good. Her cough was very severe and her mouth was sore, and she was greatly distressed. I attended upon her under the direction of the doctors, and took the cough, and had much the same symptoms. She continued to grow worse daily; the doctors gave her over, and gave her disease the name of galloping consumption, which I thought was a very appropriate name; for they are the riders, and their whip is mercury, opium and vitriol, and they galloped her out of the world in about nine weeks. She died on the 13th day of May, 1790.

I was at this time very low with the same disorder that my mother died with, and the doctor often importuned me to take some of his medicine; but I declined it, thinking I had rather die a natural death. He tried to frighten me by telling me it was the last chance of getting help, and he thought he could cure me; but I told him I had observed the effect his medicine had on my mother, for she constantly grew worse under the operation of it, and I had no desire to risk it on myself. I have always been of the opinion, that if I had followed his advice, I should have been galloped out of the world the same as my mother was; and I have never repented of my refusal to this day.

After my mother died, I undertook to doctor myself, and made some syrups of such things as I had the knowledge of, which relieved my cough; and with the warm weather, I so far recovered my health, as to be able to work some time in June. Being without women's help, I was obliged to hire such as I could get, which proved a disadvantage to my interest, and I thought it would be best to find some person who would take an interest in saving my property. On the 7th day of July, 1790, I was married to Susan Allen. We were both young, and had great hardships to encounter, but we got along very well, and both enjoyed good health until our first child was born, which was on the fourth day of July following. My wife was taken ill on Saturday, and sent for help; she lingered along till Sunday night, when she became very bad; her situation was dangerous, and she was in hand constantly the whole night, until sunrise the next morning, when she was delivered; but her senses were gone. During the whole night it was one continued struggle of forcing nature, which produced so great an injury to the nervous system, as to cause strong convulsion fits in about an hour after her delivery. The witnessing of this horrid scene of human butchery, was one great cause of my paying attention to midwifery, and my practice has since been very successful in it.

Her fits continued and grew worse; there were six doctors attended her that day, and a seventh was sent for; but she grew worse under their care; for one would give her medicine, and another said that he did wrong; another would bleed her, and the other would say he had done wrong; and so on through the whole. I heard one of them say that his experience in this case was worth fifty dollars. I found that they were trying their practice by experiments; and was so dissatisfied with their conduct, that at night I told them what I thought; and that I had heard them accusing each other of doing wrong; but I was convinced that they had all told the truth, for they had all done wrong. They all gave her over to die, and I dismissed them, having seen enough of their conduct to convince me that they were doing more hurt than good.

After they were gone, I sent for Dr. Watts and Dr. Fuller, who were called root doctors. They attended her through the night, and in the morning about the same hour that they began, the fits left her. She had in the whole, eighteen of the most shocking convulsion fits that had been ever seen by any one present. The spasms were so violent that it jarred the whole house. After the fits had left her, she was entirely senseless, and was raving distracted for three days; and then became perfectly stupid, and lay in that situation for three days; she then laughed three days, and then cried three days; after which she seemed to awake like a person from sleep, and had no knowledge of what had passed, or that she had been sick, or had a

child. These two doctors continued to attend her, and used all
the means in their power to strengthen the nervous system. She
gained very slowly, and it was a long time before she got about;
but she never got entirely over it. This sickness put me back in
my business very much, and the expense was above two hundred dollars. . . .

My mind was bent on learning the medical properties of
such vegetables as I met with, and was constantly in the habit
of tasting every thing of the kind I saw; and having a retentive
memory, I have always recollected the taste and use of all that
were ever shown me by others, and likewise of all that I discovered myself. This practice of tasting of herbs and roots has
been of great advantage to me, as I have always been able to
ascertain what is useful for any particular disease, by that
means. I was often told that I should poison myself by tasting
every thing I saw; but I thought I ought to have as much
knowledge as a beast, for they possess an instinct to discover
what is good for food, and what is necessary for medicine. I
had but very little knowledge of disease at this time; but had a
great inclination to learn whatever I had an opportunity; and
my own experience, which is the best school, had often called
my attention to the subject.

The herb which I had discovered when four years old, I had
often met with; but it had never occurred to me that it was of
any value as medicine, until about this time, when mowing in
the field with a number of men, one day, I cut a sprig of it, and
gave to the man next to me, who ate it; when we had got to the
end of the piece, which was about six rods, he said that he
believed what I had given him would kill him, for he never felt
so in his life. I looked at him and saw that he was in a most
profuse perspiration, being as wet all over as he could be; he
trembled very much, and there was no more color in him than a
corpse. I told him to go to the spring and drink some water; he
attempted to go, and got as far as the wall, but was unable to
get over it, and laid down on the ground and vomited several
times. He said he thought he threw off his stomach two quarts. I
then helped him into the house, and in about two hours he ate a
very hearty dinner, and in the afternoon was able to do a good
half day's labor. He afterwards told me that he never had any

thing do him so much good in his life; his appetite was remarkably good, and he felt better than he had for a long time. This circumstance gave me the first idea of the medical virtues of this valuable plant, which I have since found by forty years experience, in which time I have made use of it in every disease I have met with, to great advantage, that it is a discovery of the greatest importance.

In March, 1794, my second daughter was born; and my wife had no medical assistance except what I could do for her, with the advice of the doctor who lived on my farm. . . .

I was in the habit at this time of gathering and preserving in the proper season, all kinds of medical herbs and roots that I was acquainted with, in order to be able at all times to prevent as well as to cure disease; for I found by experience, that one ounce of prevention was better than a pound of cure. Only the simple article of mayweed, when a person has taken a bad cold, by taking a strong cup of the tea when going to bed, will prevent more disease in one night, with one cent's expense, than would be cured by the doctor in one month, and one hundred dollars' expense in their charges, apothecaries' drugs, and nurses.

I had not the most distant idea at this time of ever engaging in the practice of medicine, more than to assist my own family; and little did I think what those severe trials and sufferings I experienced in the cases that have been mentioned, and which I was drove to by necessity, were to bring about. It seemed as a judgment upon me, that either myself or family, or some one living with me, were sick most of the time the doctor lived on my farm, which was about seven years. Since I have had more experience, and become better acquainted with the subject, I am satisfied in my own mind of the cause. Whenever any of the family took a cold, the doctor was sent for, who would always either bleed or give physic. Taking away the blood reduces the heat, and gives power to the cold they had taken, which increases the disorder, and the coldness of the stomach causes canker; the physic drives all the determining powers from the surface inwardly, and scatters the canker through the stomach and bowels, which holds the cold inside, and drives the heat on the outside. The consequence is, that perspiration ceases, because internal heat is the sole cause of this important evacuation; and a settled fever takes place, which will continue as long as the cold keeps the upper hand. My experience has taught me that by giving hot medicine, the internal heat was increased, and by applying the steam externally, the natural perspiration was restored; and by giving medicine to clear the stomach and bowels from canker, till the cold is driven out and the heat returns, which is the turn of the fever, they will recover the digestive powers, so that food will keep the heat where it naturally belongs, which is the fuel that continues the fire or life of man.

After the doctor, who lived on my farm, moved away, I had very little sickness in my family. On the birth of my second son, which was about two years from the birth of the first son, we had no occasion for a doctor; my wife did well, and the child was much more healthy than the others had been; and I have never employed a doctor since; for I had found from sad experience, that they made much more sickness than they cured. Whenever any of my family were sick, I had no difficulty in restoring them to health by such means as were within my own knowledge. As fast as my children arrived at years of discretion, I instructed them how to relieve themselves, and they have all enjoyed good health ever since. If parents would adopt the same plan, and depend more upon themselves, and less upon the doctors, they would avoid much sickness in their families, as well as save the expense attending the employment of one of the regular physicians, whenever any trifling sickness occurs, whose extravagant charges is a grievous and heavy burthen upon the people. I shall endeavor to instruct them all in my power, by giving a plain and clear view of the experience I have had, that they may benefit by it. If they do not, the fault will not be mine, for I shall have done my duty. I am certain of the fact, that there is medicine enough in the country, within the reach of every one, to cure all the disease incident to it, if timely and properly administered.

At the birth of our third son, my wife was again given over by the midwife. Soon after the child was born, she was taken with ague fits and cramp in the stomach; she was in great pain, and we were much alarmed at her situation. I proposed giving her some medicines, but the midwife was much opposed to it;

she said she wished to have a doctor, and the sooner the better. I immediately sent for one, and tried to persuade her to give something which I thought would relieve my wife until the doctor could come; but she objected to it, saying that her case was a very difficult one, and would not allow to be trifled with; she said she was sensible of the dangerous situation my wife was in, for not one out of twenty lived through it, and probably she would not be alive in twenty-four hours from that time. We were thus kept in suspense until the man returned and the doctor could not be found, and there was no other within six miles. I then came to the determination of hearing to no one's advice any longer, but to pursue my own plan. I told my wife, that as the midwife said she could not live more than twenty-four hours, her life could not be cut short more than that time, therefore there would be no hazard in trying what I could do to relieve her. I gave her some warm medicine to raise the inward heat, and then applied the steam, which was very much opposed by the midwife; but I persisted in it according to the best of my judgment, and relieved her in about one hour, after she had laid in that situation above four hours, without any thing being done. The midwife expressed a great deal of astonishment at the success I had met with, and said that I had saved her life, for she was certain that without the means I had used, she could not have lived. She continued to do well, and soon recovered. This makes the fifth time I had applied to the mother of invention for assistance, and in all of them was completely successful.

These things began to be taken some notice of about this time, and caused much conversation in the neighborhood. My assistance was called for by some of the neighbors, and I attended several cases with good success. I had previous to this time, paid some attention to the farrier business, and had been useful in that line. This, however, gave occasion for the ignorant and credulous to ridicule me and laugh at those whom I attended; but these things had little weight with me, for I had no other object in view but to be serviceable to my fellow creatures, and I was too firmly fixed in my determination to pursue that course, which I considered was pointed out as my duty, by the experience and many hard trials I had suffered, to be deterred by the foolish remarks of the envious or malicious part of society.

The last sickness of my wife, I think took place in the year 1799, and about two years after she had another son and did well, making five sons that she had in succession; she afterwards had another daughter, which was the last, making eight children in the whole that she was the mother of; five sons and three daughters. I mention these particulars, in order that the reader may the better understand many things that took place in my family, which will give some idea of the experience and trouble I had to encounter in bringing up so large a family, especially with the many trials I had to go through in the various cases of sickness and troubles, which are naturally attendant on all families, and of which I had a very large share. The knowledge and experience, however, which I gained by these trying scenes, I have reason to be satisfied with, as it has proved to be a blessing, not only to me, but many hundreds who have been relieved from sickness and distress through my means; and I hope and trust that it will eventually be the cause of throwing off the veil of ignorance from the eyes of the good people of this country, and do away the blind confidence they are so much in the habit of placing in those who call themselves physicians, who fare sumptuously every day; living in splendor and magnificence, supported by the impositions they practise upon a deluded and credulous people; for they have much more regard for their own interest than they have for the health and happiness of those who are so unfortunate as to have any thing to do with them. If this was the worst side of the picture, it might be borne with more patience; but their practice is altogether experimental, to try the effect of their poisons upon the constitutions of their patients, and if they happen to give more than nature can bear, they either die or become miserable invalids the rest of their lives, and their friends console themselves with the idea that it is the will of God, and it is their duty to submit; the doctor gets well paid for his services, and that is an end of the tragedy. It may be thought by some that this is a highly colored picture, and that I am uncharitable to apply it to all who practise as physicians; but the truth of the statements, as respects what are called regular physicians, or those who get diplomas from the medical society, will not be doubted by any who are acquainted with the subject, and will throw aside prejudice and reflect seriously upon it—those whom the coat fits I am willing should wear it. . . .

Sometime in the month of November, 1802, my children had the measles, and some of them had them very bad. The want of knowing how to treat them gave me a great deal of trouble, much more than it would at the present time, for experience has taught me that they are very easy to manage. One of the children took the disease and gave it to the rest, and I think we had four down with them at the same time. My third son had the disorder very bad; they would not come out, but turned in, and he became stupid. The canker was much in the throat and mouth, and the rosemary would have no effect. Putrid symptoms made their appearance, and I was under the necessity of inventing something for that, and for the canker. I used the steam of vinegar to guard against putrefaction, and gold thread, or yellow root, with red oak acorns pounded and steeped together, for the canker. These had the desired effect; and by close attention he soon got better. The second son was then taken down pretty much in the same manner, and I pursued the same mode of treatment, with similar success; but the disease had so affected his lungs, that I feared it would leave him in a consumption, as was the case with my mother. He could not speak loud for three weeks. I could get nothing that would help him for some time, till at last I gave him several portions of the emetic herb, which relieved him and he soon got well. During this sickness we suffered much from fatigue and want of sleep; for neither my wife nor myself had our clothes off for twelve nights. This was a good fortnight's school to me, in which I learned the nature of the measles; and found it to be canker and putrefaction. This experience enabled me to relieve many others in this disease, and likewise in the canker-rash; in these two disorders, and the small pox, I found a looking-glass, in which we may see the nature of every other disease. I had the small pox in the year 1798, and examined its symptoms with all the skill I was capable of, to ascertain the nature of the disease; and found that it was the highest stage of canker and putrefaction that the human system was capable of receiving; the

measles the next, and the canker-rash the third; and other disorders partake more or less of the same, which I am satisfied is
a key to the whole; for by knowing how to cure this, is a general rule to know how to cure all other cases; as the same means
that will put out a large fire will put out a candle. . . .

In the spring of the year 1805, I was sent for to go to Wood-
stock, in Vermont, to attend a young woman, who was considered in a decline, and the doctors could not help her. I found
her very low, not being able to set up but very little. I staid and
attended her about a week, and then left her, with medicines
and directions what to do, and returned home. In about a
month, I went again to see her, and found her much better, so
that she was able to ride to her father's, which was above
twenty miles. All this time I had not formed an idea that I
possessed any knowledge of disorder or of medicine, more than
what I had learned by accident; and all the cases I had attended were from necessity; but the success I had met with, and
the extraordinary cures I had performed, made much talk, and
were heard of for fifty miles around.

I began to be sent for by the people of this part of the country so much, that I found it impossible to attend to my farm
and family as I ought; for the cases I had attended, I had received very little or nothing, not enough to compensate me for
my time; and I found it to be my duty to give up practice
altogether, or to make a business of it. I consulted with my wife
and asked the advice of my friends, what was best for me to do;
they all agreed, that as it seemed to be the natural turn of my
mind, if I thought myself capable of such an important undertaking, it would be best to let my own judgment govern me, and
to do as I thought best. I maturely weighed the matter in my
mind, and viewed it as the greatest trust that any one could
engage in. I considered my want of learning and my ignorance
of mankind, which almost discouraged me from the undertaking; yet I had a strong inclination for the practice, of which it
seemed impossible to divest my mind; and I had always had a
very strong aversion to working on a farm, as every thing of the
kind appeared to me to be a burthen; the reason of which I
could not account for, as I had carried on the business to good
advantage, and had as good a farm as any in the neighborhood.
I finally concluded to make use of that gift which I thought

nature, or the God of nature, had implanted in me; and if I possessed such a gift, I had no need of learning, for no one can learn that gift. I thought of what St. Paul says in his epistle to the Corinthians, concerning the different gifts by the same spirit; one had the gift of prophecy; another, the gift of healing; another, the working of miracles. I am satisfied in my own mind, that every man is made and capacitated for some particular pursuit in life, in which, if he engages, he will be more useful than he would if he happens to be so unfortunate as to follow a calling or profession, that was not congenial to his disposition. This is a very important consideration for parents, not to make their sons learn trades or professions, which are contrary to their inclinations and the natural turn of their minds; for it is certain if they do, they never can be useful or happy in following them.

I am convinced myself that I possess a gift in healing the sick, because of the extraordinary success I have met with, and the protection and support I have been afforded, against the attacks of all my enemies. Whether I should have been more useful had it been my lot to have had an education, and learned the profession in the fashionable way, is impossible for me to say with certainty; probably I should have been deemed more honorable in the world; but honor obtained by learning, without a natural gift, or capacity, can never, in my opinion, make a man very useful to his fellow creatures. I wish my readers to understand me, that I do not mean to convey the idea, that learning is not necessary and essential in obtaining a proper knowledge of any profession or art; but that going to college will make a wise man of a fool, is what I am ready to deny; or that a man cannot be useful and even great in a profession, or in the arts and sciences, without a classical education, is what I think no one will have the hardihood to attempt to support, as it is contrary to reason and common sense. We have many examples of some of the greatest philosophers, physicians, and divines the world ever knew, who were entirely self-taught; and who have done more honor, and been greater ornaments to society, than a million of those who have nothing to recommend them but having their heads crammed with learning, without sense enough to apply it to any great or useful purpose. . . .

There can be no good reason given why all the technical

terms in medical works are kept in a dead language, except it
be to deceive and keep the world ignorant of their doings, that
they may the better impose upon the credulity of the people;
for if they were to be written in our own language, every body
would understand them, and judge for themselves; and their
poisonous drugs would be thrown into the fire before their patients would take them. . . .

After I had come to the determination to make a business of
the medical practice, I found it necessary to fix upon some system or plan for my future government in the treatment of disease; for what I had done had been as it were from accident,
and the necessity arising out of the particular cases that came
under my care, without any fixed plan; in which I had been
governed by my judgment and the advantages I had received
from experience. I deemed it necessary, not only as my own
guide, but that whatever discoveries I should make in my practice, they might be so adapted to my plan that my whole system
might be easily taught to others, and preserved for the benefit
of the world. I had no other assistance than my own observations, and the natural reflections of my own mind, unaided by
learning or the opinions of others. I took nature for my guide,
and experience as my instructer; and after seriously considering every part of the subject, I came to certain conclusions concerning disease, and the whole animal economy, which more
than forty years' experience has perfectly satisfied me is the
only correct theory. My practice has invariably been conform-
able to the general principles upon which my system is
founded, and in no instance have I had reason to doubt the
correctness of its application to cure all cases of disease when
properly attended to; for that all disease is the effect of one
general cause, and may be removed by one general remedy, is
the foundation upon which I have erected my fabric, and which
I shall endeavor to explain in as clear and concise a manner as
I am capable, with a hope that it may be understood by my
readers, and that they may be convinced of its correctness.

I found, after maturely considering the subject, that all animal bodies are formed of the four elements, earth, air, fire, and
water. Earth and water constitute the solids, and air and fire, or
heat, are the cause of life and motion. That cold, or lessening

the power of heat, is the cause of all disease; that to restore heat
to its natural state, was the only way by which health could be
produced; and that, after restoring the natural heat, by clearing
the system of all obstructions and causing a natural perspiration, the stomach would digest the food taken into it, by which
means the whole body is nourished and invigorated, and heat
or nature is enabled to hold its supremacy; that the constitutions of all mankind being essentially the same, and differing
only in the different temperament of the same materials of
which they are composed; it appeared clearly to my mind, that
all disease proceeded from one general cause, and might be
cured by one general remedy; that a state of perfect health
arises from a due balance or temperature of the four elements;
but if it is by any means destroyed, the body is more or less
disordered. And when this is the case, there is always an actual
diminution or absence of the element of fire, or heat; and in
proportion to this diminution or absence, the body is affected
by its opposite, which is cold. And I found that all disorders
which the human family were afflicted with, however various
the symptoms, and different the names by which they are called,
arise directly from obstructed perspiration, which is always
caused by cold, or want of heat; for if there is a natural heat, it
is impossible but that there must be a natural perspiration.

Having fixed upon these general principles, as the only solid
foundation upon which a correct and true understanding of the
subject can be founded, my next business was to ascertain what
kinds of medicine and treatment would best answer the purpose
in conformity to this universal plan of curing disease; for it
must, I think, be certain and self-evident to every one, that
whatever will increase the internal heat, remove all obstructions
of the system, restore the digestive powers of the stomach, and
produce a natural perspiration, is universally applicable in all
cases of disease, and therefore may be considered as a general
remedy.

The first and most important consideration was to find a
medicine that would establish a natural internal heat, so as to
give nature its proper command. My emetic herb (No. 1) I
found would effectually cleanse the stomach, and would very
effectually aid in raising the heat and promoting perspiration;

but would not hold it long enough to effect the desired object, so but that the cold would return again and assume its power. It was like a fire made of shavings; a strong heat for a short time, and then all go out. After much experience and trying every thing within my knowledge, to gain this important point, I fixed upon the medicine which I have called No. 2, in my patent, for that purpose; and after using it for many years, I am perfectly convinced that it is the best thing that can be made use of to hold the heat in the stomach until the system can be cleared of obstructions, so as to produce a natural digestion of the food, which will nourish the body, establish perspiration and restore the health of the patient. I found it to be perfectly safe in all cases, and never knew any bad effects from administering it.

My next grand object was to get something that would clear the stomach and bowels from canker, which are more or less affected by it in all cases of disease to which the human family are subject. Canker and putrefaction are caused by cold, or want of heat; for whenever any part of the body is so affected by cold as to overpower the natural heat, putrefaction commences, and if not checked by medicine, or if the natural constitution is not strong enough to overcome its progress, it will communicate to the blood, when death will end the contest between heat and cold, by deciding in favor of the latter. I have made use of a great many articles, which are useful in removing canker; but my preparation called No. 3, is the best for that purpose, that has come to my knowledge; though many other things may be made use of to good effect, all of which I shall give particular a description in my general directions hereafter.

Having endeavored to convey to my readers, in a brief manner, a correct idea of the general principles upon which I formed my system of practice, I shall now give some account of the success I met with in the various cases that came under my care, and the difficulties and opposition that I have had to encounter, in maintaining it till this time, against all my enemies.

My general plan of treatment has been in all cases of disease, to cleanse the stomach by giving No. 1, and produce as great an internal heat as I could, by giving No. 2, and when necessary, made use of steaming, in which I have always found great benefit, especially in fevers; after this, I gave No. 3, to clear off the canker; and in all cases where patients had not previously become so far reduced as to have nothing to build upon, I have been successful in restoring them to health. I found that fever was a disturbed state of the heat, or more properly, that it was caused by the efforts which nature makes to throw off disease, and therefore ought to be aided in its cause, and treated as a friend; and not as an enemy, as is the practice of the physicians. In all cases of disease, I have found that there is more or less fever, according to the state of the system; but that all fevers proceed from the same cause, differing only in the symptoms; and may be managed and brought to a crisis with much less trouble than is generally considered practicable, by increasing the internal heat, till the cold is driven out, which is the cause of it. Thus keeping the fountain above the stream, and every thing will take its natural course.

During the year 1805, a very alarming disease prevailed in Alstead and Walpole, which was considered the yellow fever, and was fatal to many who were attacked by it. I was called on, and attended with very great success, not losing one patient that I attended; at the same time, nearly one half of those who had regular physicians, died. This disease prevailed for about forty days, during which time, I was not at home but eight nights. I was obliged to be nurse as well as doctor, and do every thing myself, for the people had no knowledge of my mode of practice, and I could not depend upon what any person did, except what was under my own immediate inspection. I pursued the same general plan that I had before adopted; but the experience I had from this practice, suggested to me many improvements, which I had not before thought of, as respects the manner of treatment of patients to effect the objects I aimed at in curing the disease, which was to produce a natural perspiration. I found great benefit in steaming in the manner that I had discovered and practised with my little daughter; but I found by experience, that by putting a hot stone into a spider or iron basin, and then wetting the top of the stone with vinegar, was an important improvement; and with this simple method, with a little medicine of my own preparing, answered a much better purpose, than all the bleeding and poisonous physic of the doctors. While I was attending those who were sick, and they found that my mode of treatment relieved them from their distress, they were very ready to flatter and give great credit for my practice; but after I had worn myself out in their service, they began to think that it was not done in a fashionable way; and the doctors made use of every means in their power to ridicule me and my practice, for the purpose of maintaining their own credit with the people. This kind of treatment was a new thing to me, as I did not at that time so well understand the craft, as I have since, from hard earned experience. The word quackery, when used by the doctor against me, was a very important charm to prejudice the people against my practice; but I would ask all the candid and reflecting part of the people, the following questions, and I will leave them to their consciences to give an answer; which is the greatest quack, the one who relieves them from their sickness by the most simple and safe means, without any pretensions to infallibility or skill, more than what nature and experience has taught him, or the one who, instead of curing the disease, increases it by administering poisonous medicines, which only tend to prolong the distress of the patient, till either the strength of his natural constitution, or death relieves him? . . .

In the spring of 1805, a Mrs. Richardson was brought to my house. She was brought in her bed from Westford, Vermont, about 130 miles, and was attended by a son and daughter, the one 21, and the other 18 years of age. The mother had lain in her bed most part of the time for ten years. All the doctors in that part of the country had been applied to without any advantage; and they had spent nearly all their property. I undertook with her more from a charitable feeling for the young man and woman, than from any expectation of a cure. Their conduct towards their helpless mother, was the greatest example of affection of children to a parent that I ever witnessed. The young man stated to me that his mother had been a year together without opening her eyes; that when she could open them, they thought her almost well. She was perfectly helpless, not being able to do the least thing; not even to brush off a fly, any more than an infant. She had laid so long that her knee joints had become stiff.

I began with her by cleansing her stomach, and promoting perspiration; after which, I used to try to give her some exercise. The first trial I made was to put her bed into a wheelbarrow and lay her on it: when I would run her out, till she appeared to be weary; sometimes I would make a misstep and fall, pretending that I had hurt me; in order to try to get her to move herself by frightening her. After exercising her in this way for a few days, I put her in a wagon, sitting on a bed, and drove her about in that manner; and when her joints became more limber, I sat her on the seat of the wagon. She insisted that she should fall off, for she said she could not use her feet; but the driver would sometimes drive on ground that was sideling, and rather than turn over, she would start her foot unexpectedly. After exercising her in this way some time, I put her on a horse behind her son; she at first insisted that she should fall off; but when I told her she was at liberty to fall, if she chose, she would not, choosing rather to exert herself to hold on. When she had rode a few times in this way, I put her on the horse alone, and after a few trials she would ride very well, so that in the course of two months she would ride four miles out and back every day. She used to be tired after riding, and would lay down and not move for six hours. I continued to give her medicine to keep up perspiration, and restore the digestive powers, and to strengthen the nervous system. I attended her in this way for three months, and then went with her and her son and daughter to Manchester; she rode upwards of thirty miles in a day, and stood the journey very well. I never received any pay for all my trouble and expense of keeping them for three months, except what the two young people did more than take care of their mother; but I accomplished what I undertook, and relieved these two unfortunate orphans from their burthen; which was more satisfaction to me than to have received a large sum of money, without doing any good. I saw this woman three years after at the wedding of her son, and she was quite comfortable, and has enjoyed a tolerable degree of health to this time, (1822, the date of the first edition,) being able to wait on herself. . . .

About this time I was called on to attend a woman in the town where I lived. She was an old maid, and had lately been

married to a widower, who was very fond of her. She had been
much disordered for many years, and was very spleeny; she
had been under the care of several doctors without receiving
any benefit. I visited her several times and gave general satisfaction; so much so that she allowed that I had done her more
good than all the others that had attended her. A short time
after I had done visiting her, the old man came out one morning to my house at sunrise, and I being about six miles from
home, he came with all speed where I was, and said he wished
me to come to his house as soon as possible, for his wife was
very sick. I told him to return, and I would be there as soon as
he could. I soon after set out, and we both arrived there about
the same time; and I was very much astonished to find his wife
about her work. I was asked into another room by the old man
and his wife, and he said she had something to say to me. She
then said that, "if I could not attend her without giving her
love powder, she did not wish me to attend her at all." I was
very much astonished at her speech, and asked what she meant.
She said that ever since she had taken my medicine she had felt
so curiously, that she did not know what to make of it. The old
man affirmed to the same, and he thought that I had given her
love powder, and did not know what the event might be.

This foolish whim of the old man and his wife, caused a
great bluster, and was food for those idle minds, who seem to
take delight in slandering their neighbors; and was made a
great handle of by the doctors, who spread all kinds of ridiculous stories about me during my absence in the summer of
1806. In the autumn, when I had returned home, I found that a
certain doctor of Alstead, had circulated some very foolish and
slanderous reports about me and the old woman, and had given
to them so much importance, that many people believed them. I
found that I could prove his assertions, and sued him for defa-
mation; supposing that by appealing to the laws of my country
I could get redress; but I was disappointed in my expectations,
for I was persuaded to leave the case to a reference, and he had
raised such a strong prejudice in the minds of the people
against me, that they were more ready to favor a man whom
they considered great and learned, because he had been to college, than to do justice to me; so they gave the case against me,
and I had to pay the cost. After this, I refused to attend those

people who had assisted in injuring me, and gave them up to their fashionable doctor. A curse seemed to follow them and his practice; for the spotted fever prevailed in this place soon after, and the doctor took charge of those who had sided with him against me, and if he had been a butcher and used the knife, there would not have been more destruction among them. Two men who swore falsely in his favor, and by whose means he got his cause, were among his first victims; and of the whole that he attended, about nine tenths died. He lost upwards of sixty patients in the town of Alstead in a short time. . . .

Among those doctors who seemed so much enraged against me, for no other reason that I could learn, than because I had cured people whom they had given over, and instructed them to assist themselves when sick, without having to apply to them; there was none that made themselves so conspicuous as Dr. French. I had considerable practice in his neighborhood, and was very successful in every case; this seemed to excite his malice against me to the greatest pitch; he made use of every means in his power, and took every opportunity to insult and abuse me both to my face and behind my back. A few of the inhabitants who were his friends, joined with him, and became his instruments to injure me; but a large proportion of the people were friendly to me, and took great interest in my safety and success. The doctor and his adherents spread all kinds of ridiculous reports concerning me and my practice, giving me the name of the old wizzard; and that my cures were done under the power of witchcraft. This foolish whim was too ridiculous for me to undertake to contradict, and I therefore rather favored it merely for sport; many remarkable circumstances took place tending to strengthen this belief, and some of the silly and weak-minded people really believed that I possessed supernatural powers. This will not appear so strange, when we take into view, that the people generally were ignorant of my system of practice, and when they found that I could cure those diseases that the doctors, in whom they had been in the habit of putting all their confidence, pronounced as incurable; and that I could turn a fever in two days, which would often take them as many months, they were led to believe that there was something supernatural in it.

A man who was one of the friends of Dr. French, and who

had been very inimical to me, doing all in his power to injure and ridicule me, sent word one day by a child, that his calf was sick, and he wanted me to come and give it a green powder and a sweat. Knowing that his object was to insult, I returned for answer, that he must send for Dr. French, and if he could not cure it, I would come, for that was the way that I had to practise here. It so happened that the calf died soon after, and his youngest child was taken suddenly and very dangerously sick. Not long after, he found another calf dead in the field, and about the same time his oldest son was taken sick. These things happening in such an extraordinary manner, caused him to reflect on his conduct towards me, and his conscience condemned him, for trying to injure me without cause. He had the folly to believe, or the wickedness to pretend to believe, that it was the effect of witchcraft; and wishing to make his peace with me, sent me word, that if I would let his family alone, he would never do or say any thing more to my injury. This I readily assented to; and his children soon after getting well, though there was nothing very extraordinary in it, as it might all be easily accounted for by natural causes; yet it afforded much conversation among the gossips, and idle busy-bodies in the neighborhood; and was made use of by my enemies to prejudice the people against me. Being in company with a young woman who belonged to a family that were my enemies, she, to insult me, asked me to tell her fortune. I consented, and knowing her character not to be the most virtuous, and to amuse myself at her expense, told what had taken place between her and a certain young man the night before. She seemed struck with astonishment; and said that she was convinced that I was a wizzard, for it was impossible that I could have known it without the devil had told me. She did not wish me to tell her any more.

I practised in this place and vicinity a few months and returned home to attend to my farm for the rest of the season. While at home I was sent for, and attended in different parts of the country, and was very successful in my mode of practice, particularly in places where the dysentery and fevers were most prevalent; never failing in any instance of giving relief, and completely putting a check to those alarming epidemics, which caused so much terror in many places in the interior of the country. . . .

In the fall of the year 1808, I was sent for to go to Beverly. . . . While practising in Beverly, was called on by a Mr. Lovett, to attend his son, who was sick, as they supposed with a bad cold; some thought it a typhus fever. I was very much engaged in attending upon the sick at the time, and could not go with him; he came after me three times before I could go. On seeing him, found that he complained of a stiff neck, and appeared to be very stupid, and had no pain. His aunt, who took care of him, said that he would certainly die, for he had the same symptoms as his mother, who died a short time before. I gave some medicine which relieved him; the next day carried him through a course of the medicine, and he appeared to be doing well. Being called on to go to Salem, I left him in the care of Mr. Raymond, with particular directions to keep in the house and not expose himself. This was on Wednesday, and I heard nothing from him, and knew not but what he was doing well, till the Sunday afternoon following, when I was informed that he was worse. I immediately inquired of Mr. Raymond, and learned from him that he had got so much better, he had been down on the side of the water, and returned on Friday night; that the weather was very cold, being in the month of December; that he had been chilled with the cold, and soon after his return had been taken very ill; he staid with him on Saturday night, and that he was raving distracted all night; that he had not given any medicine, thinking he was too dangerously sick for him to undertake with.

I told the young man's father, that it was very doubtful whether I could do any thing that would help him; but that I would try, and do all I could. I found that the patient was so far gone that the medicine would have no effect, and in two hours told him that I could not help his son, and advised him to call some other advice; this was said in presence of Elder Williams, and Mr. Raymond. Mr. Lovett made answer that if I could not help his son, he knew of none who could; and was very desirous for me to stay with him all night, which I did, and stood by his bed the whole time. He was much deranged in his mind till morning, when he came to himself, and was quite

sensible. I then again requested the father to send for some
other doctor, as I was sensible that I could do nothing for him
that would be any benefit. He immediately sent for two doctors,
and as soon as they arrived, I left him in their care. The two
doctors attended him till the next night about ten o'clock, when
he died. I have been more particular in giving the history of
this case, because two years after it was brought as a charge
against me for murdering this young man. The father and
friends expressed no dissatisfaction at the time, in regard to my
conduct, except they thought I ought not to have neglected the
patient so long; but it was a well known fact, that I attended as
soon as I knew of his being worse, and that the whole cause of
his second attack was owing to his going out and exposing himself, and could not be imputed as any fault of mine. . . .

Some time this season I was sent for to attend Captain
Trickey, who was very sick. I examined him and was confident
that I could not help him, and took my hat in order to leave the
house. His family insisted on my stopping and doing something for him; but I told them that I thought he was in a dying
state, and medicine would do no good. I told his son that in all
probability, he would not be alive over twenty-four hours, and
that he had better go for some other help, for I could do him
no good. I told the wife that I should give no medicine myself,
but as they had some in the house that they knew the nature of,
she might give some of it to her husband, which she did. Two
doctors were sent for; the first one that arrived bled him, and
he soon breathed very short, and grew worse; the other doctor
came, and said that his breathing short was in consequence of
the medicine I had given him; but by this he did not gain
credit, for all the family knew to the contrary; and the woman
soon after told me of his speech. The patient continued till the
next day about ten o'clock, and died. Soon as he was dead, the
doctors and their friends spared no pains to spread the report
in every direction, that I had killed this man with my screw
auger, a cant name given to my emetic herb, in consequence
of one of my patients, when under the operation of it, saying
that it twisted in him like a screw auger. This was readily
seized upon by the doctors, and made use of for the purpose of
trying to destroy the reputation of this medicine by ridicule.

They likewise gave similar names to several other articles of my medicine, for the same purpose; and represented them as the names by which I called them. They had likewise given me several names and titles, by way of reproach; such as the sweating and steaming doctor; the Indian doctor; the old wizzard; and sometimes the quack. Such kind of management had a great effect on the minds of many weak minded people; they were so afraid of ridicule, that those whom I had cured were unwilling to own it, for fear of being laughed at for employing me.

The circumstance of the death of the above mentioned Capt. Trickey, was seized upon by the doctors and their friends, and the most false and absurd representations made by them through the country, with the intention of stopping my practice, by getting me indicted for murder, or to drive me off; but my friends made out a correct statement of the facts, and had them published, which put a stop to their career for that time. I continued my practice, and had a great number of the most desperate cases, in most of which I was successful. The extraordinary cures I had performed, had the tendency to make many people believe, that I could cure every one who had life in them, let their disease be ever so bad; and where I had attended on those who were given over as incurable, and they died, whether I gave them any medicine or not, the report was immediately circulated that they were killed by me, at the same time the regular doctors would lose their patients every day, without there being any notice taken of it. When their patients died, if appearances were ever so much against their practice, it was said to be the will of the Lord, and submitted to without a murmur; but if one happened to die that I had any thing to do with, it was readily reported by those interested in destroying my credit with the people, that I killed them. . . .

After practising in those parts* through the season of 1809, I went home to Surry, where I remained a few weeks, and returned back to Salisbury. On my way there, I made several stops in different places where I had before practised, to see my friends and to give information to those who made use of my medicine and practice. On my arrival at Salisbury, my friends

* Kittery, Maine, to Portsmouth, New Hampshire.

informed me that Dr. French had been very busily employed in my absence, and that he and a Deacon Pecker, who was one of the grand jury, had been to Salem, to the court, and on their return had said that there had been a bill of indictment found against me for wilful murder. They advised me to go off, and keep out of the way; but I told them I should never do that; for if they had found a bill against me, the government must prove the charges, or I must be honorably acquitted. About ten o'clock at night Dr. French came to the place where I stopped, with a constable, and made me a prisoner in behalf of the commonwealth. I asked the constable to read the warrant, which he did; by this I found that Dr. French was the only complainant, and the justice who granted the warrant, ordered me before him to be examined, the next morning. I was then taken by the constable to Dr. French's house, and keepers were placed over me to prevent me from escaping. While at his house and a prisoner, Dr. French took the opportunity to abuse and insult me in the most shameful manner that can be conceived of, without any provocation on my part. He continued his abuse to me till between two and three o'clock, when he took his horse and set out for Salem to get the indictment. After he was gone, I found on inquiry of the constable, that after he had been before the grand jury and caused me to be indicted, he came home before the bill was made out, and finding that I was at Salisbury, fearing I might be gone, and he should miss the chance of gratifying his malicious revenge against me, he went to a brother doctor, who was a justice of the peace, before whom he made oath, that he had probable ground to suspect, and did suspect, that I had with malice aforethought, murdered sundry persons in the course of the year past, whose names were unknown to the complainant; upon which a warrant was issued against me, and I was arrested as before stated, in order to detain and keep me in custody, till the indictment could be obtained.

In the morning I was brought before the said justice, and he not being ready to proceed in my examination, the court was adjourned till one o'clock; when I was again brought before him, and he said he could not try me until the complainant was present, and adjourned the court again till near night. The constable took me to his house in the mean time, and put me in a

back room and left me alone, all of them leaving the house.
When they came back, some of them asked me why I did not
make my escape, which I might very easily have done out of a
back window; but I told them that I stood in no fear of the
consequence, having done nothing whereby I ought to be punished; that I was taken up as a malefactor, and was determined
to be convicted as such, or honorably acquitted. Just before
night, Dr. French arrived with a Sheriff, and ordered me to be
delivered up by the constable to the Sheriff; and after Dr.
French had again vented his spleen upon me by the most savage
abuse that language could express, saying that I was a mur-
derer, and that I had murdered fifty, and he could prove it; that
I should be either hung or sent to the State prison for life, and
he would do all in his power to have me convicted. I was then
put in irons by the sheriff, and conveyed to the jail in Newburyport, and confined in a dungeon, with a man who had been
convicted of an assault on a girl six years of age, and sentenced
to solitary confinement for one year. He seemed to be glad of
company; and reminded me of the old saying, that misery loves
company. I was not allowed a chair or a table, and nothing but
a miserable straw bunk on the floor, with one poor blanket
which had never been washed. I was put into this prison on the
10th day of November, 1809; the weather was very cold, and
no fire, and not even the light of the sun, or a candle; and to
complete the whole, the filth ran from the upper rooms into our
cell, and was so offensive that I was almost stifled with the
smell. I tried to rest myself as well as I could, but got no sleep
that night, for I felt something crawling over me, which caused
an itching, and not knowing what the cause was, inquired of
my fellow sufferer; he said that it was the lice, and that there
was enough of them to shingle a meeting-house.

In the morning there was just light enough shone through
the iron grates, to show the horror of my situation. My spirits
and the justness of my cause prevented me from making any
lamentation, and I bore my sufferings without complaint. At
breakfast time I was called on through the grates to take our
miserable breakfast; it consisted of an old tin pot of musty
coffee, without sweetening or milk, and was so bad as to be
unwholesome; with a tin pan containing a hard piece of Indian

bread, and the nape of a fish, which was so hard I could not eat it. This had to serve us till three o'clock in the afternoon, when we had about an equal fare, which was all we had till the next morning. The next day Mr. Osgood came from Salisbury to see me, and on witnessing my miserable situation, he was so much affected, that he could scarcely speak. He brought me some provisions, which I was very glad to receive; and when I described to him my miserable lodgings, and the horrid place I was in, he wept like a child. He asked liberty of the jailor to furnish me with a bed, which was granted, and brought me one, and other things to make me more comfortable. The next day I wrote letters to my family, to Dr. Fuller, and to Judge Rice, stating to them my situation.

The bed which was brought me, I put on the old one, and allowed my fellow sufferer a part of it, for which he was very thankful. I had provisions enough brought me by my friends for us both, and I gave him what I did not want; the crusts and scraps that were left, his poor wife would come and beg, to carry to her starving children, who were dependent on her. Her situation and that of her husband were so much worse than mine, that it made me feel more reconciled to my fate; and I gave her all I could spare, besides making his condition much more comfortable, for which they expressed a great deal of gratitude.

In a few days after my confinement, Judge Rice came to see me, and brought with him a lawyer. On consulting upon the case, they advised me to petition to the Judges of the Supreme Court to hold a special court to try my cause, as there would be no court held by law, at which it could be tried, till the next fall, and as there could be no bail for an indictment for murder, I should have to lay in prison nearly a year, whether there was any thing against me or not. This was the policy of my enemies, thinking that they could keep me in prison a year, and in all probability I should not live that time, and their ends would be fully answered.

I sent on a petition agreeably to the advice of my friends, and Judge Rice undertook to attend to the business and do every thing to get the prayer of the petition granted. He followed the business up with great zeal, and did every thing that could be done to effect the object. I think he told me that he or the lawyer, Mr. Bartlett, had rode from Newburyport to Boston fifteen times in the course of three weeks, on the business. At length Judge Parsons agreed to hold a special court at Salem, on the 10th day of December, to try the cause, which was one month from the day I was committed. My friends were very attentive and zealous in my cause, and every preparation was made for the trial.

During this time the weather was very cold, and I suffered greatly from that cause, and likewise from the badness of the air in our miserable cell, so that I had not much life or ambition. Many of my friends came to see me, and some of them were permitted to come into the cell; but the air was so bad and the smell so offensive, that they could not stay long. My friend, Dr. Shephard, came to see me, and was admitted into our dungeon. He staid a short time, but said it was so offensive he must leave me; that he would not stay in the place a week for all Newburyport. On Thanksgiving day we were taken out of our cell and put in a room in the upper story, with the other prisoners, and took supper together; they consisted of murderers, robbers, thieves, and poor debtors. All of us tried to enjoy our supper and be in as good spirits as our condition would permit. The most of their complaints were of the filthiness and bad condition of the prison, in which we all agreed. Before it was dark I and my companion were waited upon to our filthy den again. There was nothing in the room to sit upon higher than the thickness of our bed; and when I wrote any thing, I had to lay on my belly, in which situation I wrote the Medical Circular, and several other pieces, which were afterwards printed.

After I had been in prison about two weeks, my son-in-law came to see me. I had before my imprisonment sent for him to come to Portsmouth on some business, and on hearing of my being in prison, he immediately came to Newburyport to see me. He seemed much more troubled about my situation than I was myself. I felt perfectly conscious of my innocence and was satisfied that I had done nothing to merit such cruel treatment; therefore my mind was free from reproach; for I had pursued the course of duty, which I conceived was allotted me by my

Maker, and done every thing in my power to benefit my fellow-creatures. These reflections supported me in my troubles and persecutions, and I was perfectly resigned to my fate.

About this time, a lawyer came into the prison and read to me the indictment, which was in the common form, that I, with malice aforethought, not having the fear of God before my eyes, but moved by the instigation of the devil, did kill and murder the said Lovett, with lobelia, a deadly poison, &c.; but feeling so perfectly innocent of the charges, which the bill alleged against me, it had very little effect upon my feelings; knowing them to be false, and that they had been brought against me by my enemies, without any provocation on my part.

In the morning of the day that was appointed for me to be removed to Salem for trial, I was taken out of my loathsome cell by the jailor, who gave me water to wash myself with, and I was permitted to take my breakfast by a fire, which was the first time I had seen any for thirty days, and could not bear to sit near it in consequence of its causing me to feel faint. As soon as I had eaten my breakfast, the iron shackles were brought and put on my hands, which I was obliged to wear till I got to Salem. The weather was very cold, and the going bad; we stopped but once on the way, the distance being about twenty-six miles. On our arrival, I was delivered over to the care of the keeper of the prison in Salem, and was confined in a room in the second story, which was more comfortable than the one I had left. I was soon informed that Judge Parsons was sick, and had put off my trial for ten days; so I had to reconcile myself to the idea of being confined ten days more without fire. However I was not without friends; Elder Booles and Capt. Russell came to see me the first night, and Mrs. Russell sent her servant twice every day with warm coffee, and other things for my comfort, for which I have always been grateful; and Mrs. Perkins, whom I had cured of a dropsy, sent for my clothes to wash against the day of my trial. . . .

On the 20th day of December, 1809, the Supreme Court convened to hear my trial, at which Judge Parsons presided, with Judges Sewall and Parker, assistant Judges. The case was called about ten o'clock in the morning, and the chief justice ordered me to be brought from the prison and arraigned at the bar for trial. I was waited on by two constables, one on my right and the other on my left, in which situation I was brought from the jail to the court-house and placed in the bar. The court-house was so crowded with the people, that it was with much difficulty we could get in. After I was placed in the criminal seat, a chair was handed me and I sat down to wait for further orders. Here I was the object for this great concourse of people to look at; some with pity, others with scorn. In a few minutes I was directed to rise and hold up my right hand, to hear the indictment read, which the grand jury had upon their oaths presented against me. It was in common form, stating that I had with malice aforethought, murdered Ezra Lovett, with lobelia, a deadly poison. I was then directed by the court to plead to the indictment, guilty, or not guilty; I plead not guilty, and the usual forms, in such cases, were passed through, the jury called and sworn, and the trial commenced.

The Solicitor General arose, and opened the case on the part of the Commonwealth, and made many hard statements against me, which he said he was about to prove; he stated that I had at sundry times killed my patients with the same poison. The first witness called to the stand, on the part of the government, was Mr. Lovett, the father of the young man that I was accused of killing. He made a tolerable fair statement of the affair in general, particularly of coming after me several times before I could attend; though I think he exaggerated many things against me, and told over several fictitious and ridiculous names, which people had given my medicine, by way of ridicule, such as bull-dog, ram-cat, screw-auger, and belly-my-grizzle; all of which had a tendency to prejudice the court and jury against me; and I also thought that he omitted to tell many things in my favor, that must have been within his knowledge; but there was nothing in his evidence that in the least criminated me, or supported the charges in the indictment.

The next witness called, was Dr. Howe, to prove that I had administered the poison alleged in the indictment. He stated that I gave the poison to the said Lovett, and produced a sample of it, which he said was the root of lobelia. The Judge asked him if he was positive that it was lobelia; he said he was, and that I called it coffee. The sample was handed round for the

court to examine, and they all appeared to be afraid of it, and
after they had all satisfied their curiosity, Judge Rice took it in
his hand and ate it, which very much surprised them. The Solicitor General asked him if he meant to poison himself in presence of the court. He said it would not hurt him to eat a peck of
it, which seemed to strike the court with astonishment. Dr.
Howe was then called at my request for cross-examination, and
Mr. Story asked him to describe lobelia, how it looked when
growing, as he had sworn to it by the taste and smell. This
seemed to put him to a stand, and after being speechless for
several minutes, he said he had not seen any so long, he should
not know it if he should see it at this time. This so completely
contradicted and did away all that he had before stated, that he
went off the stand quite cast down.

Dr. Cutler was called on to inform the court what the medicine was that Dr. Howe had declared so positively to be lobelia,
and after examining it, he said that it appeared to him to be
marsh-rosemary, which was the fact. So far, all they had proved
against me was, that I had given the young man some marsh-
rosemary, which Dr. Cutler had declared to be a good medicine.

Some young women were brought forward as witnesses,
whom I had no knowledge of ever seeing before. They made
some of the most absurd and ridiculous statements about the
medicine, that they said I gave the young man, that were probably ever made in a court of justice before; some of which were
too indecent to be here repeated. One of them said that I
crowded my puke down his throat, and he cried murder till he
died. This was well known to be a falsehood, and that the story
was wholly made up by my enemies, as well as what had been
before stated by those women, for the purpose of trying to make
out something against me. I had two unimpeachable witnesses
in court, ready to swear that I never saw the young man for
more than fourteen hours before he died, during all which time
he was in the care of Dr. Howe; but by not having an opportunity to make my defence, in consequence of the government
not making out their case against me, could not bring them
forward.

John Lemon was the next witness brought forward on the

part of the Commonwealth, and was directed to state what he knew about the prisoner at the bar. He stated that he had been out of health for two years, being much troubled with a pain in his breast, and was so bad that he was unable to work; that he could get no help from the doctors; that he applied to me and I had cured him in one week; and that was all he knew about the prisoner at the bar. By this time Judge Parsons appeared to be out of patience, and said he wondered what they had for a grand jury, to find a bill on such evidence. The Solicitor General said he had more evidence which he wished to bring forward.

Dr. French was called, and as he had been the most busy actor in the whole business of getting me indicted, and had been the principal cause, by his own evidence, as I was informed, of the grand jury finding a bill against me, it was expected that his evidence now would be sufficient to condemn me at once; but it turned out like the rest, to amount to nothing. He was asked if he knew the prisoner at the bar; he said he did. He was then directed to state what he knew about him. He said the prisoner had practised in the part of the country where he lived, with good success; and his medicine was harmless, being gathered by the children for the use of the families. The Judge was about to charge the jury, when the Solicitor General arose and said, that if it was not proved to be murder, it might be found for manslaughter. The Judge said, you have nothing against the man, and again repeated that he wondered what they had for a grand jury.

In his charge to the jury, the Judge stated that the prisoner had broken no law, common or statute, and quoted Hale, who says, any person may administer medicine with an intention to do good; and if it has the contrary effect from his expectation, and kills the patient, it is not murder, nor even manslaughter. If doctors must risk the lives of their patients, who would practise? He quoted another clause of law from Blackstone, who says, where no malice is, no action lies.

The charge being given to the jury, they retired for about five minutes, and returned into court and gave in their verdict of Not Guilty. . . .

When I had maturely considered the subject in all its bear-

ings, and exercised my best abilities in devising some plan by
which I could extricate myself from the dangers which threatened me on every hand; and to prevent those rights, which
twenty years' labor, with much suffering and great expense had
given me a just claim to, from being wrested from me; I finally
came to the conclusion that there was only one plan for me to
pursue with any chance of success; and that was to go on to
Washington, and obtain a patent for my discoveries; and put
myself and medicine under the protection of the laws of my
country, which would not only secure to me the exclusive right
to my system and medicine, but would put me above the reach
of the laws of any state.

After coming to the conclusion to go on to the seat of government and apply for a patent, I made all necessary preparation for the journey, and started from Portsmouth on the 7th of
February, and arrived at Washington on the 23d. The next day
after my arrival, I waited on Capt. Nicholas Gilman, of Exeter,
showed him my credentials, and asked his advice, what I must
do to obtain my object. He said that he thought it could not be
made explicit enough to combine the system and practice,
without being too long; he however advised me to carry my
petition to the patent office; which was then under the control
of Mr. Monroe, Secretary of State. I went to the patent office,
and found that Dr. Thornton was the Clerk, and presented him
my petition. He asked me many questions, and then said I must
call again; I called again the next day, and he said the petition
was not right; that I must specify the medicine, and what disorder it must be used in; he said that those medicines in general terms to cure every thing, was quackery; that I must particularly designate the medicine, and state how it must be used,
and in what disease. I then waited on Martin Chittenden, late
governor of Vermont, who was at Washington, and asked his
assistance; he was from the same town where my father lived,
and readily consented. We made out the specifications in as
correct a manner as we could, and the next day I carried them
to the patent office, and gave them to Dr. Thornton; he complained much about its being too short a system, and put me off
once more. I applied again and asked him for my patent; but
he said I had not got the botanic names for the articles, and

referred me to Dr. Mitchell, of New York, who was in the
House of Representatives. I applied to him, and requested him
to give the botanic names to the articles mentioned in my petition. He wrote them, and I carried them to Dr. Thornton; but
he was unable to read some of the names, one in particular; he
said I must go again to Dr. Mitchell, and get him to give it in
some other words, and not tell him that he could not read it. I
went, and the doctor wrote the same word again, and then
wrote, or "Snap-dragon;" which I carried to Dr. Thornton, and
requested him to put in the patent my names, and record it for
himself, snap-dragon, or any other name he chose. He then
talked about sending me to Philadelphia, to Dr. Barton, to get
his names.

I found he was determined to give me all the trouble he
could, and if possible to defeat my getting a patent, and I inti-
mated that I should go with my complaint to Mr. Monroe, upon
which he seemed a little more disposed to grant my request,
and said he would do without Dr. Barton's names. He then
went to work to make out the patent, and when he came to the
article of myrrh, he found much fault about that, and said it
was good for nothing. I told him that I paid for the patent, and
if it was good for nothing it was my loss. After much trouble, I
got it made out according to my request, and the medicine to
be used in fevers, colics, dysenteries and rheumatisms; he then
asked me if I wanted any additions, and I told him to add, "the
three first numbers may be used in any other case to promote
perspiration, or as an emetic," which he did. I then had to go to
the treasury office and pay my money and bring him duplicate
receipts. After all this trouble, I at length succeeded in obtaining my patent according to my request, which was completed
and delivered to me on the third day of March, 1813. . . .

I formed those who purchased the rights, into a society; and
they chose a committee, whom I authorized as agents to sell
rights and medicine; but this caused a jealousy among the rest
of the members, who said I gave privileges to some more than
to others.

I have formed four societies, and given them certain privileges, by allowing them part of the profits on the sale of rights
and medicine; but as soon as there was any funds, it has always

created uneasiness among the members. Some of the ignorant and selfish, would call for their dividends, as though it was bank stock, instead of feeling grateful for the advantages they enjoy by having their diseases cured, and their minds relieved from the alarming consequences of a disease, with a trifling expense. I have since altered my plan, and now have but one society. Every one who purchases a right for himself and family, becomes a member of the Friendly Botanic Society, and is entitled to all the privileges of a free intercourse with each other, and to converse with any one who has bought a right, for instruction and assistance in sickness, as each one is bound to give his assistance, by advice or otherwise, when called on by a member. In this way much more good can be done, and there will be much more good-will towards each other, than where there is any money depending.

I had now been in practice, constantly attending upon those laboring under disease, whenever called on, for about thirty years; had suffered much both in body and mind, from the persecutions I had met with, and my unwearied exertions to relieve the sick; and to establish my system of practice upon a permanent basis, that the people might become satisfied of its superiority over that which is practised by those styled regular physicians; putting it in their power to become their own physicians, by enabling every one to relieve themselves and friends, from all disease incident to our country, by making use of those vegetable medicines, the produce of our own country, which are perfectly safe and easily obtained. . . .

EDWARD HICKS

(1780–1849)

Memoirs of the Life and Religious Labors of Edward Hicks, Late of Newtown, Bucks County, Pennsylvania. Written by Himself. Merrihew & Thompson, Printers, No. 7 Carter's Alley, Philadelphia, 1851. 365 pp.

The wolf also shall dwell with the lamb, and the leopard shall lie down with the kid; and the calf and the young lion and the fatling together; and a little child shall lead them.

"And the cow and the bear shall feed; their young ones shall lie down together: and the lion shall eat straw like the ox. . . .

"They shall not hurt nor destroy in all my holy mountain: for the earth shall be full of the knowledge of the Lord. . . .

To Edward Hicks, Quaker minister and sign painter, these lines from the Book of Isaiah suggested "Peaceable Kingdom." Like variations on a theme, this subject was used over and over; forty canvases are extant. I saw one in Newtown, Pennsylvania, the village where he lived and died. The holy mountain, which Hicks had colored richly, rose through a timeless light. On the timberline, gnarled storm-tossed trees flung branches against a luminous sky. Lower, a giant freckled roan ox gazed with gentle intelligent eyes. Front and center lay a long-bodied leopard, while its mate, behind, thrust an armlike leg toward it. Old bulls stood in shadow, as placid as cows. A wolf, a lamb, and a kid looked uneasy together. An amazingly hungry-faced bear munched on corn while a little child led an odd-looking creature. A plump William Penn, who had just debarked from the ship in the river, conferred with Indians in the background. Amid the throng, but also standing apart, gray hairs cascading from his ears, appeared a noble-maned lion.

The lion's face, a veritable portrait of Hicks himself, was the focal point of the painting. The anxious visage and furrowed brow were evidence of inner conflict. While Hicks the minister longed to become a lamb, Hicks the painter created the lion in his own image.

Though many know and love Hicks's paintings, few have read his book—for good reason, the reason being one can take his limited little world on canvas better than on the printed page. And yet his writing is like his painting—an expression of simple faith that all will work out somehow.

Memoirs of the Life and Religious Labors says little concerning the artist but a great deal about the man. "My constitutional nature," Hicks wrote, "has presented formidable obstacles to the attainment of that truly desirable character, a consistent and exemplary member of the Religious Society of Friends; one of which is an excessive fondness for painting, a trade to which I was brought up, being connected with coach making, and followed the greatest part of my life; having been unsuccessful in every attempt to make an honest and honorable living by a more consistent business. . . ."

In the diary jottings, or "memorandum of passing events," which Hicks began when he was sixty-six, he noted, on April 14 and 15, 1846, "Diligent in business and somewhat fervent in spirit, desiring to serve the Lord; but nothing to boast of, save a sense of great weakness of body and mind." On the seventeenth, he wrote, "Diligent in business, but I fear not sufficiently fervent in spirit. . . ." And on the eighteenth, "Diligent in business, and if not fervent in spirit, seriously thoughtful about death and eternity. Oh! how awful the consideration; I have nothing to depend upon but the mercy and forgiveness of God, for I have no works of righteousness of my own; I am nothing but a poor old worthless insignificant painter."

Published two years after his death, *Memoirs of the Life and Religious Labors of Edward Hicks* has never been reprinted.

MEMOIR.

Newtown, 4th mo. 4th, 1843.

I AM, this day, sixty-three years of age, and I have thought right to attempt, at least, to write a short narrative of my life. . . .

I was born in the village of Attleborough,* Middletown township, Bucks county, Pennsylvania, the fourth of the Fourth month, called April, 1780. My parents were Isaac and Catharine Hicks, both regularly descended from Thomas Hicks, spoken of in the Journal of our ancient friend Samuel Bownas, as was also my late distinguished kinsman, Elias Hicks. I am thus particular, as I write principally for my children, and do not wish that some peculiar circumstances, in relation to our family, should be lost. . . .

My grandfather, Gilbert Hicks, (my father's father) married the daughter of Joseph Rodman, of Long Island, a consistent, active member of the Society of Friends, and the young man, not being a member, the marriage, of course, was clandestine, which was a cause of sorrow to the dear old friend. Notwithstanding this, he could not be inexorable, for he was a Christian. He therefore received his daughter, with her husband, as his dear children, and thus addressed them, "I am old, and you are young, and would wish to be settled in life; I therefore propose, that you go into the new countries, [as Pennsylvania was then called,] and settle on a tract of land, of about six hundred acres, that I own, near the river Delaware, on the Neshaminy creek, twenty miles east of Philadelphia, and as it is worth at least three hundred pounds, more than would be a just proportion of your share of my estate, you must give me a bond for that sum, on my executing a deed that shall give you a substantial title."

The proposition of the good old Friend, was acceded to by

* Present-day Langhorne.

his children, and in the winter of 1747 and '48, they came on, and found a part of the land cleared, and a comfortable log house, where they were hospitably received by a family of the name of Vansant, and where my father was born, the twenty-first of the fourth month, 1748, (old style). After building for themselves a comfortable dwelling, the first thing they did, was to sell off two hundred acres of the land, to Lawrence Growden, for three hundred pounds, with which they payed their father, and found themselves snugly settled on a farm of four hundred acres of first rate land, clear of all incumbrance; enhancing in value daily, by the astonishing influx of European settlers.

Whether it was their wealth, or their intelligence, or both, they certainly appear to have obtained a respectable standing; for my grandfather received a commission from the royal government, as one of the justices of the peace for the county of Bucks.

Either a fondness for public business, or getting tired of the labor and care of so large a farm, induced my grandfather to sell his large farm of four hundred acres, and to purchase a small one, coming to a point, in the south-east corner of what was then called Four-lanes-end, (now Attleborough), of one hundred acres. Here he built a spacious brick house, that is still standing; and moreover, it appears, that having become wealthy, he devoted himself almost exclusively to public business, being promoted to the office of Chief Justice of the Court of Common Pleas. And now I shall record the circumstances of my grandfather's passing judgment upon two colored men, who were tried before him for some act that transported them to the West Indies, for life, as slaves.

Notwithstanding the evidence against them appeared conclusive, my grandfather had conscientious scruples as to the justice of the sentence. It appears that the voice of the spirit of truth, addressed to the ear of his soul, showed him plainly that he had better sacrifice his lucrative and honorable office, and all the favor of the royal government, than pass the sentence of the law on the poor fugitives before him; a sentence that must separate them from all their nearest and dearest connections in life, and send them as exiles, to die by the hand of oppression, in a foreign land. But my poor grandfather was then basking in the sunshine of prosperity, increasing in wealth. He was a politician, he had been an office-hunter, and was now an office-holder, and therefore would not give up to the heavenly vision. The consequence was, that in the return of retributive justice, in less than seven years, he lost the object of his youthful affections, the wife of his bosom, the mother of his children; and by continuing his attachment to his royal master, in opposition to the American patriots, whom he imprudently insulted, he was driven from his home, his country, and property, and from every near and dear connection in life, becoming an exile in a foreign land, where his days were suddenly ended by the hand of an assassin; and his property being all confiscated, his family was reduced to indigence, if not to penury. Such was the end of my dear grandfather.

Whilst he found an asylum with the British army at New York, my father paid him his last visit, and on parting, my grandfather gave his son his last advice, in a language like this, "You are a young man, and as you may be exposed to many temptations, my last and most serious advice to you is, never act contrary to your conscientious feelings; never disobey the voice of eternal truth in your own soul. Sacrifice property, personal liberty, and even life itself, rather than be disobedient to a Heavenly vision. I disobeyed this inward monitor, and am now suffering the due reward of my deeds." Such were the last words of my dear old grandfather to his son, on leaving New York with the British army, at the close of the Revolution, for Nova Scotia. My venerable father, at the age of four score, related the circumstance to me, in such an impressive manner, that I had no doubt that he wished it handed down to posterity. . . .

My uncle William, after all the pains that was taken to give him a great scholastic education, was heard to lament in a language like this, "Ah, my poor deluded parents, they have only been concerned to put me in possession of all kinds of sense, but common sense!" He was unfit to fill, with propriety, the social and relative duties of life, and notwithstanding he had warmly espoused the cause of the proprietors, and was such a favorite with the Penn family, that they put him into the Prothonotary's office, then the most lucrative office in the county of Bucks, his education had so fostered his natural pride and extravagance, that the want of common sense kept him poor, and, to add to his difficulties, his father, who was a merchant in New York, failed in his business, and became poor, no doubt from the same causes, that is, pride, extravagance and a want of common sense.

Having been furnished recently, through the kindness of Doctor Gordon, with several letters written by my uncles William and Edward, I have been led to compare them with letters written by their cousin Elias Hicks, who was brought up in the path of humble industry. They are inferior in every characteristic of good writing, and no marvel that it should be so, for mark the difference in their education. While the pretty boys and best scholars, as George Dilwyn called them, were going to high schools and colleges, those nurseries of pride, indolence and effeminency, the bane of true republicanism, and most efficient contrivance of Satan, for the destruction of primitive Christianity, Elias was laboring hard through the day, at the useful and highly honorable trade of a carpenter, improving himself in the evening in useful knowledge, when others were asleep. The consequence was, the former, overwhelmed with pride, luxury, idleness and disease, sunk unnoticed, into an untimely grave. The latter arose from the path of humble industry, by virtue, knowledge, temperance, patience, godliness, brotherly kindness, and charity, to be one of the most dignified practical Christians, Christendom ever saw, and after living for more than four score years, passed out of time into eternity, to be joined to the spirits of just men made perfect, to the general assembly and church of the first born, whose names are written in heaven; and leaving behind him a savour, grateful to surviving generations; a name, I hope, that stands gloriously enrolled on the records of eternity.

My dear mother appears to have received, what I would call a bad education for a woman. She was brought up in pride, and idleness, and was the very reverse of a perfect woman, as set forth by the inspired poet, in the last chapter of Proverbs. It was such an education as was calculated to make, what the high church would call, a lady; a friend to kings and priests.

But the tremendous turnings and overturnings that took

place in the time of the Revolution, produced a great change in my mother's family, and the success of the American patriots, in laying the foundation of the present excellent government, deprived the royal aristocrats of their lucrative offices, reducing our family to comparative poverty. But the afflicting dispensation appears to have had a good effect upon my mother. . . . And from the best information I am in possession of, and which seems confirmed by the impressions of my mind, my precious mother, on her death bed, was fully convinced of the blessed *Truth*, as held by Friends. For I understood she requested that there should be no superfluity about her corpse or her coffin, and that there should be no monument of any kind placed at her grave, which appears to have been complied with, for when I went into what is called St. Mary's church-yard, in Burlington, to look for her grave, I could not find it. This seems the more extraordinary, as she had been educated and brought up a regular member of the Episcopal church, and the rest of her family that had died, had been buried in vaults, in the high church style.

Thus ended the earthly pilgrimage of my mother, Catharine Hicks, on the 19th of the 10th month, 1781, in the 36th year of her age, in Burlington, N. J., leaving her poor little feeble infant under the care of her colored woman, Jane, who had been a slave in the family, and being left to shift for herself, took me with her like her own child, for my father was now broken up, having no home of his own, or any business by which he could support and keep his children together.

This colored woman, Jane, worked about among the farmers in the neighborhood of Four-lanes-end, or Attleborough and Newtown, for a living, taking me with her. Being at the house of a friend, by the name of Janney, at the last-mentioned place, where Elizabeth, the wife of David Twining, was in the habit of visiting, she noticed a poor sickly-looking white child, who appeared to be under the care of a colored woman that seemed cross to it, and was led to inquire whose child it was. When informed that it was the youngest child of her dear deceased friend, Kitty Hicks, that she had seen about a year before in its mother's arms, dressed in rich and gay apparel; her sympathy for the child and love for the mother, caused her to express herself on this wise: "Oh! that my husband was willing, I would take this child and bring it up as my own." My father was soon informed of this circumstance, and begged of her to take his poor little son as a boarder, which she agreed to do, with her husband's consent.

David Twining was one of the most respectable, intelligent, and wealthy farmers in the county of Bucks, having been chosen one of the Provincial Assembly, though an exemplary member of the Society of Friends. His wife, Elizabeth, was just such a woman as is described in the last chapter of Proverbs. . . . She was certainly the best example of humble industry I ever knew for so wealthy a woman. It was this woman that it seems was providentially appointed to adopt me as a son, and to be to me a delegated shepherdess, under the great Shepherd and Bishop of souls. She had the simplicity and almost the innocence of a child. Being deprived of her parents in her childhood, and left poor, she received no scholastic education, only learning to read after she was grown up; yet she read the Scriptures with a sweetness, solemnity, and feeling I never heard equalled. . . .

I continued under the care of my adopted mother, as a boarder, until I was turned of thirteen; when my father finding himself disappointed in his prospect of making a great man out of a weak little boy, by scholastic learning or education, did the best thing that he could have done, by binding me out an apprentice to an industrious mechanic; for here the propensity to idleness, for which I had a natural turn, was necessarily counteracted. What a pity other parents and guardians do not follow his example. . . .

I say, what a pity that parents and guardians could not see what my father might have seen, that the more scholastic learning is wasted on a weak boy, the bigger blockhead he will become. Whether he made this discovery or not, at that time, I must leave; one thing is certain, he was disappointed in my not taking learning, for he intended me for a lawyer, as he had made a doctor of my only brother Gilbert. But his ambitious views were baffled in us both, and our precious mother's dying prayers were answered. . . .

My father might have succeeded more to his mind in the

education of my only sister, two years older than myself, for she was put to a boarding school, and brought up in the gay world in pride and idleness. But, marrying a young man, who was in the path of humble industry, coming up on foot, she joined him in his journey, and they had advanced so far in the estimation of the people, that her husband had become high sheriff of the county; and she herself, according to his testimony, looking towards uniting with her brother, when, by a sudden and affecting death, her course in this world was stopped.

In the latter part of the 7th month, 1817, in the evening of the day, she had prepared supper, and stepped out to call her eldest son, a lad about six years old, who had become very fond of playing in a creek that ran near their dwelling, when she heard him cry for help. On running to the creek, where it was deep and the bank high, she saw him in the water, apparently drowning. A few feet up stream she crossed, and ran to his assistance. Her screams of distress alarmed her neighbors, and particularly her husband, who was writing in his office. When he came to the bank, six or seven feet above the water, and saw his wife and child in the deep below, he immediately jumped in to their assistance; but, being no swimmer, they were all three immersed together in a hole in the water, not more than ten feet wide and ten feet deep.

I think it is most likely my dear sister sunk soon after getting into the deep water, never to rise alive, for she was within a month or two of her confinement. Her husband and child struggled longer, but were nearly gone, when a young man, about sixteen years of age, saved the child; and the dying father, as he was sinking for the last time, laid hold of a board that had been run into the water by a colored man, and by which he was drawn to the shore, nearly dead, and was with some difficulty brought to.

My poor dear sister's lifeless corpse was at last brought from the bottom of the deep hole, by the manly exertions of a sailor, but every attempt at resuscitation was in vain. Such was the tragical end of my dear sister Eliza Violetta Kennedy, in the fortieth year of her age.

At this sorrowful and affecting time I was sitting in a reli-

gious meeting, appointed for me at five o'clock in Rahway, between forty and fifty miles off in New Jersey. I dare not say I
had an impression that something sorrowful had happened to
me, but I think I recollect it was nearly a silent meeting, and I
told the people that, for some reason or other, I had but little to
communicate to them. And I very well remember that the
friend from New York, that was with me, took me by the hand
after the meeting broke, and said most emphatically, whilst his
eyes were overflowing with tears, "Edward, what is the matter?" And I think that my prospect changed in that meeting,
and instead of visiting a number of meetings in New Jersey, I
concluded to come immediately home, and had I not been im-
properly detained at Kingston, I should have got to my dear
sister's funeral.

There are two considerations connected with her sudden and
afflicting death that are relieving, and they are: a hope that she
was looking towards Heaven, and that she died in the highest
exercise of the finest feelings of her nature. . . .

I return again to my dear father, whose disappointment in
his son's not being sufficiently learned for the law, induced him
to bind me at the age of thirteen to a coachmaker, for seven
years. But his attachment to scholastic education was embraced
in the indenture that I should have one year's schooling.

In the Fourth month, 1793, I left my dear old adopted
mother in tears, and went to live with William and Rachael
Tomlinson, at Four-lanes-end, now Attleborough.

They were young married people, comfortably established in
the coachmaking business. William was in partnership with his
brother, Henry Tomlinson, a man I very much loved.

My master was an example of humble industry worthy to be
imitated. He led his hands to work and to meals, and only
asked them to follow his example. Indeed I do not know that I
ever saw him idle whilst he had a shop and business.

But the change was very great for a poor little weak boy, who
was brought up thus far as a gentleman's son, to sit at the table
as a boarder as long as he pleased, and had only to ask for what
he wanted, to get it. Then to sit down quickly and eat such as
was set before him, asking no questions, with a voracious set of
men and boys, who seemed to eat for their lives, and rise with

the master, was hard, and to go to work was still harder. And, as too often is the case at such establishments, both men and boys gave way to a kind of low slang and vulgarity of conversation and conduct, which came directly in contact with my respectable religious education, and I, of course, became the butt of their insignificant wit. But the tenderness of my religious impressions too soon wore off, and, instead of weeping and praying, I soon got to laughing and swearing; and having what may be truly called a natural fund of nonsense, I soon became a kind of favorite with my shopmates.

In less than six months (I think) after I went to the trade, the establishment was destroyed by fire, and we were thrown out of the coachmaking business; and the tavern next door to where my master lived being vacant by the absconding of the landlord, he moved into it and continued there, if I am not mistaken, till the spring of 1795, when our shops were all completed, and we moved into a house adjoining them.

While at the tavern I served in the capacity of lackey, shoeblack, hostler, and bar-tender; too often exposed to the worst of company, to see that kind of conduct that debases rational beings below brutality, and blots out of their very nature all that is good and beautiful. And what increased the evil, it was the time of what is called the Western expedition, when there was a great deal of military parade and excitement. But in the midst of all this exposure the heavenly Shepherd, under whose care a dying mother had left me, extended the crook of His love, and preserved me from gross evils, awakening at times serious impressions, particularly at the death of my mistress's first born child, a dear little girl that I had attended much, and for whom I felt a strong attachment.

I very well remember the tender sympathy, sorrow, and love I felt on the occasion, especially for my mistress, who appeared to be very solemnly and seriously impressed. Our feelings being similar, it caused a spiritual attachment or love, that has continued down to the present day, and I hope will extend beyond the confines of time into a never ending eternity. I think that my mistress was qualified to be such a woman as is described in the last chapter of Proverbs.

Although I was removed from the tavern when about fifteen,

and employed steadily in the coachmaking business, I was unfortunately introduced to those places of diversion called cutting apple frolics, spinning frolics, raffling matches, and indeed all kind of low convivial parties, so peculiarly calculated to nourish the seeds of vanity and lies. Thus the garden of my heart was too soon overrun with those noxious weeds—licentiousness, intemperance, angry passions, and devilishness, which obstruct the growth of those precious plants of the Heavenly Father's right hand planting: virtue, knowledge, temperance, patience, and godliness. Hence it was I entered the wide gate, and was travelling in the broad way that leads to destruction. . . .

This appears to me to have been the most critical period of my life, when growing up from a boy to a man, and forming the channel in which life was to run, if not determining its everlasting issue.

And what increased the tremendous danger of a poor weak youth, was the free use of spirituous liquors; for it was then the ridiculous custom of those who got new carriages to treat the hands with liquor, sometimes three or four gallons; and, during my seven years' apprenticeship, I do not know that there was a day when there was not more or less liquor about; but although I used it freely with my shopmates, through mercy I was preserved from forming the distressing artificial appetite of the habitual drunkard; for it appears that intemperance was not my besetting sin, and, therefore, I claim but little merit for my temperate habits; though I may say, what too few can say, that I have used no spirituous liquors as a drink in private, in company, or in business for near forty years, and but very seldom as a medicine.

But licentious lewdness was much more a besetting sin, and my preservation from ruin in this way appears to me as a miracle, for I certainly indulged in licentious thoughts till their corrupting tendency led to what was still worse, lewd conversation; and had I broken through the barriers of virtue, I have reason to believe, from the strength of my passion and the weakness of my resolution, I should have plunged into that vortex of dissipation that might have sealed my eternal ruin. . . .

On this subject I would wish to say more, but am at a loss to find language sufficiently chaste and sufficiently forcible adequately to set forth what I feel. Suffice it to say I was introduced by lechers and debauchees into the worst of company and the worst of places, both in city and country. . . .

Although I had scarcely reached my eighteenth year, the sound of war being heard in our land, I enrolled myself as a soldier, delighted with the martial music, and the feathered foppery of the regimentaled dandy.

Had I at this time obtained a commission in the army, I might have followed my companions to an untimely grave.

But in the midst of all this sanguine cheer, and streamers gay, when I had cut my cable and launched into the world, my SAVIOUR did not forsake me, for I was not a reprobate, therefore he was still *in* me, and had only retired as it were to the hinder part of my little ship, and was apparently asleep. For when about the twentieth year of my age a terrible storm of sickness overtook me whilst on a frolic in the city of Philadelphia, and when my poor frail bark was sinking beneath the waves, I awoke my Saviour by my cries, and he arose and rebuked the direful disease that was ready to overwhelm my life, and I was again restored to health. Yet, notwithstanding all my promises to live a better life, such was my strong passion for music, dancing, and singing, that I was participating in all those amusements before I was able to leave the city, and ride home. Poor sanguine young man. Peter like, I was a swearer and a liar, but I was not yet ready, like Peter, to weep bitterly for sin.

My seven years' apprenticeship having expired when I was twenty, I hired as a journeyman with my old masters, Henry and William Tomlinson, and continued with them about four months, when I set up coach and house painting for myself in the place of my birth and apprenticeship; but such was my want of stability and almost every other qualification to fit me for business, that I am much astonished that I should have been employed. Yet I was employed and encouraged by respectable people, for the character of my family gave me a standing that I certainly did not merit, being in my own estimation a weak, wayward young man, susceptible of strong and tender attachments, especially to young women, of whom I had a number of favorites, and was excessively fond of their society. But they know and I know that we were innocent, and I continue to feel a brotherly affection for those who are still living.

In the fall of 1800 I went to work for Doctor Fenton at painting his house. He was a superior physician, a great mechanical genius, and to me a very agreeable and interesting man.

We soon agreed that when the weather got too cold to paint, I should come and assist him in making a new fashioned carriage. In the beginning of winter I went to live with him, and found a very agreeable home. His wife was one of those excellent women spoken of in the Scriptures, "She looketh well to the ways of her household, and eateth not the bread of idleness." They had but one child, who was an interesting little girl ten or twelve years old. They were Presbyterians, but not sour Calvinists, and I went with them to their meeting.

One day the Doctor proposed to me, in his familiar way, that I had better join their church. And as an inducement, observed that he would then use his influence in my forming an advantageous marriage with a very rich and respectable elder's daughter, who was an heiress, independent of her father. Whether he was in earnest or not I must leave.

I think I told him that I had no idea that I would ever be worthy to join any religious society, but if I should think myself fit, I should join the Quakers. He expressed his astonishment that a young man of my turn would think of joining so simple and lifeless a people, and if it ever took place he should think that miracles had not ceased; making some further remarks unfavorable to Friends, which produced excitement and brought on considerable argument, ending, in all probability as such arguments mostly do, in both of us thinking we were right. . . .

I was now approaching my twenty-first year, and had left the volunteer company I belonged to, and was in fact under the preparing hand for a change. I had often serious and even sorrowful thoughts, when alone, and was disgusted with myself and all my conduct, though I could not find that I had ever done an act which, if published before an earthly tribunal, would leave a stain on my moral character in the sight of men. But I continued exceedingly fond of singing, dancing, vain amusements, and the company of young people, and too often profanely swearing when angry or excited, although my associates were more respectable than formerly.

In the latter part of winter I went to Philadelphia on horseback, and returned through a snow-storm in company with a young friend who has since sat by my side in meeting for more than twenty years in the station of an elder. I believe the young man was almost ashamed of his company, for I sung all the way home, besides stopping at several taverns to drink. Being wet, weary, and hungry, I eat a hearty supper and went early to bed. About midnight I was awakened with the same alarming symptoms I was attacked with a year before in the city, when I was only saved from death by a miracle. The thoughts of the promises I then made and broke, and inexpressible pain and distress produced a horror which I cannot describe. My friend the doctor gave my body relief, but my mind was too solemnly impressed to be cured by anything but a heavenly physician. From this time my appearance was somewhat changed from a sanguine to a melancholy cast, and my friend the doctor told me that my frequently sighing was indicative of the approach of a serious disease, either of body or mind, and would sometimes exercise his wit to rally me off. . . .

I was now disposed rather to shun than to court young company, and spent my First days* in rambling about by myself in solitary places.

In one of these excursions I found myself within reach of Friends' meeting at Middletown, and went to it, and though I had often been there, I do not recollect that I had been at that meeting since my serious turn. Be that as it may, I think I had a precious meeting, for I continued to walk five miles to that meeting every First day, while I lived with Doctor Fenton in Northampton.

About this time I was solicited to join a respectable young friend in carrying on the coachmaking business in Milford, six or seven miles from where I then lived, and I went there to see the place, and make some arrangement. I mention this to show the state of my mind. I think I wept nearly all the way there, and yet when introduced into the company of some very re-

* Sundays.

spectable young friends, who asked me to sing, I sung for them the greater part of the night, and then went weeping home next day. It was astonishing that in company I could not refrain from my wonted cheerfulness and vivacity, when by myself I was so serious as to weep and pray.

Soon after this I went to the city on some business, and met one of my old companions, who appeared to be pleased to see me, and told me that a mutual friend, who played well on the violin, had got a new one, which he played admirably. I went with him with some reluctance, but the delightful music soon raised my natural vivacity; and I attempted, in company with two partners, to go through with a country dance. Whether I went through or not I almost forget, but I know that this was the last time I ever danced. Leaving this place and passing down the street with a heavy heart, I was overtaken by one of my juvenile companions, and an old fellow soldier, a young man of superior talents but of profligate character. He was pleased to see me, and began to talk in his usual way, but soon felt or saw that something ailed me, for I was different from what I used to be, and he left me. After my return home I quit singing, and was brought into a strait about using the plural language, and found a difficulty in adopting the plain *thee* and *thou*. As to dress I had no trouble, for I always admired a plain dress for either man or woman.

I have often thought I should have got along better had I continued to live with the Presbyterians, for then I should have kept more to myself, and been with Friends at their meetings, and only occasionally at their houses. But living altogether amongst respectable, political, worldly-minded Quakers, and, above all, being treated by them with kindness and attention, was certainly too much for such a poor, weak, trifling young man as I was, and I think proved a serious disadvantage to my spiritual state.

On the 27th of the 8th month, 1801, I went to Milford to live, and to assist Joshua C. Canby, in the coachmaking business, making my home with Samuel Hulme, one of those excellent men, who are a blessing to the neighborhood where their lot is cast, and an honor to the society to which they belong; a man whose cheerfulness and patience under the heaviest afflictions, I never saw exceeded. I owe much to that dear friend for his many acts of brotherly kindness towards me, when a poor, weak, unworthy young man. This debt I have tried to discharge by endeavoring to do to others that which he did unto me. . . .

In the fall of 1801, I agreed with my employer, Joshua C. Canby, to work at the coachmaking business, particularly the painting, for thirteen dollars per month, and he to find me my board and lodging, and give me every Fifth-day, from 9 until 2 o'clock, so that I might go to meeting, which was about two and a-half miles. I went to Middletown meeting. I had to walk, and, I think, for forty years, I have no recollection of missing a mid-week meeting, when I was well enough to go, and had I been as faithful in every thing that was required of me, I have thought I should have come out in the ministry, about the 22d year of my age. But I was unfaithful in little things, and therefore was never made ruler over much, and the impetuous waves of youthful passion, too often carried the weak, wayward young man out of the straight and narrow way, and greatly increased the difficulty of his probationary journey.

It seems unnecessary to say much, if any thing, about my business as a mechanic, for I think it has always been marked with weakness.

Early in the spring of 1803, I applied to the overseers of Middletown Monthly Meeting, to be received into membership with Friends. I was received with open arms, and the dear old Friends that were appointed to visit me, have left a savor of sweetness upon my mind. I love to think of them and hope to meet them in heaven.

On the 17th of 11th month, of the same year, I was married to Sarah, the second daughter of Joseph and Susannah Worstall, of this town, near neighbors to my father, and their daughter was the first object of my youthful affection, even whilst I was a child. I loved her with that love which an all-wise Creator has placed in every perfect nature and rational man, for a wise and good purpose, and she has conferred on me as much natural and rational happiness as any man ought to have in this world, and after a union of forty years, I am thankful in being able to say that I feel an increasing love for her, and a daily prayer that our immortal spirits may be prepared for the enjoyment of GOD in glory.

In the spring of 1804, we settled in Milford, living in a small house, for we were poor, and I had not wherewith to build or purchase, and better might it have been for us if I had not been persuaded to borrow money and build a house, when I was not able to pay for it. This was the commencement of serious pecuniary embarrassments, and having learned from the things I have suffered, I am prepared to give or leave this advice to who ever may read it, when I am gone into the eternal world: NEVER GO IN DEBT—NEVER BORROW MONEY. BE HUMBLE—BE INDUSTRIOUS, YOUR WANTS WILL THEN BE FEW, AND YOUR INDUSTRY WILL MORE THAN SUPPLY THEM.

It would be as unnecessary as it would be uninteresting, to go into a detail of the discouragements and difficulties I had to pass through; suffice it to say, my debts and dealings brought me in contact with selfish men, and my want of capacity made me a kind of prey for them. This had a tendency to chafe and sour me, and I soon got into a state like the man in the fable, who got his neighbors' faults and his own into a wallet, but in putting it on his shoulder he got his own faults behind and his neighbors' before his eyes, where he could always see them. Thus I got to be a great talker, and a great fault finder, and, if I remember right, joined a debating society, read news papers, particularly the speeches of members of Congress, went to elections, talked politics; but keeping to meeting, Friends put me forward into an office I was unfit for; a mistake that Leah-eyed friends are too apt to make, to the great injury of the individual and the cause of truth. I was moreover a very zealous temperance man, and of course denounced every one, particularly Friends, who sold or used distilled spirituous liquors; for, a short time before I had built a house without finding one drop, and I believe it was the first that was built without spirituous liquor, in the lower section of Bucks county. . . .

On the 16th of the Fourth month, 1811, we moved to Newtown, where at that time, comparatively speaking, every tenth house was a tavern, and every twentieth of bad report.

I think there were not more than about four or five families of Friends in Newtown and its vicinity, no meeting of Friends nor hardly such a thing thought of. No coachmaking and very little mechanical business of any kind, for the people of the place seemed principally to depend upon the courts and the spoil of litigious contention. The lawyers, county officers, and principal men of the place, were mostly *free masons*, among whom religion and morals were at a very low ebb. . . .

I have travelled considerably in several States of the Union, and once into Canada, and I now verily believe for the most part—with the exception of my Canadian journey—it had been better to have done as I think others had better have done, learnt the subjection of my own will at home, endeavoring to be a consistent Christian minister, a loving and faithful husband, an affectionate father, saying daily to my children, in the silent but powerful language of example, "follow me as I follow CHRIST;" in a word, filling up with propriety all the social and relative duties of life that constitute the crown and diadem of a perfect man, and in order to this essential attainment of a perfect gospel minister, followed my blessed Saviour more steadily, in the path of humble industry. I should then have never needed the assistance of my friends in a pecuniary way, a circumstance that has been the greatest yoke of bondage upon my Christian liberty, caused the most sleepless nights and wearisome days, and, in a word, the most heartfelt sorrow of all the sins I ever committed. And O, young man, especially a minister, who may read this, take my advice, NEVER GO IN DEBT—NEVER BORROW MONEY. But if thou doest, be sure to exert thyself to the utmost in the path of humble industry to pay the utmost farthing; remembering that no man or woman can ever become the child of God, much less his minister, whilst they trample under foot with impunity, Justice, one of his divine attributes.

If I had my time to go over again I would try strictly to obey the advice in our excellent discipline and so scrupulously live within the bounds of my circumstances, that if I earned but twenty cents per day I would live on ten or fifteen. Oh! this borrowing money and then borrowing again to pay the interest, or leaving it unpaid until the avaricious monster, usury, comes upon the poor debtor with accumulated ruin. . . .

In addition to a constitutional weakness, I quit the only business I understood, and for which I had a capacity, viz. painting, for the business of a farmer, which I did not understand, and for which I had no qualifications whatever. I verily thought then, and still think, *farming* more consistent with the Christian, and was willing to sacrifice all my fondness for painting. But it would not do, for notwithstanding I worked hard, I went behind hand daily. The cruel moth of usury was eating up my outward garment, soon to expose me a poor naked bankrupt; for my father, who I thought had given me forty acres of land n the vicinity of the village, altered his mind and took it from ne, leaving me with only twenty acres, for which I had given eighty-six dollars per acre at public sale, and which I had to sell for forty dollars. Thus ended my farming speculation.

If the Christian world was in the real spirit of *Christ,* I do not believe there would be such a thing as a fine painter in christendom. It appears clearly to me to be one of those trifling, insignificant arts, which has never been of any substantial advantage to mankind. But as the inseparable companion of voluptuousness and pride, it has presaged the downfall of empires and kingdoms; and in my view stands now enrolled among the premonitory symptoms of the rapid decline of the American Republic. But there is something of importance in the example of the primitive Christians and primitive Quakers, to mind their callings or business, and work with their own hands at such business as they are capable of, avoiding idleness and fanaticism. Had I had my time to go over again I think I would take the advice given me by my old friend Abraham Chapman, a shrewd, sensible lawyer that lived with me about the time I was quitting painting; "Edward, thee has now the source of independence within thyself, in thy peculiar talent for painting. Keep to it, within the bounds of innocence and usefulness, and thee can always be comfortable.". . .

But I am writing too much and saying too little, and had better mind my own business, which if I am not mistaken is to bear a simple, child-like testimony to this mercy and goodness . . . which will subject me to be pitied by the wise and prudent of this world, as a fool, or ridiculed as an enthusiast; my doctrine considered madness, and my end without honor. Yet I would not part with this child-like belief . . . for ten thousand times ten thousand worlds. . . .

CHESTER HARDING

(1792–1866)

My Egotistigraphy. By Chester Harding. Prepared for his Family and Friends by One of his Children. Press of John Wilson and Son, Cambridge, 1866. 185 pp.

An ingenious, entertaining, lighthearted title! In a long career as a portrait painter, Chester Harding studied and read many and various faces; he learned about ego and self-esteem and the motives that brought men and women to his studio to have their likenesses painted. What could be more natural, then, than that when the time came to record his own immortality, he should take a philosophical view and accept cheerfully the egotism necessary for writing about one's self. He invented a word for this kind of writing—egotistigraphy.

Harding won popular success while still a young man. In earlier years he had been desperately poor, but by the time he was thirty-one he had made enough money to go to Europe and still leave his family provided for. Age thirty-one was as far as he got in writing his *Egotistigraphy*. A daughter pieced out the rest of his story from diaries he kept and "a few particulars" he added.

A "particular," from 1827 in Boston, that I like especially is: "Among the sitters I had at this time was Timothy Pickering, of Salem. He was far advanced in years, but as bright in intellect as a man of thirty. His conversation was extremely interesting, though it mostly pertained to the early days of our Government. One day, I felt a strong desire to know how a man would feel who knew that his allotted time was nearly spent, and thought I might venture to put the question to him; so I said, 'You have lived beyond the average of human life: how do you feel upon the subject of the final departure to the other world?' His reply was, 'It was only the other day I was asking old Dr. Holyoke the same question.' The doctor was some ten years his senior."

Harding moved to Springfield, Massachusetts, in 1830. His wife, whom he married in 1815, and who bore him three daughters and six sons, died in 1845. When the Civil War came, two sons fought for the Union, two for the Confederacy.

In 1952 the Connecticut Valley Historical Museum of Springfield mounted an exhibition of his work, which it called the most comprehensive ever assembled.

Harding's daughter and editor, Margaret E. White, described him as "measuring six feet three inches in his stockings; while his frame was so finely proportioned, that his size was not fully appreciated until compared with that of an average-sized man. His muscular power was prodigious. . . . His hands and feet were so large, that he was obliged to import his gloves, and to have his boots made for him. The width between his eyes was such, that an ordinary pair of spectacles would but half cover them. During the later years of his life, he wore a full beard, which, as well as his hair, was almost white. . . . A few months before his death, he sat to an artist as a model for the head of St. Peter."

Privately printed, *My Egotistigraphy* is a rare book. A second edition, shorn of its lively title and called instead, *A Sketch of Chester Harding, Artist* . . . printed in Boston in 1890, is also scarce. So is a sumptuous "new edition" of *A Sketch of Chester Harding, Artist* . . . "with annotations by his grandson, W. P. G. Harding," Boston, 1929.

The following chapters are those that Harding himself completed.

MY EGOTISTIGRAPHY

CHAPTER I.

Of my ancestors I know nothing beyond my grandparents. My paternal grandfather was a substantial farmer in Deerfield, Mass. He lived in a two-story house, which to my youthful imagination was a palace; filled many offices of profit and trust in the town, lived to a good old age, and was gathered to his fathers with the universal respect of his neighbors.

On the maternal side, I can go no further back. My grandfather Smith was a farmer, who lived to a ripe old age, and died much respected. For many years he held the office of deacon, in the town of Whately, where he resided. I was born in the adjoining town of Conway, on the 1st of September, 1792.

My parents were poor; and, of course, I was brought up like all other poor children of that period. My first recollection is of our moving from Conway to Hatfield. I well remember the brook that ran close by the house we lived in there, and the amusement I had in catching the little fishes with a pin-hook. As I grew older, I began to fish with a real hook, and to catch trout. Like most boys of my age, I thought more of "going a-fishing" than of all other indulgences. Indeed it amounted almost to a passion with me. I would go miles on an errand, or do any amount of service, for a penny or two, that I might be able to buy my fishhooks.

From the age of eight to ten, I lived in Bernardston, with an aunt. Here again I had a brook that constantly enticed me from my daily duties, which consisted chiefly of the care of a flock of young geese. I played truant nearly every day, and as often was whipped by my aunt. I returned home at the end of two years. We were very poor, and were often in need of the necessaries of life. My father was a good man, of unexceptionable habits; but he was not thrifty, and did little towards the support of the family. He had a great inventive genius, and turned all his powers towards the discovery of perpetual motion. At the time of his death, his attic was full of machines, the making of which had occupied a large part of his life. But this brought no bread and butter to his hungry children.

One hard winter he went to Northfield, Mass., to get work, where my mother supposed he was earning something for the maintenance of the family. While there, he had the small-pox; and all the work he did was to make the body of a very large bass-viol. Imagine the disappointment of his family when they found that this monster skeleton was all he had brought home to them!

My mother was a noble woman. In all the trials of poverty, she managed to keep her children decently dressed, that they might go to meeting on Sunday, and make a respectable appearance among other boys. It is true our more prosperous cousins rather turned up their noses at us now and then, much to our mortification.

At the age of twelve, I was hired out at six dollars a month, to a Mr. Graves, in Hatfield. He was a good and religious man. I lived with him two years. I went to school in the winter, and learned to read enough to read the Bible. I partook largely of the religious sentiment that pervaded the family. I said my prayers night and morning, and was deemed a model boy. At the age of fourteen, my father moved to the western part of New-York State, into Madison County, than an unbroken wilderness. Now began my hard work and harder fare. Our first business was to build a log-house, and to clear a patch of ground, and fit it for seed. I had two brothers older than myself, the oldest of whom was a chair-maker by trade, and made common flag-bottomed chairs for the neighbors. By this means we could get an occasional piece of pork, some flour and potatoes; whilst my father and his other boys wielded the axe,—that great civilizer.

We finished the house, and in the spring we had a few acres felled and ready for burning. We planted corn and potatoes amongst the blackened stumps; fortunately, the crop needed no labor beyond that of planting. Before the season was far spent, we were all down with chills and fever. We managed somehow to live through that year, which was the hardest we had ever seen. I grew strong, and was distinguished for my skill in using the axe. I could lift a larger log than any one else, and, in short, at eighteen was considered a prodigy of strength. Our means for intellectual development were very scant. Our parents would sometimes read the Bible to us, the only book we had in the house; and occasionally we were blessed with a visit from some itinerant preacher, when the whole forest settlement would meet in some large building, either the schoolhouse or a barn, and listen to his divine teachings. At nineteen I changed my mode of life. I began to think there might be an easier way of getting a living than by cutting down and clearing up the heavily timbered forest, and worked one winter with my brother at turning stuff for chairs.

About this time, war was declared between the United States and Great Britain.* A military spirit was aroused throughout the whole of Western New York, and I imbibed as much of it as any one. I had become a distinguished drummer, and had drummed for pay, until I was obliged to do military duty. My brother, next younger than myself, was one of the first to enlist in the service for one year. The troops were soon called to active service at Oswego. After six months he was anxious to return home. I offered myself, and was accepted as a substitute. As he was a drummer, I could easily fill his place.

Nothing of importance broke in upon the monotony of camp-life until mid-winter, when we were ordered to prepare three days' provisions, and to march next morning for Sacket's Harbor. The snow was very deep, and the weather cold; yet the days of our march were holidays, when compared to camp-life. We committed many depredations on our way, such as stealing chickens, or, on rare occasions, a pig. I was on the rear section of the column one day, and with another soldier had fallen so far behind, that we had lost sight of the troops. Being uncertain which of two roads to take, we applied at a house which was near, for directions. "Oh!" said the woman, "you have only to follow the feathers."

Sacket's Harbor was threatened with an attack by the British. They had a considerable force in Canada, nearly opposite; and the lake at that point was completely frozen over. We were

* War of 1812.

constantly drilled, and kept in readiness for an attack. We had several alarms, and were often drummed out at midnight to face the foe; but he was only found in the imagination of the frightened sentinel.

Sickness now began to thin our ranks. Every hour in the day, some poor fellow would be followed to Briarfield; and the tune, "Away goes the merryman home to his grave," played on returning from the burial, was too often heard to leave the listeners indifferent to its notes. My turn came at last, and I was taken down with the prevailing disease, dysentery; but my lieutenant took me to his own quarters, instead of sending me to the hospital. He was my neighbor, and in this instance proved himself to be one in the Scripture sense. Had I gone to the hospital, I should probably have shared the fate of nearly all who went there, and have been carried to Briarfield. As soon as I recovered sufficient strength to get home, I was discharged, as my time of service was nearly up.

I suffered intensely on my way home. I was thinly clad, without overcoat or gloves. I started from camp with a lad who was taking back a horse that an officer had ridden to Sacket's Harbor: he was warmly clothed and of a very robust make. We travelled on, until I began to feel a good deal fatigued. We at last came to a house where we had been told we could find accommodation. We arrived there just at dusk; and, to our dismay, were told by the master of the house, that he could not keep us, and that he had nothing on hand for either man or beast to eat. It was six miles to the next house, and the road lay on the beach of the lake, exposed to the piercing winds which blew over it. We started off, I on foot as before, while the boy was mounted. I had to run to keep warm. At length we came in sight of a light; but what was our dismay to find an open river between us and it! I shouted to the utmost capacity of my lungs, but could get no response. What was to be done? Nothing, but to return to the shelter we had left an hour and a half before. I started back at the same speed I came; but, before we had gone half the distance, my strength gave out, leaving me no other alternative but to mount the horse with the boy. I soon found myself getting very cold, and a strong desire to go to sleep came over me. I looked at the thick clumps of evergreen that stood by our path, and thought seriously of lying down under one of them to wait until daylight. The boy was crying, and begged me to keep on, saying, "If you lie down there, you will freeze to death," which would indeed have been inevitable. I yielded to his entreaties, and we finally reached the house we had left three hours before. The boy was not much frozen, but I was badly bitten. My face, hands, and thighs were stiff. After a good deal of rapping and hallooing, the door was opened. The man of the house had been used to such scenes, and knew well what to do. He put my feet into cold water, at the same time making applications to my face, ears, and legs. Mortal never suffered more acute pain than I did through that sleepless night. I experienced the truth of our host's statement with regard to provisions. The next day at noon, we started again on our perilous journey, having been assured that we were mistaken about the river being open. Travelling more leisurely than we had done the previous night, we reached the river again; and, owing to the intense cold, it was covered with a thin coat of ice, but not thick enough to bear a man in an upright position. I got a long pole, and, by putting myself in a swimming posture, reached the opposite shore in safety, though it was frightful to feel the ice, not much thicker than a pane of window-glass, bending under me. At the house, I was told that the crossing was half a mile back. I recrossed the river; and, retracing our steps a mile, we found a blind road leading over the bluff, which soon took us in safety to a comfortable house, where we found enough to eat for ourselves and our horse. The next day I started for my home, where my sufferings were soon forgotten. I speedily recovered, and went to work with my brother. We had a contract for drum-making from the United States, which gave us employment all the following summer.

Early in the fall of this year, I embarked in a new business. A mechanic had invented and patented a spinning-head, which was thought to be a great improvement upon the old plan. I accepted an offer he made me to sell the patent in the State of Connecticut. The only thing in the way of my making a fortune was the want of capital. However, "where there's a will, there's a way." I soon contrived to get a horse and wagon, and five or six dollars in money, besides a quantity of essences, such as pepper-mint, tanzy, winter-green, &c. With this fit-out I launched forth into the wide world in pursuit of fortune. There is no period in the history of a young man which awakens so many of the finer feelings of his nature as that when he leaves his home, and for the first time assumes the position and responsibility of an independent man. All the joyful recollections of that home he is about to leave, no matter how humble it is, rush with overwhelming force upon his susceptible heart. I started with all the firmness and resolution I could call to my aid; yet, if my mother could have looked into my eyes, she would have seen them filled with big tears. I jumped into my wagon, whipped up my horse, and was soon out of sight of what, at that moment, seemed all the world to me.

I managed, in view of my small stock of money, to get along without drawing largely upon it. I often bartered my essences for a night's entertainment, and was going on swimmingly, until I came to a small town on the banks of the Mohawk. I stopped to bait my horse; and, as I was about to start, a man with a bundle of clothing in his hand wanted to get a ride as far as the next town, for which he would give me twenty-five cents. I, of course, was glad to avail myself of his offer. We had travelled perhaps a mile, when we overtook two men by the roadside, in violent dispute about a pack of cards. One was very drunk. My new friend proposed, that we should stop, and inquire into the rights of the case: so I pulled up. The drunken man was contending, that he had won a quarter of a dollar of the other; whereupon he proceeded to show us how it was done. He had bet that the top card was the jack of clubs, and was willing to bet again that the top card was the jack of clubs; at the same time showing, as if by accident, that it was on the bottom of the pack. My friend bet him a quarter, that it was not on the top; and won. He fixed his cards again very clumsily, as he was very drunk. I bet, and won. I bet a half next time; so did my friend: we lost. We now accused him of heaving two jacks in the pack, and my friend examined the pack, but found only one; and that he managed to drop into the bottom of the wagon, and covered it with his foot. The cards were again shuffled. We had no scruples about betting on a certainty, as it was to get our money back, so we each bet a dollar, but lost. In some mysterious manner the card had been taken from under the foot. There was nothing to be done but to bear this loss as well as I could; and we started on, very sad. My companion had lost every cent he had in the world. He had a loaded whip, worth two or three dollars, that he urged me to buy. In pity for the poor fellow I gave him his price, when he suddenly recollected that he had left something at the tavern, and must go back. He soon overtook the two worthies we had just left, and all three joined in a hearty laugh. My eyes were instantly opened. I clenched my new whip, determined to go back and thrash the scoundrels; but, as they were three to one, I finally thought better of it. I firmly believe, that, if I had gone back, I should have killed one of them at least, with my loaded whip. I travelled on, not much in love with myself. I bore the loss of the money better than I did the way in which it was lost. This lesson has never been forgotten. I finally reached Connecticut, the field of my future operations. I returned with more money than I started with, and had a surplus of fifty or sixty wooden clocks and several watches, which I had taken for the patent in different parts of the State.

Near the close of the war, my brother (younger than myself) and I went into the cabinet and chair manufactory in Caledonia, a small town in Livingstone County, N.Y.

At this juncture, I happened to meet with Caroline Woodruff, a lovely girl of twenty, with handsome, dark eyes, fine brunette complexion, and of an amiable disposition. I fell in love with her at first sight. I can remember the dress she wore at our first meeting as well as I do those beautiful eyes. It was a dark crimson, woollen dress, with a neat little frill about the neck. I saw but little of her; for the family soon moved to a distance of forty or fifty miles. Though she was absent, however, her image was implanted too deeply in my heart to be forgotten. It haunted me day and night. At length I took the resolution to go to see her; which was at once carried out. I set out on foot, found her and proposed, and was bid to wait a while for my answer. I went again, in the same way, and this time had the happiness to be accepted; and, three weeks after, she became my wife, and accompanied me to my home. We had hardly reached it before I was sued for a small debt, which I

could not meet: in short, business was not very flourishing, and
we were much embarrassed.

To relieve myself, I went into an entirely new business—that
of tavern-keeping. Here I paid off some old debts by making
new ones. Matters, however, did not improve: on the contrary,
creditors grew more clamorous and threatening. Nothing could
strike me with more horror than the thought of being shut up in
Batavia Jail. At that time the barbarous practice of imprisonment for debt was in full force. My mind was made up. On
Saturday night, I took leave of my wife and child, and left for
the head waters of the Alleghany River. As soon as the river
opened, I took passage on a raft, and worked my way down to
Pittsburg. Here I was at a loss what to do. Times were hard;
and, besides, I was not a good enough mechanic to get employment at the only trade I knew any thing of. I finally got a job at
house-painting; but I felt lonely and unhappy. As soon as I had
saved a few dollars, I started for my wife and child. I walked
over mountains, and through wild forests, with no guide but the
blazed trees. Bears, wolves, deer, and turkeys I met so often,
that I would hardly turn around to look at them. At last I
reached the settlement within a few miles of Caledonia. Here I
halted till night, thinking it safer to travel by moonlight than in
broad day. As it grew dark, I started, tired and foot-sore. I saw
a horse grazing in the road, and the thought struck me that he
could ease my weary limbs. I succeeded in catching and mounting him; and, by means of my staff or walking-stick, I steered
him to the street of Caledonia. I then turned him on his way
home, and bade him goodnight. I remained in close concealment three or four days, and, when all was ready, started again
for the head waters of the Alleghany, but not alone: this time
my wife and child were with me. We experienced many hardships on our way, but nothing of particular interest occurred.
At Orleans Point we embarked upon a raft, with a comfortable
shanty on board, and in a week floated down the river to Pittsburg. Before I had left Pittsburg, I had rented a tenfooter, with
two rooms in it: so we went directly there. All our availables
consisted of one bed, and a chest of clothing, and some cooking
utensils; so that we had little labor in getting settled down.

But now all my money was gone, and how to get more was

the question. I could find no work as a house-painter, and what to do I did not know. I would walk about the town, and return to find my wife in tears,—though she always had a smile for me. I went into the market the next morning, though for what purpose I could hardly tell; for I had not one cent of money. At last I ventured to ask the price of a beefsteak. I had the impudence to say to the man, that I should like that piece very much, but that I had no change with me. To my great surprise, he said I could take it, and pay for it the next time I came. As I had made the acquaintance of Mr. Sands, a barber who occupied the twin part of the house I was in, I went to his wife, and asked her to loan me half a loaf of bread, which she did cheerfully. If we went hungry that day, it was not because we had not enough to eat, and that, too, with an honest appetite.

There was an opening just now for a sign-painter. I had talked with Neighbor Sands upon the subject of my becoming one. He approved the plan, and was the means of my getting an order. A Mr. W. H. Wetherell wanted a sign painted in gold letters on both sides, so as to project it into the street. I agreed to do it; but where was the stock of gold paint and board to come from? I went into Neighbor Sands' half a dozen times, for the purpose of asking him to lend me the money to procure the materials, and as often my heart failed me. At last I made a grand effort, and said, "Neighbor Sands, I wish you would lend me twenty dollars for a few days, as I have no money by me that is current."—"Certainly, with pleasure." I could hardly believe it real. I took the money, and hurried into my room, and threw it into my wife's lap. She was frightened, fearing I had obtained it by some unlawful means. The first use I made of it was to go to the market, and to pay the credulous butcher; and to buy some vegetables, tea, sugar, and some other little luxuries. I got my signboard made, bought my gold leaf, paints, &c.; went to a printer, and got some very large impressions of the alphabet; and, having in my chair-making experience learned the art of gilding, I soon had my sign finished, and paid back my neighbor his money. He never knew that I was not flush of money; but his kindness I never forgot. I was at once established as a sign-painter, and followed that trade for a year.

CHAPTER II.

About this time, I fell in with a portrait-painter by the name of Nelson,—one of the primitive sort. He was a sign, ornamental, and portrait painter. He had for his sign a copy of the "Infant Artists" of Sir Joshua Reynolds, with this inscription, "Sign, Ornamental, and Portrait Painting executed on the shortest notice, with neatness and despatch." It was in his sanctum that I first conceived the idea of painting heads. I saw his portraits, and was enamored at once. I got him to paint me and my wife, and thought the pictures perfection. He would not let me see him paint, nor would he give me the least idea how the thing was done. I took the pictures home, and pondered on them, and wondered how it was possible for a man to produce such wonders of art. At length my admiration began to yield to an ambition to do the same thing. I thought of it by day, and dreamed of it by night, until I was stimulated to make an attempt at painting myself. I got a board; and, with such colors as I had for use in my trade, I began a portrait of my wife. I made a thing that looked like her. The moment I saw the likeness, I became frantic with delight: it was like the discovery of a new sense; I could think of nothing else. From that time, sign-painting became odious, and was much neglected.

I next painted a razeed portrait of an Englishman who was a journeyman baker, for which I received five dollars. He sent it to his mother in London. I also painted portraits of the man and his wife with whom I boarded, and for which I received, on account, twelve dollars each. This was in the winter season: the river was closed, and there was but little to be done in sign-painting.

I shall always remember the friendship of an Irish apothecary, who, at this period of my history, encouraged me in my attempts at portrait-painting, and allowed me to buy any materials I needed, on credit, from his paint and drug store. I had been painting a second picture of my wife, and asked Nelson the painter to come and see it. He declared it to be no more like my wife than like him, and said further that it was utter nonsense for me to try to paint portraits at my time of life: he had been ten years in learning the trade. To receive such a lecture, and such utter condemnation of my work, when I expected encouragement and approval, was truly disheartening. He left me; and I was still sitting before the picture, in great dejection, when my friend the doctor came in. He instantly exclaimed, with much apparent delight, "That's good; first-rate, a capital likeness," &c. I then repeated what Nelson had just said. He replied that it was sheer envy; that he never painted half so good a head, and never would. The tide of hope began to flow again, and I grew more and more fond of head-painting. I now regarded sign-painting merely as a necessity, while my whole soul was wrapped up in my new love; and neglected my trade so much that I was kept pretty short of money. I resorted to every means to eke out a living. I sometimes played the clarionet for a tight-rope dancer, and on market-days would play at the window of the museum to attract the crowd to the exhibition. For each of these performances I would get a dollar.

I was strictly temperate in my habits, and seldom spent a sixpence for any thing that we did not actually need; but I remember one occasion when my love of music and excitement got the better of my prudence. I had gone out one evening to borrow a dollar to go to market with the next morning, when, as I was sauntering about, I heard music, which attracted me to the spot. It was the performance of the orchestra of the theatre. It was a temporary building, loosely boarded; and as I looked through the cracks of the covering, I saw such a sight as I had never dreamed of. I went instantly to the door, got a ticket, and crowded my way in. By degrees, I managed to get into a box which was full. I stood for the first hour in perfect amazement at the lords and ladies, and was overwhelmed by the brilliant lights and heavenly music. At the end of one of the acts, one of the gentlemen left his seat, and went out; and I took it. He came back, and claimed his seat. I was not inclined to admit his claim. I had paid my dollar, and told him I thought I had as good a right to a seat as he had; and that he could as well stand an hour as I. He prepared to eject me by force; but, as I unfolded my dimensions, he relinquished his purpose, and bore the loss of his seat as well as he could. I did not leave the theatre until the last lamp was extinguished. The play which had so enchanted me was Scott's "Lady of the Lake." This was my first acquaintance with the stage. I do not remember how we fared the next day in our marketing; but I presume I borrowed another dollar in the morning.

Up to this time, I had never read any book but the Bible, and could only read that with difficulty. My wife, who had received a comparatively good education, and had once taught school, borrowed of one of the neighbors "The Children of the Abbey," a popular novel of that day. I was rather opposed to her reading it, as I had been taught to believe by my mother, that cards and novels were the chief instruments of the Devil in seducing mortals from the paths of virtue. However, her desire to read it was too strong to be overcome by any objections I could raise, so I had to yield; but I insisted upon her reading it aloud. One dark and rainy day, she commenced the reading. She read on till bed-time, and then proposed to leave the rest of the story until the next day; but I was altogether too eager to hear how the next chapter ended, to consent to that. She was persuaded to read the next chapter, and the next, and the next. In short, I kept her reading all night, and gave her no rest until the novel was finished. The first novel I ever read myself was "Rob Roy." I could only read it understandingly by reading it aloud, and to this day I often find myself whispering the words in the daily newspaper.

My brother Horace, the chair-maker, was established in Paris, Ky. He wrote to me that he was painting portraits, and that there was a painter in Lexington who was receiving fifty dollars a head. This price seemed fabulous to me; but I began to think seriously of trying my fortune in Kentucky. I soon settled upon the idea, and acted at once. Winding up my affairs in Pittsburg, I found that I had just money enough to take me down the river. I knew a barber, by the name of Jarvis, who was going to Lexington; and I proposed to join him in the purchase of a large skiff. He agreed to it; and we fitted it up with a sort of awning or tent, and embarked, with our wives and children. Sometimes we rowed our craft; but oftener we let her float as she pleased, while we gave ourselves up to music. He, as well as I, played the clarionet; and we had much enjoyment on our voyage. We arrived in Paris with funds rather low; but, as my brother was well known there, I found no difficulty on that score.

Here I began my career as a professional artist. I took a room, and painted the portrait of a very popular young man, and made a decided hit. In six months from that time, I had painted nearly one hundred portraits, at twenty-five dollars a head. The first twenty-five I took rather disturbed the equanimity of my conscience. It did not seem to me that the portrait was intrinsically worth that money; now, I know it was not.

I have stated previously, that I was strictly temperate. This was not from principle, but simply because I did not want any stimulant. During my stay in Paris,* I was constantly thrown into the society of those who did drink. It was the almost universal custom to take a julep before breakfast; and by degrees I fell into the habit of taking *my* julep, and sometimes two. I soon guessed where this would end, for I found that I felt uncomfortable unless I had my morning dram. I stopped short at once, and for five years never tasted a drop of ardent spirits. I was sometimes obliged to sip a glass of wine at the dinner table.

My second daughter was born in Paris, in the winter of 1818–19.

Here it was that I mingled for the first time with the tip-top of society. I went at once, on my arrival in the town, to the first-class hotel. I found unspeakable embarrassment at the table, with so many fine young gentlemen, all so elegantly dressed, with ruffled shirts, rings on their white and delicate fingers, and diamond pins in their bosoms. They, no doubt, thought me very clownish; as I undoubtedly was. I found little respect paid me by them, until I began to attract the attention of their masters. I soon became a sort of lion, and grew very popular among these clerks, especially after I was so far advanced in the ways of society as to take my morning juleps.

Up to this time, I had thought little of the profession, so far as its honors were concerned. Indeed it had never occurred to me, that it was more honorable or profitable than sign-painting. I now began to entertain more elevated ideas of the art, and to desire some means of improvement. Finding myself in funds sufficient to visit Philadelphia, I did so; and spent two months

* Paris, Kentucky.

in that city, devoting my time entirely to drawing in the Academy, and studying the best pictures, practising at the same time with the brush. I would sometimes feel a good deal discouraged as I looked at the works of older artists. I saw the labor it would cost me to emulate them, working, as I should, under great disadvantages. Then again, when I had painted a picture successfully, my spirits would rise, and I would resolve that I could and would overcome every obstacle. One good effect of my visit to Philadelphia was to open my eyes to the merits of the works of other artists, though it took away much of my self-satisfaction. My own pictures did not look as well to my own eye as they did before I left Paris. I had thought then that my pictures were far ahead of Mr. Jewitt's, the painter my brother had written me about, who received such unheard-of prices, and who really was a good artist. My estimation of them was very different now: I found they were so superior to mine, that their excellence had been beyond my capacity of appreciation.

When I returned to Kentucky, I found that the scarcity of money, from which the State was then suffering, seriously affected my business; and after struggling on for a few months, without bettering my finances, I concluded to try a new field. I first tried my fortune in Cincinnati; but, after waiting a week or two in vain for orders, I gave up all hope of succeeding there, and determined to push on to St. Louis. But how to get there was a puzzling question. I had used up all my money; but, in my palmy days in Paris, I had bought a dozen silver spoons, and a gold watch and chain for my wife. There was no way left for me now but to dispose of these superfluities. I went with them to a broker, and pawned them for money enough to take me and my family to Missouri. I had letters of introduction to St. Louis, and set off at once for that far-off city. We went as far as Louisville on a flat-boat, and there found a steamboat ready to take passengers; and in ten days we were safely landed in St. Louis. I presented one of my letters to Governor Clarke, who was then Governor of the Territory, Indian Agent, &c.; and he kindly helped me about getting a suitable room for a studio, and then offered himself as a sitter. This was an auspicious and cheering beginning. I was decidedly happy in my likeness of him, and, long before I had finished his head,

I had others engaged; and for fifteen months I was kept constantly at work.

In June of this year, I made a trip of one hundred miles for the purpose of painting the portrait of old Colonel Daniel Boone.* I had much trouble in finding him. He was living, some miles from the main road, in one of the cabins of an old block-house, which was built for the protection of the settlers against the incursions of the Indians. I found that the nearer I got to his dwelling, the less was known of him. When within two miles of his house, I asked a man to tell me where Colonel Boone lived. He said he did not know any such man. "Why, yes, you do," said his wife. "It is that white-headed old man who lives on the bottom, near the river." A good illustration of the proverb, that a prophet is not without honor save in his own country.

I found the object of my search engaged in cooking his dinner. He was lying in his bunk, near the fire, and had a long strip of venison wound around his ramrod, and was busy turning it before a brisk blaze, and using salt and pepper to season his meat. I at once told him the object of my visit. I found that he hardly knew what I meant. I explained the matter to him, and he agreed to sit. He was ninety years old, and rather infirm; his memory of passing events was much impaired, yet he would amuse me every day by his anecdotes of his earlier life. I asked him one day, just after his description of one of his long hunts, if he never got lost, having no compass. "No," said he, "I can't say as ever I was lost, but I was *bewildered* once for three days."

He was much astonished at seeing the likeness. He had a very large progeny; one grand-daughter had eighteen children, all at home near the old man's cabin: *they* were even more astonished at the picture than was the old man himself.

I will mention in this connection the fact of my painting one of the Osage chiefs. There was a deputation from this tribe on a visit to Governor Clarke. I asked some of them to go to my room, and there showed them the portrait of Governor Clarke, at the sight of which they gave several significant grunts. They

* This picture is now in possession of John L. King, Esq., of Springfield, Mass. (Footnote in original.)

were not satisfied with merely looking, but went close to the picture, rubbed their fingers across the face, looked behind it, and showed great wonder. The old chief was a fine-looking man, of great dignity of manner. I asked him to sit for his portrait. He did so; and, after giving evident signs of pleasure at seeing himself reproduced on canvas, he said that I was a god (a great spirit), and, if I would go home with him, I should be a brave, and have two wives.

The deputation went to Washington, where they staid long enough to lose much, I may say nearly all, of that which ennobles the Indian character. I saw them on their return to St. Louis. They wore, instead of their own graceful blankets, a military dress with tawdry cotton epaulettes and cotton lace; and withal had fallen into the habit of getting beastly drunk. All the interest I had felt in them was gone.

The city became very sickly, and the weather was intensely hot. I decided to leave the city for a month or two. I hired a pair of horses and a close carriage and driver, and started for the town of Franklin, about two hundred miles from St. Louis, situated on the Missouri River. The day after we started, I was taken violently ill of dysentery, and was reduced in one week to a skeleton.

We met with an adventure on our way, which I relate for the amusement of the younger portion of my readers. We stopped one day about noon to bait our horses. While waiting at the tavern, I saw the fresh skin of some wild animal, and inquired what it was. I was told that it was the skin of a panther that had been shot the night before, and that her mate was prowling about the prairie. The two had done great damage to the young cattle and hogs, and a deadly war had been waged against them. The whole settlement had turned out on the hunt, and at last had succeeded in killing one. We started to cross the prairie called the Twenty-mile Prairie, and travelled on through intense heat and swarms of flies until near night, and were within a mile of the wooded border, when the driver suddenly stopped, and called out, "My God! massa, what dat dar?" I lifted the window of the coach, and there stood an enormous panther, directly in our path, and in a half-crouching posture. The negro swung his hat, and yelled as if he were frightened out of his senses; and there was good cause for his fear, for the animal was not more than twenty feet from us. The monster gave one or two leaps into the grass, and there stood and eyed us very closely as we passed. If the driver was frightened, those within the carriage were no less so. We were none of us sorry to part company with the creature. We soon reached the tavern; and, as the landlord was beginning to take the harness from the horses, I told him the adventure. He instantly dropped the harness; and calling all the men, boys, and dogs that were near, they all started at their utmost speed. They soon found the beast, and followed him nearly all night; but he would not "tree."

We had a little adventure at this tavern, which might have shocked some of the refined boarders at the Astor House. I had observed a white counterpane spread upon the grass, covered over with fruit for the purpose of drying. On sitting down at the tea-table, the same article appeared as a table-cloth; and, on going to bed, we found it put to its legitimate use.

We arrived, at last, at the town of Franklin, which was the county seat. Where the bed of the Missouri River now lies, the Courthouse then stood. Such have been the ravages of this unreliable stream, that not a house in the then flourishing town is now standing. It was here that my oldest son was born. One other event of importance occurred. It was here that I obtained a perfect knowledge of the English language: at least, I was assured by an itinerant professor, that he could make me a thorough grammarian in twelve lessons. As I took the required number, if I am not all that he promised me, it must be his fault, and not mine.

While in St. Louis, I bought a lot of land, for which I painted five hundred dollars worth in pictures at their then current value. On leaving St. Louis, I left the lot in charge of an agent, with funds for the accruing taxes. I never thought of the lot or the agent for five years, when I met a gentleman in Washington who was well acquainted with real estate in St. Louis. I asked him if he knew any thing about my lot: he said it had, he thought, been sold for taxes. This proved to be true; but, as the limit of redemption had not expired, I empowered this gentleman to redeem it, and to sell it at once, if he could get a fair

price for it, to relieve myself from the trouble of looking after
it. He sold it for seven hundred dollars. That same lot is now
worth forty thousand. By such chances fortunes are made or
missed!

My ambition in my profession now began to take a higher
flight, and I determined to go to Europe. I had accumulated
over a thousand dollars in cash, and had bought a carriage and
pair of horses. With these I started with my family for Western
New York, where my parents were still living, by whom we
were warmly welcomed.

My success in painting, and especially the amount of money
I had saved, was the wonder of the whole neighborhood. My
grandfather Smith, at an advanced age, had followed his children to the West, and was living in the same place with my
father. He had, as yet, said nothing congratulatory upon my
success; but one day he began, "Chester, I want to speak to
you about your present mode of life. I think it is very little
better than swindling to charge forty dollars for one of those
effigies. Now, I want you to give up this course of living, and
settle down on a farm, and become a respectable man." As I did
not exactly coincide in his views, I did not become the "respectable man" according to his notions.

My failure in Caledonia for four or five hundred dollars had
caused as much surprise and excitement as would the failure of
any of our first merchants in Boston. The surprise was, at least,
as great to my creditors to find themselves paid off in full.

My plan now was to leave my wife and children with my
father and mother, and go to Europe. This plan was so far ma-
tured and carried out, that I had my trunk packed, and was to
leave on the following morning.* Just before starting, my
mother asked me to sit down by her, as she wished to have a
serious talk with me. She began, "You are now going to Europe; and how soon—if ever—you return, no one can tell. You
are leaving your wife and children with very little to live upon;
certainly, not enough to support them in the way they have
lived. To come to the point, I want you to give up your trip for

* The ship I was intending to sail in was the ill-fated "Albion." She was
wrecked, and all on board were lost except one man, an invalid, who was
thrown up a cleft in the rocks, and saved. (Footnote in original.)

the present, and buy a farm [pointing to one in the neighbor-hood that was for sale], and place your family in a comfortable position. If you go to Europe, and never return, they are then provided for; and this reflection will console you under any trials you may be called on to pass through." This appeal was too much for me. I yielded; and the next morning, instead of starting for Europe, I started for the farm, and before night had a deed of one hundred and fifty acres. I next made a con-tract with a carpenter to build a frame-house upon it; and then started for Washington, to spend the winter.

I had fairly begun work before Congress assembled, and had some happy specimens for exhibition. I spent about six months there; was full of business, and was able in the spring to pay for the new house, and make another payment on the farm.

The following summer I spent in Pittsfield and Northamp-ton. Mr. Mills,* United States Senator from Massachusetts, re-sided in the latter town. He had seen my pictures in Washing-ton, and had spoken favorably of them and of me; and I found that I had already a high reputation. I at once got orders, and in a short time my room was tolerably well filled with pictures.

While I was there, the annual cattle-show came off. I allowed my pictures to be exhibited among the mechanic arts. They elicited great admiration, and formed one of the chief attrac-tions. I went into the room one day when there was a great crowd, and was soon pointed out as the artist. Conversation ceased, and all eyes were turned upon me. This was altogether too much for my modesty, and I withdrew as quickly as possi-ble.

I one day received an invitation to a large party, to be given by Mrs. Ashmun (the stepmother of George Ashmun†), which I accepted; but, as the evening drew near, began to regret that I had done so. I finally went into my room, and sat down on the bed, before beginning to dress, and took the matter into serious consideration. Should I go? or should I not? It was a fearful ordeal to go through. I had never been to a fashionable lady's

* Elijah Hunt Mills (1776–1829) served in the United States Senate from 1820 to 1827.

† A distinguished statesman, George Ashmun (1804–1870) served in each branch of the Massachusetts legislature and in Congress from 1845 to 1851.

party, and should not know how to behave. My heart grew faint
at the thought of my ignorance and awkwardness. But then I
reflected, there must be a first time; and, with a mighty effort,
resolved that this should be it! So I went, and passed through
the trial better than I anticipated; but I was glad enough when
it was over.

While in Northampton, I painted the portraits of two gentlemen from Boston. They encouraged me to establish myself in
that city. I did so, and for six months rode triumphantly on the
top wave of fortune. I took a large room, arranged my pictures,
and fixed upon one o'clock as my hour for exhibition. As soon
as the clock struck, my bell would begin to ring; and people
would flock in, sometimes to the number of fifty. New orders
were constantly given me for pictures. I was compelled to resort
to a book for registering the names of the numerous applicants.
As a vacancy occurred, I had only to notify the next on the list,
and it was filled. I do not think any artist in this country ever
enjoyed more popularity than I did; but popularity is often
easily won, and as easily lost. Mr. Stuart,* the greatest portrait
painter this country ever produced, was at that time in his manhood's strength as a painter; yet he was idle half the winter. He
would ask of his friends, "How rages the Harding fever?"

Although I had painted about eighty portraits, I had a still
greater number of applicants awaiting their turn; but I was
determined to go to Europe, as I had money enough to pay for
my farm, and some sixteen hundred dollars besides. I had engaged to paint a few portraits in Springfield, which I did on my
way to Barre, where my family were living. After spending a
week or two there in arranging matters connected with their
comfort, I took leave of them, and started for New York City,
where I was to embark. On my way, I spent a day or two in
Northampton with my friends. While there, a lady, whose judgment I respected, advised me to send for my family, and establish them in that town; urging as a reason, that my children
would grow up wild where they were, and that my wife could
not improve in the accomplishments of refined society, but inevitably remain stationary, on the standard level of those she

* Gilbert Stuart (1755–1828) moved to Boston in 1805, where he lived and
worked for the rest of his life.

would be obliged to associate with, while I should be improving by mingling with the refined and distinguished persons my profession would throw me among. I was impressed with the good sense of this advice, and adopted it. I started at once for my wild home, and brought my family, now numbering four children, to Northampton; and saw them well settled in a very excellent boarding-house, where they remained two years. I have had good reason to thank my friend for her judicious suggestion.

And now, at last, I took my departure for a foreign land, leaving wife, children, and friends,—all indeed that I had sympathy with,—to cast in my lot, for a time, with strangers in a strange land. My heart was full of conflicting emotions. Scores of my patrons in Boston had tried to dissuade me from taking this step, some urging as a reason, that I already had such a press of business that I could lay up a considerable sum of money yearly; while others insisted that I need not go abroad, for I already painted better pictures than any artist in this country, and probably better than any in Europe. My self-esteem was not large enough, however, to listen to all this, and my desire for study and improvement was too great to be overpowered by flattery. In spite of all advice to the contrary, I sailed for England, in the good packet ship "Canada," on the first day of August, 1823.

After a favorable passage of eighteen days, we arrived safely in port, at Liverpool; and I remember feeling so ridiculously happy at setting foot on shore again, that I laughed heartily without knowing why. . . .

LINDA BRENT

(1818–1896)

Incidents in the Life of a Slave Girl. Written by Herself. Edited by L. Maria Child. Published for the Author, Boston, 1861. 306 pp.

$300 REWARD! Ran away from the subscriber, an intelligent, bright, mulatto girl, named Linda, 21 years of age. Five feet four inches high. Dark eyes, and black hair inclined to curl; but it can be made straight. Has a decayed spot on a front tooth. She can read and write, and in all probability will try to get to the Free States. All persons are forbidden, under penalty of the law, to harbor or employ said slave. $150 will be given to whoever takes her in the state, and $300 if taken out of the state and delivered to me, or lodged in jail.

DR. FLINT

There are many narratives of slave life, but Linda Brent's is one of the few told by a woman. In addition to all the horrors of living in bondage, the female was constantly subject to the terror of sexual exploitation. Desperate to escape this kind of abuse, Linda Brent hid in a tiny garret. For seven years, in unbelievably tight quarters, she roasted in summer, froze in winter, and was at all times cramped almost beyond endurance. Miraculously, she survived.

Linda Brent also suffered great mental anguish—she feared for her children. Having rebuffed her owner and then accepted another white man, she knew the former could take revenge on her children.

The father of Linda Brent's children was elected to Congress. "If the secret Memoirs of many members of Congress should be published," she wrote, "curious details would be unfolded. I once saw a letter from a member of Congress to a slave, who was the mother of six of his children. He wrote to request that she would send her children away from the great house before his return, as he expected to be accompanied by friends. The

104

woman could not read, and was obliged to employ another to read the letter. The existence of the colored children did not trouble this gentleman, it was only the fear that friends might recognize in their features a resemblance to him."

Eventually, Linda Brent crossed over Mason and Dixon's Line and was free. The father of her children cared enough about her to buy them and send them to her. "It was conjectured that he advanced the money," she wrote, "but it was not known. At the south, a gentleman may have a shoal of colored children without any disgrace; but if he is known to purchase them, with the view of setting them free, the example is thought to be dangerous . . . and he becomes unpopular."

A prominent family in the north aided Linda Brent and gave her employment. When she needed help in writing her book, she turned to Lydia Maria Francis Child (1802–1880), the respected and well-known Massachusetts abolitionist whose *Appeal in Favor of that Class of Americans Called Africans,* 1833, won many to the cause of ending slavery. In an introduction to *Incidents,* Maria Child wrote, "The author . . . is personally known to me. . . . At her request, I have revised the manuscript; but such changes as I have made have been mainly for the purpose of condensation and orderly arrangement. I have not added anything . . . or changed the import. . . . With trifling exceptions, both the ideas and the language are her own. . . . The names of both persons and places are known to me. . . ."

All the names in Linda Brent's book are fictitious, even her own; her real name was Harriet Brent Jacobs. In every other respect, however, she claimed her narrative was true. Far from being exaggerated, she said, it fell short of what she had experienced. The mores of the nineteenth century would not have permitted her to be more explicit.

Incidents in the Life of a Slave Girl has never been reprinted. Ten of its forty-one chapters follow.

INCIDENTS

IN THE

LIFE OF A SLAVE GIRL,
SEVEN YEARS CONCEALED.

———————•———————

I.

CHILDHOOD

I was born a slave; but I never knew it till six years of happy childhood had passed away. My father was a carpenter, and considered so intelligent and skilful in his trade, that, when buildings out of the common line were to be erected, he was sent for from long distances, to be head workman. On condition of paying his mistress two hundred dollars a year, and supporting himself, he was allowed to work at his trade, and manage his own affairs. His strongest wish was to purchase his children; but, though he several times offered his hard earnings for that purpose, he never succeeded. In complexion my parents were a light shade of brownish yellow, and were termed mulattoes. They lived together in a comfortable home; and, though we were all slaves, I was so fondly shielded that I never dreamed I was a piece of merchandise, trusted to them for safe keeping, and liable to be demanded of them at any moment. I had one brother, William, who was two years younger than myself—a bright, affectionate child. I had also a great treasure in my maternal grandmother, who was a remarkable woman in many respects. She was the daughter of a planter in South Carolina, who, at his death, left her mother and his three children free, with money to go to St. Augustine, where they had relatives. It was during the Revolutionary War; and they were captured on their passage, carried back, and sold to different purchasers. Such was the story my grandmother used to tell me; but I do not remember all the particulars. She was a little girl when she was captured and sold to the keeper of a large hotel. I have often heard her tell how hard she fared during childhood. But as she grew older she evinced so much intelligence, and was so faithful, that her master and mistress could not help seeing it was for their interest to take care of such a valuable piece of property. She became an indispensable personage in the household, officiating in all capacities, from cook and wet nurse to seamstress. She was much praised for her cooking; and her nice crackers became so famous in the neighborhood that many people were desirous of obtaining them. In consequence of numerous requests of this kind, she asked permission of her mistress to bake crackers at night, after all the household work was done; and she obtained leave to do it, provided she would clothe herself and her children from the profits. Upon these terms, after working hard all day for her mistress, she began her midnight bakings, assisted by her two oldest children. The business proved profitable; and each year she laid by a little, which was saved for a fund to purchase her children. Her master died, and the property was divided among his heirs. The widow had her dower in the hotel, which she continued to keep open. My grandmother remained in her service as a slave; but her children were divided among her master's children. As she had five, Benjamin, the youngest one, was sold, in order that each heir might have an equal portion of dollars and cents. There was so little difference in our ages that he seemed more like my brother than my uncle. He was a bright, handsome lad, nearly white; for he inherited the complexion my grandmother had derived from Anglo-Saxon ancestors. Though only ten years old, seven hundred and twenty dollars were paid for him. His sale was a terrible blow to my grandmother; but she was naturally hopeful, and she went to work with renewed energy, trusting in time to be able to purchase some of her children. She had laid up three hundred dollars, which her mistress one day begged as a loan, promising to pay her soon. The reader probably knows that no promise or writing given to a slave is legally binding; for, according to Southern laws, a slave, *being* property, can *hold* no property. When my grandmother lent her hard earnings to her mistress, she trusted solely to her honor. The honor of a slaveholder to a slave!

To this good grandmother I was indebted for many comforts. My brother Willie and I often received portions of the crackers, cakes, and preserves, she made to sell; and after we ceased to be children we were indebted to her for many more important services.

Such were the unusually fortunate circumstances of my early childhood. When I was six years old, my mother died; and then, for the first time, I learned, by the talk around me, that I was a slave. My mother's mistress was the daughter of my grandmother's mistress. She was the foster sister of my mother; they were both nourished at my grandmother's breast. In fact, my mother had been weaned at three months old, that the babe of the mistress might obtain sufficient food. They played together as children; and, when they became women, my mother was a most faithful servant to her whiter foster sister. On her death-bed her mistress promised that her children should never suffer for any thing; and during her lifetime she kept her word. They all spoke kindly of my dead mother, who had been a slave merely in name, but in nature was noble and womanly. I grieved for her, and my young mind was troubled with the thought who would now take care of me and my little brother. I was told that my home was now to be with her mistress; and I found it a happy one. No toilsome or disagreeable duties were imposed upon me. My mistress was so kind to me that I was always glad to do her bidding, and proud to labor for her as much as my young years would permit. I would sit by her side for hours, sewing diligently, with a heart as free from care as that of any free-born white child. When she thought I was tired, she would send me out to run and jump; and away I bounded, to gather berries or flowers to decorate her room. Those were happy days—too happy to last. The slave child had no thought for the morrow; but there came that blight, which too surely waits on every human being born to be a chattel.

When I was nearly twelve years old, my kind mistress sickened and died. As I saw the cheek grow paler, and the eye more glassy, how earnestly I prayed in my heart that she might live! I loved her; for she had been almost like a mother to me. My prayers were not answered. She died, and they buried her in the little churchyard, where, day after day, my tears fell upon her grave.

I was sent to spend a week with my grandmother. I was now old enough to begin to think of the future; and again and again I asked myself what they would do with me. I felt sure I should never find another mistress so kind as the one who was gone. She had promised my dying mother that her children should never suffer for any thing; and when I remembered that, and recalled her many proofs of attachment to me, I could not help having some hopes that she had left me free. My friends were almost certain it would be so. They thought she would be sure to do it, on account of my mother's love and faithful service. But, alas! we all know that the memory of a faithful slave does not avail much to save her children from the auction block.

After a brief period of suspense, the will of my mistress was read, and we learned that she had bequeathed me to her sister's daughter, a child of five years old. So vanished our hopes. My mistress had taught me the precepts of God's Word: "Thou shalt love thy neighbor as thyself." "Whatsoever ye would that men should do unto you, do ye even so unto them." But I was her slave, and I suppose she did not recognize me as her neighbor. I would give much to blot out from my memory that one great wrong. As a child, I loved my mistress; and, looking back on the happy days I spent with her, I try to think with less bitterness of this act of injustice. While I was with her, she taught me to read and spell; and for this privilege, which so rarely falls to the lot of a slave, I bless her memory.

She possessed but few slaves; and at her death those were all distributed among her relatives. Five of them were my grandmother's children, and had shared the same milk that nourished her mother's children. Notwithstanding my grandmother's long and faithful service to her owners, not one of her children escaped the auction block. These God-breathing machines are no more, in the sight of their masters, than the cotton they plant, or the horses they tend.

II.

THE NEW MASTER AND MISTRESS

Dr. Flint, a physician in the neighborhood, had married the sister of my mistress, and I was now the property of their little daughter. It was not without murmuring that I prepared for my new home; and what added to my unhappiness, was the fact that my brother William was purchased by the same family. My father, by his nature, as well as by the habit of transacting business as a skilful mechanic, had more of the feelings of a freeman than is common among slaves. My brother was a spirited boy; and being brought up under such influences, he early detested the name of master and mistress. One day, when his father and his mistress both happened to call him at the same time, he hesitated between the two; being perplexed to know which had the strongest claim upon his obedience. He finally concluded to go to his mistress. When my father reproved him for it, he said, "You both called me, and I didn't know which I ought to go to first."

"You are *my* child," replied our father, "and when I call you, you should come immediately, if you have to pass through fire and water."

Poor Willie! He was now to learn his first lesson of obedience to a master. Grandmother tried to cheer us with hopeful words, and they found an echo in the credulous hearts of youth.

When we entered our new home we encountered cold looks, cold words, and cold treatment. We were glad when the night came. On my narrow bed I moaned and wept, I felt so desolate and alone.

I had been there nearly a year, when a dear little friend of mine was buried. I heard her mother sob, as the clods fell on the coffin of her only child, and I turned away from the grave, feeling thankful that I still had something left to love. I met my grandmother, who said, "Come with me, Linda;" and from her tone I knew that something sad had happened. She led me apart from the people, and then said, "My child, your father is dead." Dead! How could I believe it? He had died so suddenly I had not even heard that he was sick. I went home with my grandmother. My heart rebelled against God, who had taken from me mother, father, mistress, and friend. The good grandmother tried to comfort me. "Who knows the ways of God?" said she. "Perhaps they have been kindly taken from the evil days to come." Years afterwards I often thought of this. She promised to be a mother to her grandchildren, so far as she might be permitted to do so; and strengthened by her love, I returned to my master's. I thought I should be allowed to go to my father's house the next morning; but I was ordered to go for flowers, that my mistress's house might be decorated for an evening party. I spent the day gathering flowers and weaving them into festoons, while the dead body of my father was lying within a mile of me. What cared my owners for that? he was merely a piece of property. Moreover, they thought he had spoiled his children, by teaching them to feel that they were human beings. This was blasphemous doctrine for a slave to teach; presumptuous in him, and dangerous to the masters.

The next day I followed his remains to a humble grave beside that of my dear mother. There were those who knew my father's worth, and respected his memory.

My home now seemed more dreary than ever. The laugh of the little slave-children sounded harsh and cruel. It was selfish to feel so about the joy of others. My brother moved about with a very grave face. I tried to comfort him, by saying, "Take courage, Willie; brighter days will come by and by."

"You don't know any thing about it, Linda," he replied. "We shall have to stay here all our days; we shall never be free."

I argued that we were growing older and stronger, and that perhaps we might, before long, be allowed to hire our own time, and then we could earn money to buy our freedom. William declared this was much easier to say than to do; moreover, he did not intend to *buy* his freedom. We held daily controversies upon this subject.

Little attention was paid to the slaves' meals in Dr. Flint's house. If they could catch a bit of food while it was going, well and good. I gave myself no trouble on that score, for on my various errands I passed my grandmother's house, where there was always something to spare for me. I was frequently threatened with punishment if I stopped there; and my grandmother, to avoid detaining me, often stood at the gate with something for my breakfast or dinner. I was indebted to *her* for all my comforts, spiritual or temporal. It was *her* labor that supplied my scanty wardrobe. I have a vivid recollection of the linsey-woolsey dress given me every winter by Mrs. Flint. How I hated it! It was one of the badges of slavery.

While my grandmother was thus helping to support me from

her hard earnings, the three hundred dollars she had lent her mistress were never repaid. When her mistress died, her son-in-law, Dr. Flint, was appointed executor. When grandmother applied to him for payment, he said the estate was insolvent, and the law prohibited payment. It did not, however, prohibit him from retaining the silver candelabra, which had been purchased with that money. I presume they will be handed down in the family, from generation to generation.

My grandmother's mistress had always promised her that, at her death, she should be free; and it was said that in her will she made good the promise. But when the estate was settled, Dr. Flint told the faithful old servant that, under existing circumstances, it was necessary she should be sold.

On the appointed day, the customary advertisement was posted up, proclaiming that there would be a "public sale of negroes, horses, &c." Dr. Flint called to tell my grandmother that he was unwilling to wound her feelings by putting her up at auction, and that he would prefer to dispose of her at private sale. My grandmother saw through his hypocrisy; she understood very well that he was ashamed of the job. She was a very spirited woman, and if he was base enough to sell her, when her mistress intended she should be free, she was determined the public should know it. She had for a long time supplied many families with crackers and preserves; consequently, "Aunt Marthy," as she was called, was generally known, and every body who knew her respected her intelligence and good character. Her long and faithful service in the family was also well known, and the intention of her mistress to leave her free. When the day of sale came, she took her place among the chattels, and at the first call she sprang upon the auction-block. Many voices called out, "Shame! Shame! Who is going to sell *you*, aunt Marthy? Don't stand there! That is no place for *you*." Without saying a word, she quietly awaited her fate. No one bid for her. At last, a feeble voice said, "Fifty dollars." It came from a maiden lady, seventy years old, the sister of my grandmother's deceased mistress. She had lived forty years under the same roof with my grandmother; she knew how faithfully she had served her owners, and how cruelly she had been defrauded of her rights; and she resolved to protect her.

The auctioneer waited for a higher bid; but her wishes were respected; no one bid above her. She could neither read nor write; and when the bill of sale was made out, she signed it with a cross. But what consequence was that, when she had a big heart overflowing with human kindness? She gave the old servant her freedom.

At that time, my grandmother was just fifty years old. Laborious years had passed since then; and now my brother and I were slaves to the man who had defrauded her of her money, and tried to defraud her of her freedom. One of my mother's sisters, called Aunt Nancy, was also a slave in his family. She was a kind, good aunt to me; and supplied the place of both housekeeper and waiting maid to her mistress. She was, in fact, at the beginning and end of every thing.

Mrs. Flint, like many southern women, was totally deficient in energy. She had not strength to superintend her household affairs; but her nerves were so strong, that she could sit in her easy chair and see a woman whipped, till the blood trickled from every stroke of the lash. She was a member of the church; but partaking of the Lord's supper did not seem to put her in a Christian frame of mind. If dinner was not served at the exact time on that particular Sunday, she would station herself in the kitchen, and wait till it was dished, and then spit in all the kettles and pans that had been used for cooking. She did this to prevent the cook and her children from eking out the meagre fare with the remains of the gravy and other scrapings. The slaves could get nothing to eat except what she chose to give them. Provisions were weighed out by the pound and ounce, three times a day. I can assure you she gave them no chance to eat wheat bread from her flour barrel. She knew how many biscuits a quart of flour would make, and exactly what size they ought to be.

Dr. Flint was an epicure. The cook never sent a dinner to his table without fear and trembling; for if there happened to be a dish not to his liking, he would either order her to be whipped, or compel her to eat every mouthful of it in his presence. The poor, hungry creature might not have objected to eating it; but she did object to having her master cram it down her throat till she choked.

They had a pet dog, that was a nuisance in the house. The cook was ordered to make some Indian mush for him. He refused to eat, and when his head was held over it, the froth flowed from his mouth into the basin. He died a few minutes after. When Dr. Flint came in, he said the mush had not been well cooked, and that was the reason the animal would not eat it. He sent for the cook, and compelled her to eat it. He thought that the woman's stomach was stronger than the dog's; but her sufferings afterwards proved that he was mistaken. This poor woman endured many cruelties from her master and mistress; sometimes she was locked up, away from her nursing baby, for a whole day and night.

When I had been in the family a few weeks, one of the plantation slaves was brought to town, by order of his master. It was near night when he arrived, and Dr. Flint ordered him to be taken to the work house, and tied up to the joist, so that his feet would just escape the ground. In that situation he was to wait till the doctor had taken his tea. I shall never forget that night. Never before, in my life, had I heard hundreds of blows fall, in succession, on a human being. His piteous groans, and his "O, pray don't, massa," rang in my ear for months afterwards. There were many conjectures as to the cause of this terrible punishment. Some said master accused him of stealing corn; others said the slave had quarrelled with his wife, in presence of the overseer, and had accused his master of being the father of her child. They were both black, and the child was very fair.

I went into the work house next morning, and saw the cowhide still wet with blood, and the boards all covered with gore. The poor man lived, and continued to quarrel with his wife. A few months afterwards Dr. Flint handed them both over to a slave-trader. The guilty man put their value into his pocket, and had the satisfaction of knowing that they were out of sight and hearing. When the mother was delivered into the trader's hands, she said, "You *promised* to treat me well." To which he replied, "You have let your tongue run too far; damn you!" She had forgotten that it was a crime for a slave to tell who was the father of her child.

From others than the master persecution also comes in such cases. I once saw a young slave girl dying soon after the birth of a child nearly white. In her agony she cried out, "O Lord, come and take me!" Her mistress stood by, and mocked at her like an incarnate fiend. "You suffer, do you?" she exclaimed. "I am glad of it. You deserve it all, and more too."

The girl's mother said, "The baby is dead, thank God; and I hope my poor child will soon be in heaven, too."

"Heaven!" retorted the mistress. "There is no such place for the like of her and her bastard."

The poor mother turned away, sobbing. Her dying daughter called her, feebly, and as she bent over her, I heard her say, "Don't grieve so, mother; God knows all about it; and HE will have mercy upon me."

Her sufferings, afterwards, became so intense, that her mistress felt unable to stay; but when she left the room, the scornful smile was still on her lips. Seven children called her mother. The poor black woman had but the one child, whose eyes she saw closing in death, while she thanked God for taking her away from the greater bitterness of life. . . .

V.

THE TRIALS OF GIRLHOOD

During the first years of my service in Dr. Flint's family, I was accustomed to share some indulgences with the children of my mistress. Though this seemed to me no more than right, I was grateful for it, and tried to merit the kindness by the faithful discharge of my duties. But I now entered on my fifteenth year—a sad epoch in the life of a slave girl. My master began to whisper foul words in my ear. Young as I was, I could not remain ignorant of their import. I tried to treat them with indifference or contempt. The master's age, my extreme youth, and the fear that his conduct would be reported to my grandmother, made him bear this treatment for many months. He was a crafty man, and resorted to many means to accomplish his purposes. Sometimes he had stormy, terrific ways, that made his victims tremble; sometimes he assumed a gentleness that he thought must surely subdue. Of the two, I preferred his stormy moods, although they left me trembling. He tried his utmost to corrupt the pure principles my grandmother had instilled. He peopled my young mind with unclean images, such as only a vile monster could think of. I turned from him with disgust and hatred. But he was my master. I was compelled to live under the same roof with him—where I saw a man forty years my senior daily violating the most sacred commandments of nature. He told me I was his property; that I must be subject to his will in all things. My soul revolted against the mean tyranny. But where could I turn for protection? No matter whether the slave girl be as black as ebony or as fair as her mistress. In either case, there is no shadow of law to protect her from insult, from violence, or even from death; all these are inflicted by fiends who bear the shape of men. The mistress, who ought to protect the helpless victim, has no other feelings towards her but those of jealousy and rage. The degradation, the wrongs, the vices, that grow out of slavery, are more than I can describe. They are greater than you would willingly believe. Surely, if you credited one half the truths that are told you concerning the helpless millions suffering in this cruel bondage, you at the north would not help to tighten the yoke. You surely would refuse to do for the master, on your own soil, the mean and cruel work which trained bloodhounds and the lowest class of whites do for him at the south.

Every where the years bring to all enough of sin and sorrow; but in slavery the very dawn of life is darkened by these shadows. Even the little child, who is accustomed to wait on her mistress and her children, will learn, before she is twelve years old, why it is that her mistress hates such and such a one among the slaves. Perhaps the child's own mother is among those hated ones. She listens to violent outbreaks of jealous passion, and cannot help understanding what is the cause. She will become prematurely knowing in evil things. Soon she will learn to tremble when she hears her master's footfall. She will be compelled to realize that she is no longer a child. If God has bestowed beauty upon her, it will prove her greatest curse. That which commands admiration in the white woman only hastens the degradation of the female slave. I know that some are too much brutalized by slavery to feel the humiliation of their position; but many slaves feel it most acutely, and shrink from the memory of it. I cannot tell how much I suffered in the presence of these wrongs, nor how I am still pained by the retrospect. My master met me at every turn, reminding me that I belonged to him, and swearing by heaven and earth that he would compel me to submit to him. If I went out for a breath of fresh air, after a day of unwearied toil, his footsteps dogged me. If I knelt by my mother's grave, his dark shadow fell on me even there. The light heart which nature had given me became heavy with sad forebodings. The other slaves in my master's house noticed the change. Many of them pitied me; but none dared to ask the cause. They had no need to inquire. They knew too well the guilty practices under that roof; and they were aware that to speak of them was an offence that never went unpunished.

I longed for some one to confide in. I would have given the world to have laid my head on my grandmother's faithful bosom, and told her all my troubles. But Dr. Flint swore he would kill me, if I was not as silent as the grave. Then, although my grandmother was all in all to me, I feared her as well as loved her. I had been accustomed to look up to her with a respect bordering upon awe. I was very young, and felt shamefaced about telling her such impure things, especially as I knew her to be very strict on such subjects. Moreover, she was a woman of a high spirit. She was usually very quiet in her demeanor; but if her indignation was once roused, it was not very easily quelled. I had been told that she once chased a white gentleman with a loaded pistol, because he insulted one of her daughters. I dreaded the consequences of a violent outbreak; and both pride and fear kept me silent. But though I did not confide in my grandmother, and even evaded her vigilant watchfulness and inquiry, her presence in the neighborhood was some protection to me. Though she had been a slave, Dr. Flint was afraid of her. He dreaded her scorching rebukes. Moreover, she was known and patronized by many people; and he did not wish to have his villainy made public. It was lucky for me that I did not live on a distant plantation, but in a town not so large that the inhabitants were ignorant of each other's affairs. Bad as are the laws and customs in a slaveholding community, the doctor, as a professional man, deemed it prudent to keep up some outward show of decency.

O, what days and nights of fear and sorrow that man caused me! Reader, it is not to awaken sympathy for myself that I am telling you truthfully what I suffered in slavery. I do it to kindle a flame of compassion in your hearts for my sisters who are still in bondage, suffering as I once suffered.

I once saw two beautiful children playing together. One was a fair white child; the other was her slave, and also her sister. When I saw them embracing each other, and heard their joyous laughter, I turned sadly away from the lovely sight. I foresaw the inevitable blight that would fall on the little slave's heart. I knew how soon her laughter would be changed to sighs. The fair child grew up to be a still fairer woman. From childhood to womanhood her pathway was blooming with flowers, and over-arched by a sunny sky. Scarcely one day of her life had been clouded when the sun rose on her happy bridal morning.

How had those years dealt with her slave sister, the little playmate of her childhood? She, also, was very beautiful; but the flowers and sunshine of love were not for her. She drank the cup of sin, and shame, and misery, whereof her persecuted race are compelled to drink.

In view of these things, why are ye silent, ye free men and women of the north? Why do your tongues falter in mainte-nance of the right? Would that I had more ability! But my heart is so full, and my pen is so weak! There are noble men and women who plead for us, striving to help those who cannot help themselves. God bless them! God give them strength and courage to go on! God bless those, every where, who are labor-ing to advance the cause of humanity!

VI.

THE JEALOUS MISTRESS

I would ten thousand times rather that my children should be the half-starved paupers of Ireland than to be the most pam-pered among the slaves of America. I would rather drudge out my life on a cotton plantation, till the grave opened to give me rest, than to live with an unprincipled master and a jealous mistress. The felon's home in a penitentiary is preferable. He may repent, and turn from the error of his ways, and so find peace; but it is not so with a favorite slave. She is not allowed to have any pride of character. It is deemed a crime in her to wish to be virtuous.

Mrs. Flint possessed the key to her husband's character before I was born. She might have used this knowledge to counsel and to screen the young and the innocent among her slaves; but for them she had no sympathy. They were the objects of her constant suspicion and malevolence. She watched her husband with unceasing vigilance; but he was well practised in means to evade it. What he could not find opportunity to say in words he manifested in signs. He invented more than were ever thought of in a deaf and dumb asylum. I let them pass, as if I did not understand what he meant; and many were the curses and threats bestowed on me for my stupidity. One day he caught me teaching myself to write. He frowned, as if he was not well pleased; but I suppose he came to the conclusion that such an accomplishment might help to advance his favorite scheme. Before long, notes were often slipped into my hand. I would return them, saying, "I can't read them, sir." "Can't you?" he replied; "then I must read them to you." He always finished the reading by asking, "Do you understand?" Sometimes he would complain of the heat of the tea room, and order his supper to be placed on a small table in the piazza. He would seat himself there with a well-satisfied smile, and tell me to stand by and brush away the flies. He would eat very slowly, pausing between the mouthfuls. These intervals were employed in describing the happiness I was so foolishly throwing away, and in threatening me with the penalty that finally awaited my stubborn disobedience. He boasted much of the forbearance he had exercised towards me, and reminded me that there was a limit to his patience. When I succeeded in avoiding opportunities for him to talk to me at home, I was ordered to come to his office, to do some errand. When there, I was obliged to stand and listen to such language as he saw fit to address to me. Sometimes I so openly expressed my contempt for him that he would become violently enraged, and I wondered why he did not strike me. Circumstanced as he was, he probably thought it was better policy to be forbearing. But the state of things grew worse and worse daily. In desperation I told him that I must and would apply to my grandmother for protection. He threatened me with death, and worse than death, if I made any complaint to her. Strange to say, I did not despair. I was naturally of a buoyant disposition, and always I had a hope of somehow getting out of his clutches. Like many a poor, simple slave before me, I trusted that some threads of joy would yet be woven into my dark destiny.

I had entered my sixteenth year, and every day it became more apparent that my presence was intolerable to Mrs. Flint. Angry words frequently passed between her and her husband. He had never punished me himself, and he would not allow any body else to punish me. In that respect, she was never satisfied; but, in her angry moods, no terms were too vile for her to bestow upon me. Yet I, whom she detested so bitterly, had far more pity for her than he had, whose duty it was to make her life happy. I never wronged her, or wished to wrong her; and one word of kindness from her would have brought me to her feet.

After repeated quarrels between the doctor and his wife, he announced his intention to take his youngest daughter, then four years old, to sleep in his apartment. It was necessary that a servant should sleep in the same room, to be on hand if the child stirred. I was selected for that office, and informed for what purpose that arrangement had been made. By managing to keep within sight of people, as much as possible, during the day time, I had hitherto succeeded in eluding my master, though a razor was often held to my throat to force me to change this line of policy. At night I slept by the side of my great aunt, where I felt safe. He was too prudent to come into her room. She was an old woman, and had been in the family many years. Moreover, as a married man, and a professional man, he deemed it necessary to save appearances in some degree. But he resolved to remove the obstacle in the way of his scheme; and he thought he had planned it so that he should evade suspicion. He was well aware how much I prized my refuge by the side of my old aunt, and he determined to dispossess me of it. The first night the doctor had the little child in his room alone. The next morning, I was ordered to take my station as nurse the following night. A kind Providence interposed

in my favor. During the day Mrs. Flint heard of this new arrangement, and a storm followed. I rejoiced to hear it rage.

After a while my mistress sent for me to come to her room.
Her first question was, "Did you know you were to sleep in the
doctor's room?"

"Yes, ma'am."

"Who told you?"

"My master."

"Will you answer truly all the questions I ask?"

"Yes, ma'am."

"Tell me, then, as you hope to be forgiven, are you innocent
of what I have accused you?"

"I am."

She handed me a Bible, and said, "Lay your hand on your
heart, kiss this holy book, and swear before God that you tell
me the truth."

I took the oath she required, and I did it with a clear conscience.

"You have taken God's holy word to testify your innocence,"
said she. "If you have deceived me, beware! Now take this
stool, sit down, look me directly in the face, and tell me all that
has passed between your master and you."

I did as she ordered. As I went on with my account her color
changed frequently, she wept, and sometimes groaned. She
spoke in tones so sad, that I was touched by her grief. The tears
came to my eyes; but I was soon convinced that her emotions
arose from anger and wounded pride. She felt that her marriage vows were desecrated, her dignity insulted; but she had
no compassion for the poor victim of her husband's perfidy.
She pitied herself as a martyr; but she was incapable of feeling
for the condition of shame and misery in which her unfortunate, helpless slave was placed.

Yet perhaps she had some touch of feeling for me; for when
the conference was ended, she spoke kindly, and promised to
protect me. I should have been much comforted by this assur-
ance if I could have had confidence in it; but my experiences in
slavery had filled me with distrust. She was not a very refined
woman, and had not much control over her passions. I was an
object of her jealousy, and, consequently, of her hatred; and I

knew I could not expect kindness or confidence from her under the circumstances in which I was placed. I could not blame her. Slaveholders' wives feel as other women would under similar circumstances. The fire of her temper kindled from small sparks, and now the flame became so intense that the doctor was obliged to give up his intended arrangement.

I knew I had ignited the torch, and I expected to suffer for it afterwards; but I felt too thankful to my mistress for the timely aid she rendered me to care much about that. She now took me to sleep in a room adjoining her own. There I was an object of her especial care, though not of her especial comfort, for she spent many a sleepless night to watch over me. Sometimes I woke up, and found her bending over me. At other times she whispered in my ear, as though it was her husband who was speaking to me, and listened to hear what I would answer. If she startled me, on such occasions, she would glide stealthily away; and the next morning she would tell me I had been talking in my sleep, and ask who I was talking to. At last, I began to be fearful for my life. It had been often threatened; and you can imagine, better than I can describe, what an unpleasant sensation it must produce to wake up in the dead of night and find a jealous woman bending over you. Terrible as this experience was, I had fears that it would give place to one more terrible.

My mistress grew weary of her vigils; they did not prove satisfactory. She changed her tactics. She now tried the trick of accusing my master of crime, in my presence, and gave my name as the author of the accusation. To my utter astonishment, he replied, "I don't believe it; but if she did acknowledge it, you tortured her into exposing me." Tortured into exposing him! Truly, Satan had no difficulty in distinguishing the color of his soul! I understood his object in making this false representation. It was to show me that I gained nothing by seeking the protection of my mistress; that the power was still all in his own hands. I pitied Mrs. Flint. She was a second wife, many years the junior of her husband; and the hoary-headed miscreant was enough to try the patience of a wiser and better woman. She was completely foiled, and knew not how to proceed. She would gladly have had me flogged for my supposed false oath; but, as I have already stated, the doctor never allowed any one to whip me. The old sinner was politic. The application of the lash might have led to remarks that would have exposed him in the eyes of his children and grandchildren. How often did I rejoice that I lived in a town where all the inhabitants knew each other! If I had been on a remote plantation, or lost among the multitude of a crowded city, I should not be a living woman at this day.

The secrets of slavery are concealed like those of the Inquisition. My master was, to my knowledge, the father of eleven slaves. But did the mothers dare to tell who was the father of their children? Did the other slaves dare to allude to it, except in whispers among themselves? No, indeed! They knew too well the terrible consequences.

My grandmother could not avoid seeing things which excited her suspicions. She was uneasy about me, and tried various ways to buy me; but the neverchanging answer was always repeated: "Linda does not belong to *me*. She is my daughter's property, and I have no legal right to sell her." The conscientious man! He was too scrupulous to *sell* me; but he had no scruples whatever about committing a much greater wrong against the helpless young girl placed under his guardianship, as his daughter's property. Sometimes my persecutor would ask me whether I would like to be sold. I told him I would rather be sold to anybody than to lead such a life as I did. On such occasions he would assume the air of a very injured individual, and reproach me for my ingratitude. "Did I not take you into the house, and make you the companion of my own children?" he would say. "Have I ever treated you like a negro? I have never allowed you to be punished, not even to please your mistress. And this is the recompense I get, you ungrateful girl!" I answered that he had reasons of his own for screening me from punishment, and that the course he pursued made my mistress hate me and persecute me. If I wept, he would say, "Poor child! Don't cry! don't cry! I will make peace for you with your mistress. Only let me arrange matters in my own way. Poor, foolish girl! you don't know what is for your own good. I would cherish you. I would make a lady of you. Now go, and think of all I have promised you."

I did think of it.

Reader, I draw no imaginary pictures of southern homes. I am telling you the plain truth. Yet when victims make their escape from this wild beast of Slavery, northerners consent to act the part of bloodhounds, and hunt the poor fugitive back into his den, "full of dead men's bones, and all uncleanness." Nay, more, they are not only willing, but proud, to give their daughters in marriage to slaveholders. The poor girls have romantic notions of a sunny clime, and of the flowering vines that all the year round shade a happy home. To what disappointments are they destined! The young wife soon learns that the husband in whose hands she has placed her happiness pays no regard to his marriage vows. Children of every shade of complexion play with her own fair babies, and too well she knows that they are born unto him of his own household. Jealousy and hatred enter the flowery home, and it is ravaged of its loveliness.

Southern women often marry a man knowing that he is the father of many little slaves. They do not trouble themselves about it. They regard such children as property, as marketable as the pigs on the plantation; and it is seldom that they do not make them aware of this by passing them into the slave-trader's hands as soon as possible, and thus getting them out of their sight. I am glad to say there are some honorable exceptions.

I have myself known two southern wives who exhorted their husbands to free those slaves towards whom they stood in a "parental relation;" and their request was granted. These husbands blushed before the superior nobleness of their wives' natures. Though they had only counselled them to do that which it was their duty to do, it commanded their respect, and rendered their conduct more exemplary. Concealment was at an end, and confidence took the place of distrust.

Though this bad institution deadens the moral sense, even in white women, to a fearful extent, it is not altogether extinct. I have heard southern ladies say of Mr. Such a one, "He not only thinks it no disgrace to be the father of those little niggers, but he is not ashamed to call himself their master. I declare, such things ought not to be tolerated in any decent society!"

VII.

THE LOVER

Why does the slave ever love? Why allow the tendrils of the heart to twine around objects which may at any moment be wrenched away by the hand of violence? When separations come by the hand of death, the pious soul can bow in resignation, and say, "Not my will, but thine be done, O Lord!" But when the ruthless hand of man strikes the blow, regardless of the misery he causes, it is hard to be submissive. I did not reason thus when I was a young girl. Youth will be youth. I loved, and I indulged the hope that the dark clouds around me would turn out a bright lining. I forgot that in the land of my birth the shadows are too dense for light to penetrate. A land

"Where laughter is not mirth; nor thought the mind;
Nor words a language; nor e'en men mankind.
Where cries reply to curses, shrieks to blows,
And each is tortured in his separate hell."

There was in the neighborhood a young colored carpenter; a free born man. We had been well acquainted in childhood, and frequently met together afterwards. We became mutually attached, and he proposed to marry me. I loved him with all the ardor of a young girl's first love. But when I reflected that I was a slave, and that the laws gave no sanction to the marriage of such, my heart sank within me. My lover wanted to buy me; but I knew that Dr. Flint was too wilful and arbitrary a man to consent to that arrangement. From him, I was sure of experiencing all sorts of opposition, and I had nothing to hope from my mistress. She would have been delighted to have got rid of me, but not in that way. It would have relieved her mind of a burden if she could have seen me sold to some distant state, but if I was married near home I should be just as much in her husband's power as I had previously been,—for the husband of a slave has no power to protect her. Moreover, my mistress, like many others, seemed to think that slaves had no right to any family ties of their own; that they were created merely to wait upon the family of the mistress. I once heard her abuse a young slave girl, who told her that a colored man wanted to make her his wife. "I will have you peeled and pickled, my lady," said she, "if I ever hear you mention that subject again. Do you suppose that I will have you tending *my* children with the children of that nigger?" The girl to whom she said this had a mulatto child, of course not acknowledged by its father. The poor black man who loved her would have been proud to acknowledge his helpless offspring.

Many and anxious were the thoughts I revolved in my mind. I was at a loss what to do. Above all things, I was desirous to spare my lover the insults that had cut so deeply into my own soul. I talked with my grandmother about it, and partly told her my fears. I did not dare to tell her the worst. She had long suspected all was not right, and if I confirmed her suspicions I knew a storm would rise that would prove the overthrow of all my hopes.

This love-dream had been my support through many trials; and I could not bear to run the risk of having it suddenly dissipated. There was a lady in the neighborhood, a particular friend of Dr. Flint's, who often visited the house. I had a great respect for her, and she had always manifested a friendly interest in me. Grandmother thought she would have great influence with the doctor. I went to this lady, and told her my story. I told her I was aware that my lover's being a free-born man would prove a great objection; but he wanted to buy me; and if Dr. Flint would consent to that arrangement, I felt sure he would be willing to pay any reasonable price. She knew that Mrs. Flint disliked me; therefore, I ventured to suggest that perhaps my mistress would approve of my being sold, as that would rid her of me. The lady listened with kindly sympathy, and promised to do her utmost to promote my wishes. She had an interview with the doctor, and I believe she pleaded my cause earnestly; but it was all to no purpose.

How I dreaded my master now! Every minute I expected to be summoned to his presence; but the day passed, and I heard nothing from him. The next morning, a message was brought to me: "Master wants you in his study." I found the door ajar, and I stood a moment gazing at the hateful man who claimed a right to rule me, body and soul. I entered, and tried to appear calm. I did not want him to know how my heart was bleeding. He looked fixedly at me, with an expression which seemed to say, "I have half a mind to kill you on the spot." At last he broke the silence, and that was a relief to both of us.

"So you want to be married, do you?" said he, "and to a free nigger."

"Yes, sir."

"Well, I'll soon convince you whether I am your master, or the nigger fellow you honor so highly. If you *must* have a husband, you may take up with one of my slaves."

What a situation I should be in, as the wife of one of *his* slaves, even if my heart had been interested!

I replied, "Don't you suppose, sir, that a slave can have some preference about marrying? Do you suppose that all men are alike to her?"

"Do you love this nigger?" said he, abruptly.

"Yes, sir."

"How dare you tell me so!" he exclaimed, in great wrath. After a slight pause, he added, "I supposed you thought more of yourself; that you felt above the insults of such puppies."

I replied, "If he is a puppy I am a puppy, for we are both of the negro race. It is right and honorable for us to love each other. The man you call a puppy never insulted me, sir; and he would not love me if he did not believe me to be a virtuous woman."

He sprang upon me like a tiger, and gave me a stunning blow. It was the first time he had ever struck me; and fear did not enable me to control my anger. When I had recovered a little from the effects, I exclaimed, "You have struck me for answering you honestly. How I despise you!"

There was silence for some minutes. Perhaps he was deciding what should be my punishment; or, perhaps, he wanted to give me time to reflect on what I had said, and to whom I had said it. Finally, he asked, "Do you know what you have said?"

"Yes, sir; but your treatment drove me to it."

"Do you know that I have a right to do as I like with you,— that I can kill you, if I please?"

"You have tried to kill me, and I wish you had; but you have no right to do as you like with me."

"Silence!" he exclaimed, in a thundering voice. "By heavens, girl, you forget yourself too far! Are you mad? If you are, I will soon bring you to your senses. Do you think any other master would bear what I have borne from you this morning? Many masters would have killed you on the spot. How would you like to be sent to jail for your insolence?"

"I know I have been disrespectful, sir," I replied; "but you drove me to it; I couldn't help it. As for the jail, there would be more peace for me there than there is here."

"You deserve to go there," said he, "and to be under such treatment, that you would forget the meaning of the word *peace*. It would do you good. It would take some of your high notions out of you. But I am not ready to send you there yet, notwithstanding your ingratitude for all my kindness and forbearance. You have been the plague of my life. I have wanted to make you happy, and I have been repaid with the basest ingratitude; but though you have proved yourself incapable of appreciating my kindness, I will be lenient towards you, Linda. I will give you one more chance to redeem your character. If you behave yourself and do as I require, I will forgive you and treat you as I always have done; but if you disobey me, I will punish you as I would the meanest slave on my plantation. Never let me hear that fellow's name mentioned again. If I ever know of your speaking to him, I will cowhide you both; and if I catch him lurking about my premises, I will shoot him as soon as I would a dog. Do you hear what I say? I'll teach you a lesson about marriage and free niggers! Now go, and let this be the last time I have occasion to speak to you on this subject."

Reader, did you ever hate? I hope not. I never did but once; and I trust I never shall again. Somebody has called it "the atmosphere of hell;" and I believe it is so.

For a fortnight the doctor did not speak to me. He thought to mortify me; to make me feel that I had disgraced myself by receiving the honorable addresses of a respectable colored man, in preference to the base proposals of a white man. But though his lips disdained to address me, his eyes were very loquacious. No animal ever watched its prey more narrowly than he watched me. He knew that I could write, though he had failed to make me read his letters; and he was now troubled lest I should exchange letters with another man. After a while he became weary of silence; and I was sorry for it. One morning, as he passed through the hall, to leave the house, he contrived to thrust a note into my hand. I thought I had better read it, and spare myself the vexation of having him read it to me. It expressed regret for the blow he had given me, and reminded me that I myself was wholly to blame for it. He hoped I had become convinced of the injury I was doing myself by incurring his displeasure. He wrote that he had made up his mind to go to Louisiana; that he should take several slaves with him, and intended I should be one of the number. My mistress would remain where she was; therefore I should have nothing to fear from that quarter. If I merited kindness from him, he assured me that it would be lavishly bestowed. He begged me to think over the matter, and answer the following day.

The next morning I was called to carry a pair of scissors to his room. I laid them on the table, with the letter beside them. He thought it was my answer, and did not call me back. I went as usual to attend my young mistress to and from school. He met me in the street, and ordered me to stop at his office on my way back. When I entered, he showed me his letter, and asked me why I had not answered it. I replied, "I am your daughter's property, and it is in your power to send me, or take me, wherever you please." He said he was very glad to find me so willing to go, and that we should start early in the autumn. He had a large practice in the town, and I rather thought he had made up the story merely to frighten me. However that might be, I was determined that I would never go to Louisiana with him.

Summer passed away, and early in the autumn Dr. Flint's eldest son was sent to Louisiana to examine the country, with a view to emigrating. That news did not disturb me. I knew very well that I should not be sent with *him*. That I had not been taken to the plantation before this time, was owing to the fact that his son was there. He was jealous of his son; and jealousy of the overseer had kept him from punishing me by sending me into the fields to work. Is it strange that I was not proud of these protectors? As for the overseer, he was a man for whom I had less respect than I had for a bloodhound.

Young Mr. Flint did not bring back a favorable report of

Louisiana, and I heard no more of that scheme. Soon after this, my lover met me at the corner of the street, and I stopped to speak to him. Looking up, I saw my master watching us from his window. I hurried home, trembling with fear. I was sent for, immediately, to go to his room. He met me with a blow. "When is mistress to be married?" said he, in a sneering tone. A shower of oaths and imprecations followed. How thankful I was that my lover was a free man! that my tyrant had no power to flog him for speaking to me in the street!

Again and again I revolved in my mind how all this would end. There was no hope that the doctor would consent to sell me on any terms. He had an iron will, and was determined to keep me, and to conquer me. My lover was an intelligent and religious man. Even if he could have obtained permission to marry me while I was a slave, the marriage would give him no power to protect me from my master. It would have made him miserable to witness the insults I should have been subjected to. And then, if we had children, I knew they must "follow the condition of the mother." What a terrible blight that would be on the heart of a free, intelligent father! For *his* sake, I felt that I ought not to link his fate with my own unhappy destiny. He was going to Savannah to see about a little property left him by an uncle; and hard as it was to bring my feelings to it, I earnestly entreated him not to come back. I advised him to go to the Free States, where his tongue would not be tied, and where his intelligence would be of more avail to him. He left me, still hoping the day would come when I could be bought. With me the lamp of hope had gone out. The dream of my girlhood was over. I felt lonely and desolate.

Still I was not stripped of all. I still had my good grandmother, and my affectionate brother. When he put his arms round my neck, and looked into my eyes, as if to read there the troubles I dared not tell, I felt that I still had something to love. But even that pleasant emotion was chilled by the reflection that he might be torn from me at any moment, by some sudden freak of my master. If he had known how we loved each other, I think he would have exulted in separating us. We often planned together how we could get to the north. But, as William remarked, such things are easier said than done. My movements were very closely watched, and we had no means of getting any money to defray our expenses. As for grandmother, she was strongly opposed to her children's undertaking any such project. She had not forgotten poor Benjamin's sufferings, and she was afraid that if another child tried to escape, he would have a similar or a worse fate. To me, nothing seemed more dreadful than my present life. I said to myself, "William *must* be free. He shall go to the north, and I will follow him." Many a slave sister has formed the same plans. . . .

X.

A PERILOUS PASSAGE IN THE SLAVE GIRL'S LIFE

After my lover went away, Dr. Flint contrived a new plan. He seemed to have an idea that my fear of my mistress was his greatest obstacle. In the blandest tones, he told me that he was going to build a small house for me, in a secluded place, four miles away from the town. I shuddered; but I was constrained to listen, while he talked of his intention to give me a home of my own, and to make a lady of me. Hitherto, I had escaped my dreaded fate, by being in the midst of people. My grandmother had already had high words with my master about me. She had told him pretty plainly what she thought of his character, and there was considerable gossip in the neighborhood about our affairs, to which the open-mouthed jealousy of Mrs. Flint contributed not a little. When my master said he was going to build a house for me, and that he could do it with little trouble and expense, I was in hopes something would happen to frustrate his scheme; but I soon heard that the house was actually begun. I vowed before my Maker that I would never enter it. I had rather toil on the plantation from dawn till dark; I had rather live and die in jail, than drag on, from day to day, through such a living death. I was determined that the master, whom I so hated and loathed, who had blighted the prospects of my youth, and made my life a desert, should not, after my long struggle with him, succeed at last in trampling his victim under his feet. I would do any thing, every thing, for the sake of defeating him. What *could* I do? I thought and thought, till I became desperate, and made a plunge into the abyss.

And now, reader, I come to a period in my unhappy life,

which I would gladly forget if I could. The rememberance fills me with sorrow and shame. It pains me to tell you of it; but I have promised to tell you the truth, and I will do it honestly, let it cost me what it may. I will not try to screen myself behind the plea of compulsion from a master; for it was not so. Neither can I plead ignorance or thoughtlessness. For years, my master had done his utmost to pollute my mind with foul images, and to destroy the pure principles inculcated by my grandmother, and the good mistress of my childhood. The influences of slavery had had the same effect on me that they had on other young girls; they had made me prematurely knowing, concerning the evil ways of the world. I knew what I did, and I did it with deliberate calculation.

But, O, ye happy women, whose purity has been sheltered from childhood, who have been free to choose the objects of your affection, whose homes are protected by law, do not judge the poor desolate slave girl too severely! If slavery had been abolished, I, also, could have married the man of my choice; I could have had a home shielded by the laws; and I should have been spared the painful task of confessing what I am now about to relate; but all my prospects had been blighted by slavery. I wanted to keep myself pure; and, under the most adverse circumstances, I tried hard to preserve my self-respect; but I was struggling alone in the powerful grasp of the demon Slavery; and the monster proved too strong for me. I felt as if I was forsaken by God and man; as if all my efforts must be frustrated; and I became reckless in my despair.

I have told you that Dr. Flint's persecutions and his wife's jealousy had given rise to some gossip in the neighborhood. Among others, it chanced that a white unmarried gentleman had obtained some knowledge of the circumstances in which I was placed. He knew my grandmother, and often spoke to me in the street. He became interested for me, and asked questions about my master, which I answered in part. He expressed a great deal of sympathy, and a wish to aid me. He constantly sought opportunities to see me, and wrote to me frequently. I was a poor slave girl, only fifteen years old.

So much attention from a superior person was, of course, flattering; for human nature is the same in all. I also felt grate-

ful for his sympathy, and encouraged by his kind words. It
seemed to me a great thing to have such a friend. By degrees, a
more tender feeling crept into my heart. He was an educated
and eloquent gentleman; too eloquent, alas, for the poor slave
girl who trusted in him. Of course I saw whither all this was
tending. I knew the impassable gulf between us; but to be an
object of interest to a man who is not married, and who is not
her master, is agreeable to the pride and feelings of a slave, if
her miserable situation has left her any pride or sentiment. It
seems less degrading to give one's self, than to submit to compulsion. There is something akin to freedom in having a lover
who has no control over you, except that which he gains by
kindness and attachment. A master may treat you as rudely as
he pleases, and you dare not speak; moreover, the wrong does
not seem so great with an unmarried man, as with one who has
a wife to be made unhappy. There may be sophistry in all this;
but the condition of a slave confuses all principles of morality,
and, in fact, renders the practice of them impossible.

When I found that my master had actually begun to build
the lonely cottage, other feelings mixed with those I have described. Revenge, and calculations of interest, were added to
flattered vanity and sincere gratitude for kindness. I knew
nothing would enrage Dr. Flint so much as to know that I favored another; and it was something to triumph over my tyrant
even in that small way. I thought he would revenge himself by
selling me, and I was sure my friend, Mr. Sands, would buy
me. He was a man of more generosity and feeling than my master, and I thought my freedom could be easily obtained from
him. The crisis of my fate now came so near that I was desperate. I shuddered to think of being the mother of children that
should be owned by my old tyrant. I knew that as soon as a new
fancy took him, his victims were sold far off to get rid of them;
especially if they had children. I had seen several women sold,
with his babies at the breast. He never allowed his offspring by
slaves to remain long in sight of himself and his wife. Of a man
who was not my master I could ask to have my children well
supported; and in this case, I felt confident I should obtain the
boon. I also felt quite sure that they would be made free. With
all these thoughts revolving in my mind, and seeing no other

way of escaping the doom I so much dreaded, I made a head-
long plunge. Pity me, and pardon me, O virtuous reader! You
never knew what it is to be a slave; to be entirely unprotected
by law or custom; to have the laws reduce you to the condition
of a chattel, entirely subject to the will of another. You never
exhausted your ingenuity in avoiding the snares, and eluding the
power of a hated tyrant; you never shuddered at the sound of
his footsteps, and trembled within hearing of his voice. I know
I did wrong. No one can feel it more sensibly than I do. The
painful and humiliating memory will haunt me to my dying
day. Still, in looking back, calmly, on the events of my life, I
feel that the slave woman ought not to be judged by the same
standard as others.

The months passed on. I had many unhappy hours. I secretly
mourned over the sorrow I was bringing on my grandmother,
who had so tried to shield me from harm. I knew that I was the
greatest comfort of her old age, and that it was a source of
pride to her that I had not degraded myself, like most of the
slaves. I wanted to confess to her that I was no longer worthy of
her love; but I could not utter the dreaded words.

As for Dr. Flint, I had a feeling of satisfaction and triumph
in the thought of telling *him*. From time to time he told me of
his intended arrangements, and I was silent. At last, he came
and told me the cottage was completed, and ordered me to go to
it. I told him I would never enter it. He said, "I have heard
enough of such talk as that. You shall go, if you are carried by
force; and you shall remain there."

I replied, "I will never go there. In a few months I shall be
a mother."

He stood and looked at me in dumb amazement, and left the
house without a word. I thought I should be happy in my triumph over him. But now that the truth was out, and my relatives would hear of it, I felt wretched. Humbled as were their
circumstances, they had pride in my good character. Now, how
could I look them in the face? My self-respect was gone! I had
resolved that I would be virtuous, though I was a slave. I had
said, "Let the storm beat! I will brave it till I die." And now,
how humiliated I felt!

I went to my grandmother. My lips moved to make confes-
sion, but the words stuck in my throat. I sat down in the shade

of a tree at her door and began to sew. I think she saw something unusual was the matter with me. The mother of slaves is very watchful. She knows there is no security for her children. After they have entered their teens she lives in daily expectation of trouble. This leads to many questions. If the girl is of a sensitive nature, timidity keeps her from answering truthfully, and this well-meant course has a tendency to drive her from maternal counsels. Presently, in came my mistress, like a mad woman, and accused me concerning her husband. My grandmother, whose suspicions had been previously awakened, believed what she said. She exclaimed, "O Linda! has it come to this? I had rather see you dead than to see you as you now are. You are a disgrace to your dead mother." She tore from my fingers my mother's wedding ring and her silver thimble. "Go away!" she exclaimed, "and never come to my house, again." Her reproaches fell so hot and heavy, that they left me no chance to answer. Bitter tears, such as the eyes never shed but once, were my only answer. I rose from my seat, but fell back again, sobbing. She did not speak to me; but the tears were running down her furrowed cheeks, and they scorched me like fire. She had always been so kind to me! *So* kind! How I longed to throw myself at her feet, and tell her all the truth! But she had ordered me to go, and never to come there again. After a few minutes, I mustered strength, and started to obey her. With what feelings did I now close that little gate, which I used to open with such an eager hand in my childhood! It closed upon me with a sound I never heard before.

Where could I go? I was afraid to return to my master's. I walked on recklessly, not caring where I went, or what would become of me. When I had gone four or five miles, fatigue compelled me to stop. I sat down on the stump of an old tree. The stars were shining through the boughs above me. How they mocked me, with their bright, calm light! The hours passed by, and as I sat there alone a chilliness and deadly sickness came over me. I sank on the ground. My mind was full of horrid thoughts. I prayed to die; but the prayer was not answered. At last, with great effort I roused myself, and walked some distance further, to the house of a woman who had been a friend of my mother. When I told her why I was there, she spoke soothingly to me; but I could not be comforted. I thought I

could bear my shame if I could only be reconciled to my grandmother. I longed to open my heart to her. I thought if she could
know the real state of the case, and all I had been bearing for
years, she would perhaps judge me less harshly. My friend advised me to send for her. I did so; but days of agonizing suspense passed before she came. Had she utterly forsaken me?
No. She came at last. I knelt before her, and told her the things
that had poisoned my life; how long I had been persecuted;
that I saw no way of escape; and in an hour of extremity I had
become desperate. She listened in silence. I told her I would
bear any thing and do any thing, if in time I had hopes of
obtaining her forgiveness. I begged of her to pity me, for my
dead mother's sake. And she did pity me. She did not say, "I
forgive you;" but she looked at me lovingly, with her eyes full
of tears. She laid her old hand gently on my head, and mur-
mured, "Poor child! Poor child!" . . .

XIV.
ANOTHER LINK TO LIFE.

I had not returned to my master's house since the birth of
my child. The old man raved to have me thus removed from
his immediate power; but his wife vowed, by all that was good
and great, she would kill me if I came back; and he did not
doubt her word. Sometimes he would stay away for a season.
Then he would come and renew the old threadbare discourse
about his forbearance and my ingratitude. He labored, most
unnecessarily, to convince me that I had lowered myself. The
venomous old reprobate had no need of descanting on that
theme. I felt humiliated enough. My unconscious babe was the
ever-present witness of my shame. I listened with silent contempt when he talked about my having forfeited *his* good opinion; but I shed bitter tears that I was no longer worthy of being
respected by the good and pure. Alas! slavery still held me in
its poisonous grasp. There was no chance for me to be respectable. There was no prospect of being able to lead a better life.

Sometimes, when my master found that I still refused to accept what he called his kind offers, he would threaten to sell my
child. "Perhaps that will humble you," said he.

Humble *me!* Was I not already in the dust? But his threat lacerated my heart. I knew the law gave him power to fulfil it; for slaveholders have been cunning enough to enact that "the child shall follow the condition of the *mother*," not of the *father;* thus taking care that licentiousness shall not interfere with avarice. This reflection made me clasp my innocent babe all the more firmly to my heart. Horrid visions passed through my mind when I thought of his liability to fall into the slave trader's hands. I wept over him, and said, "O my child! perhaps they will leave you in some cold cabin to die, and then throw you into a hole, as if you were a dog."

When Dr. Flint learned that I was again to be a mother, he was exasperated beyond measure. He rushed from the house, and returned with a pair of shears. I had a fine head of hair; and he often railed about my pride of arranging it nicely. He cut every hair close to my head, storming and swearing all the time. I replied to some of his abuse, and he struck me. Some months before, he had pitched me down stairs in a fit of passion; and the injury I received was so serious that I was unable to turn myself in bed for many days. He then said, "Linda, I swear by God I will never raise my hand against you again;" but I knew that he would forget his promise.

After he discovered my situation, he was like a restless spirit from the pit. He came every day; and I was subjected to such insults as no pen can describe. I would not describe them if I could; they were too low, too revolting. I tried to keep them from my grandmother's knowledge as much as I could. I knew she had enough to sadden her life, without having my troubles to bear. When she saw the doctor treat me with violence, and heard him utter oaths terrible enough to palsy a man's tongue, she could not always hold her peace. It was natural and mother-like that she should try to defend me; but it only made matters worse.

When they told me my new-born babe was a girl, my heart was heavier than it had ever been before. Slavery is terrible for men; but it is far more terrible for women. Superadded to the burden common to all, *they* have wrongs, and sufferings, and mortifications peculiarly their own.

Dr. Flint had sworn that he would make me suffer, to my last day, for this new crime against *him*, as he called it; and as long as he had me in his power he kept his word. On the fourth day after the birth of my babe, he entered my room suddenly, and commanded me to rise and bring my baby to him. The nurse who took care of me had gone out of the room to prepare some nourishment, and I was alone. There was no alternative. I rose, took up my babe, and crossed the room to where he sat. "Now stand there," said he, "till I tell you to go back!" My child bore a strong resemblance to her father, and to the deceased Mrs. Sands, her grandmother. He noticed this; and while I stood before him, trembling with weakness, he heaped upon me and my little one every vile epithet he could think of. Even the grandmother in her grave did not escape his curses. In the midst of his vituperations I fainted at his feet. This recalled him to his senses. He took the baby from my arms, laid it on the bed, dashed cold water in my face, took me up, and shook me violently, to restore my consciousness before any one entered the room. Just then my grandmother came in, and he hurried out of the house. I suffered in consequence of this treatment; but I begged my friends to let me die, rather than send for the doctor. There was nothing I dreaded so much as his presence. My life was spared; and I was glad for the sake of my little ones. Had it not been for these ties to life, I should have been glad to be released by death, though I had lived only nineteen years.

Always it gave me a pang that my children had no lawful claim to a name. Their father offered his; but, if I had wished to accept the offer, I dared not while my master lived. Moreover, I knew it would not be accepted at their baptism. A Christian name they were at least entitled to; and we resolved to call my boy for our dear good Benjamin, who had gone far away from us.

My grandmother belonged to the church; and she was very desirous of having the children christened. I knew Dr. Flint would forbid it, and I did not venture to attempt it. But chance favored me. He was called to visit a patient out of town, and was obliged to be absent during Sunday. "Now is the time," said my grandmother; "we will take the children to church, and have them christened."

When I entered the church, recollections of my mother came

over me, and I felt subdued in spirit. There she had presented me for baptism, without any reason to feel ashamed. She had been married, and had such legal rights as slavery allows to a slave. The vows had at least been sacred to *her,* and she had never violated them. I was glad she was not alive, to know under what different circumstances her grandchildren were presented for baptism. Why had my lot been so different from my mother's? *Her* master had died when she was a child; and she remained with her mistress till she married. She was never in the power of any master; and thus she escaped one class of the evils that generally fall upon slaves.

When my baby was about to be christened, the former mistress of my father stepped up to me, and proposed to give it her Christian name. To this I added the surname of my father, who had himself no legal right to it; for my grandfather on the paternal side was a white gentleman. What tangled skeins are the genealogies of slavery! I loved my father; but it mortified me to be obliged to bestow his name on my children.

When we left the church, my father's old mistress invited me to go home with her. She clasped a gold chain round my baby's neck. I thanked her for this kindness; but I did not like the emblem. I wanted no chain to be fastened on my daughter, not even if its links were of gold. How earnestly I prayed that she might never feel the weight of slavery's chain, whose iron entereth into the soul!

XV.
CONTINUED PERSECUTIONS.

My children grew finely; and Dr. Flint would often say to me, with an exulting smile, "These brats will bring me a handsome sum of money one of these days."

I thought to myself that, God being my helper, they should never pass into his hands. It seemed to me I would rather see them killed than have them given up to his power. The money for the freedom of myself and my children could be obtained; but I derived no advantage from that circumstance. Dr. Flint loved money, but he loved power more. After much discussion, my friends resolved on making another trial. There was a slaveholder about to leave for Texas, and he was commissioned to buy me. He was to begin with nine hundred dollars, and go up to twelve. My master refused his offers. "Sir," said he, "she don't belong to me. She is my daughter's property, and I have no right to sell her. I mistrust that you come from her paramour. If so, you may tell him that he cannot buy her for any money; neither can he buy her children."

The doctor came to see me the next day, and my heart beat quicker as he entered. I never had seen the old man tread with so majestic a step. He seated himself and looked at me with withering scorn. My children had learned to be afraid of him. The little one would shut her eyes and hide her face on my shoulder whenever she saw him; and Benny, who was now nearly five years old, often inquired, "What makes that bad man come here so many times? Does he want to hurt us?" I would clasp the dear boy in my arms, trusting that he would be free before he was old enough to solve the problem. And now, as the doctor sat there so grim and silent, the child left his play and came and nestled up by me. At last my tormentor spoke. "So you are left in disgust, are you?" said he. "It is no more than I expected. You remember I told you years ago that you would be treated so. So he is tired of you? Ha! ha! ha! The virtuous madam don't like to hear about it, does she? Ha! ha! ha!" There was a sting in his calling me virtuous madam. I no longer had the power of answering him as I had formerly done. He continued: "So it seems you are trying to get up another intrigue. Your new paramour came to me, and offered to buy you; but you may be assured you will not succeed. You are mine; and you shall be mine for life. There lives no human being that can take you out of slavery. I would have done it; but you rejected my kind offer."

I told him I did not wish to get up any intrigue; that I had never seen the man who offered to buy me.

"Do you tell me I lie?" exclaimed he, dragging me from my chair. "Will you say again that you never saw that man?"

I answered, "I do say so."

He clinched my arm with a volley of oaths. Ben began to scream, and I told him to go to his grandmother.

"Don't you stir a step, you little wretch!" said he. The child drew nearer to me, and put his arms round me, as if he wanted to protect me. This was too much for my enraged master. He caught him up and hurled him across the room. I thought he was dead, and rushed towards him to take him up.

"Not yet!" exclaimed the doctor. "Let him lie there till he comes to."

"Let me go! Let me go!" I screamed, "or I will raise the whole house." I struggled and got away; but he clinched me again. Somebody opened the door, and he released me. I picked up my insensible child, and when I turned my tormentor was gone. Anxiously I bent over the little form, so pale and still; and when the brown eyes at last opened, I don't know whether I was very happy.

All the doctor's former persecutions were renewed. He came morning, noon, and night. No jealous lover ever watched a rival more closely than he watched me and the unknown slaveholder, with whom he accused me of wishing to get up an intrigue. When my grandmother was out of the way he searched every room to find him.

In one of his visits, he happened to find a young girl, whom he had sold to a trader a few days previous. His statement was, that he sold her because she had been too familiar with the overseer. She had had a bitter life with him, and was glad to be sold. She had no mother, and no near ties. She had been torn from all her family years before. A few friends had entered into bonds for her safety, if the trader would allow her to spend with them the time that intervened between her sale and the gathering up of his human stock. Such a favor was rarely granted. It saved the trader the expense of board and jail fees, and though the amount was small, it was a weighty consideration in a slave-trader's mind.

Dr. Flint always had an aversion to meeting slaves after he had sold them. He ordered Rose out of the house; but he was no longer her master, and she took no notice of him. For once the crushed Rose was the conqueror. His gray eyes flashed angrily upon her; but that was the extent of his power. "How came this girl here?" he exclaimed. "What right had you to allow it, when you knew I had sold her?"

I answered "This is my grandmother's house, and Rose came

to see her. I have no right to turn any body out of doors, that comes here for honest purposes."

He gave me the blow that would have fallen upon Rose if she had still been his slave. My grandmother's attention had been attracted by loud voices, and she entered in time to see a second blow dealt. She was not a woman to let such an outrage, in her own house, go unrebuked. The doctor undertook to explain that I had been insolent. Her indignant feelings rose higher and higher, and finally boiled over in words. "Get out of my house!" she exclaimed. "Go home, and take care of your wife and children, and you will have enough to do, without watching my family."

He threw the birth of my children in her face, and accused her of sanctioning the life I was leading. She told him I was living with her by compulsion of his wife; that he needn't accuse her, for he was the one to blame; he was the one who had caused all the trouble. She grew more and more excited as she went on. "I tell you what, Dr. Flint," said she, "you ain't got many more years to live, and you'd better be saying your prayers. It will take 'em all, and more too, to wash the dirt off your soul."

"Do you know whom you are talking to?" he exclaimed.

She replied, "Yes, I know very well who I am talking to."

He left the house in a great rage. I looked at my grandmother. Our eyes met. Their angry expression had passed away, but she looked sorrowful and weary—weary of incessant strife. I wondered that it did not lessen her love for me; but if it did she never showed it. She was always kind, always ready to sympathize with my troubles. There might have been peace and contentment in that humble home if it had not been for the demon Slavery.

The winter passed undisturbed by the doctor. The beautiful spring came; and when Nature resumes her loveliness, the human soul is apt to revive also. My drooping hopes came to life again with the flowers. I was dreaming of freedom again; more for my children's sake than my own. I planned and I planned. Obstacles hit against plans. There seemed no way of overcoming them; and yet I hoped.

Back came the wily doctor. I was not at home when he called.

A friend had invited me to a small party, and to gratify her I went. To my great consternation, a messenger came in haste to say that Dr. Flint was at my grandmother's, and insisted on seeing me. They did not tell him where I was, or he would have come and raised a disturbance in my friend's house. They sent me a dark wrapper; I threw it on and hurried home. My speed did not save me; the doctor had gone away in anger. I dreaded the morning, but I could not delay it; it came, warm and bright. At an early hour the doctor came and asked me where I had been last night. I told him. He did not believe me, and sent to my friend's house to ascertain the facts. He came in the afternoon to assure me he was satisfied that I had spoken the truth. He seemed to be in a facetious mood, and I expected some jeers were coming. "I suppose you need some recreation," said he, "but I am surprised at your being there, among those negroes. It was not the place for *you*. Are you *allowed* to visit such people?"

I understood this covert fling at the white gentleman who was my friend; but I merely replied, "I went to visit my friends, and any company they keep is good enough for me."

He went on to say, "I have seen very little of you of late, but my interest in you is unchanged. When I said I would have no more mercy on you I was rash. I recall my words. Linda, you desire freedom for yourself and your children, and you can obtain it only through me. If you agree to what I am about to propose, you and they shall be free. There must be no communication of any kind between you and their father. I will procure a cottage, where you and the children can live together. Your labor shall be light, such as sewing for my family. Think what is offered you, Linda—a home and freedom! Let the past be forgotten. If I have been harsh with you at times, your wilfulness drove me to it. You know I exact obedience from my own children, and I consider you as yet a child."

He paused for an answer, but I remained silent.

"Why don't you speak?" said he. "What more do you wait for?"

"Nothing, sir."

"Then you accept my offer?"

"No, sir."

His anger was ready to break loose; but he succeeded in curbing it, and replied, "You have answered without thought. But I must let you know there are two sides to my proposition; if you reject the bright side, you will be obliged to take the dark one. You must either accept my offer, or you and your children shall be sent to your young master's plantation, there to remain till your young mistress is married; and your children shall fare like the rest of the negro children. I give you a week to consider of it."

He was shrewd; but I knew he was not to be trusted. I told him I was ready to give my answer now.

"I will not receive it now," he replied. "You act too much from impulse. Remember that you and your children can be free a week from to-day if you choose."

On what a monstrous chance hung the destiny of my children! I knew that my master's offer was a snare, and that if I entered it escape would be impossible. As for his promise, I knew him so well that I was sure if he gave me free papers, they would be so managed as to have no legal value. The alternative was inevitable. I resolved to go to the plantation. But then I thought how completely I should be in his power, and the prospect was appalling. Even if I should kneel before him, and implore him to spare me, for the sake of my children, I knew he would spurn me with his foot, and my weakness would be his triumph.

Before the week expired, I heard that young Mr. Flint was about to be married to a lady of his own stamp. I foresaw the position I should occupy in his establishment. I had once been sent to the plantation for punishment, and fear of the son had induced the father to recall me very soon. My mind was made up; I was resolved that I would foil my master and save my children, or I would perish in the attempt. I kept my plans to myself; I knew that friends would try to dissuade me from them, and I would not wound their feelings by rejecting their advice.

On the decisive day the doctor came, and said he hoped I had made a wise choice.

"I am ready to go to the plantation, sir," I replied.

"Have you thought how important your decision is to your children?" said he.

I told him I had.

"Very well. Go to the plantation, and my curse go with you," he replied. "Your boy shall be put to work, and he shall soon be sold; and your girl shall be raised for the purpose of selling well. Go your own ways!" He left the room with curses, not to be repeated.

As I stood rooted to the spot, my grandmother came and said, "Linda, child, what did you tell him?"

I answered that I was going to the plantation.

"*Must* you go?" said she. "Can't something be done to stop it?"

I told her it was useless to try; but she begged me not to give up. She said she would go to the doctor, and remind him how long and how faithfully she had served in the family, and how she had taken her own baby from her breast to nourish his wife. She would tell him I had been out of the family so long they would not miss me; that she would pay them for my time, and the money would procure a woman who had more strength for the situation than I had. I begged her not to go; but she persisted in saying, "He will listen to *me*, Linda." She went, and was treated as I expected. He coolly listened to what she said, but denied her request. He told her that what he did was for my good, that my feelings were entirely above my situation, and that on the plantation I would receive treatment that was suitable to my behavior.

My grandmother was much cast down. I had my secret hopes; but I must fight my battle alone. I had a woman's pride, and a mother's love for my children; and I resolved that out of the darkness of this hour a brighter dawn should rise for them. My master had power and law on his side; I had a determined will. There is might in each.

XVII.

THE FLIGHT.

Mr. Flint was hard pushed for house servants, and rather than lose me he had restrained his malice. I did my work faithfully, though not, of course, with a willing mind. They were evidently afraid I should leave them. Mr. Flint wished that I should sleep in the great house instead of the servants' quarters.

His wife agreed to the proposition, but said I mustn't bring my
bed into the house, because it would scatter feathers on her carpet. I knew when I went there that they would never think of
such a thing as furnishing a bed of any kind for me and my
little one. I therefore carried my own bed, and now I was forbidden to use it. I did as I was ordered. But now that I was
certain my children were to be put in their power, in order to
give them a stronger hold on me, I resolved to leave them that
night. I remembered the grief this step would bring upon my
dear old grandmother; and nothing less than the freedom of my
children would have induced me to disregard her advice. I went
about my evening work with trembling steps. Mr. Flint twice
called from his chamber door to inquire why the house was not
locked up. I replied that I had not done my work. "You have
had time enough to do it," said he. "Take care how you answer
me!"

I shut all the windows, locked all the doors, and went up to
the third story, to wait till midnight. How long those hours
seemed, and how fervently I prayed that God would not forsake
me in this hour of utmost need! I was about to risk every thing
on the throw of a die; and if I failed, O what would become of
me and my poor children? They would be made to suffer for
my fault.

At half past twelve I stole softly down stairs. I stopped on
the second floor, thinking I heard a noise. I felt my way down
into the parlor, and looked out of the window. The night was so
intensely dark that I could see nothing. I raised the window
very softly and jumped out. Large drops of rain were falling,
and the darkness bewildered me. I dropped on my knees, and
breathed a short prayer to God for guidance and protection. I
groped my way to the road, and rushed towards the town with
almost lightning speed. I arrived at my grandmother's house,
but dared not see her. She would say, "Linda, you are killing
me;" and I knew that would unnerve me. I tapped softly at the
window of a room, occupied by a woman, who had lived in the
house several years. I knew she was a faithful friend, and could
be trusted with my secret. I tapped several times before she
heard me. At last she raised the window, and I whispered,
"Sally, I have run away. Let me in, quick." She opened the

Samuel Thomson

Title page of his book

NEW

GUIDE TO HEALTH;

OR

BOTANIC FAMILY PHYSICIAN.

CONTAINING

A COMPLETE SYSTEM OF PRACTICE,

ON A PLAN ENTIRELY NEW:

WITH A DESCRIPTION OF THE VEGETABLES MADE
USE OF, AND DIRECTIONS FOR PREPARING AND
ADMINISTERING THEM, TO CURE DISEASE

TO WHICH IS PREFIXED,

A NARRATIVE

OF THE

LIFE AND MEDICAL DISCOVERIES

OF THE AUTHOR.

BY SAMUEL THOMSON.

BOSTON:
Printed for the Author, and sold by his General Agent, at
the Office of the Boston Investigator.
J. Q. Adams, Printer.
1835.

Lucy P. Vincent Smith

*Dukes County Historical
Society, Edgartown, Mass.*

A page from her journal

*Nicholson Whaling
Collection, Providence
Public Library*

Joshua Slocum

Cover of Joshua
Slocum's book

Albert Pinkham Ryder
Portrait by Kenneth Hayes Miller (1876-1952)

door softly, and said in low tones, "For God's sake, don't. Your grandmother is trying to buy you and de chillern. Mr. Sands was here last week. He tole her he was going away on business, but he wanted her to go ahead about buying you and de chillern, and he would help her all he could. Don't run away, Linda. Your grandmother is all bowed down wid trouble now."

I replied, "Sally, they are going to carry my children to the plantation to-morrow; and they will never sell them to any body so long as they have me in their power. Now, would you advise me to go back?"

"No, chile, no," answered she. "When dey finds you is gone, dey won't want de plague ob de chillern; but where is you going to hide? Dey knows ebery inch ob dis house."

I told her I had a hiding-place, and that was all it was best for her to know. I asked her to go into my room as soon as it was light, and take all my clothes out of my trunk, and pack them in hers; for I knew Mr. Flint and the constable would be there early to search my room. I feared the sight of my children would be too much for my full heart; but I could not go out into the uncertain future without one last look. I bent over the bed where lay my little Benny and baby Ellen. Poor little ones! fatherless and motherless! Memories of their father came over me. He wanted to be kind to them; but they were not all to him, as they were to my womanly heart. I knelt and prayed for the innocent little sleepers. I kissed them lightly, and turned away.

As I was about to open the street door, Sally laid her hand on my shoulder, and said, "Linda, is you gwine all alone? Let me call your uncle."

"No, Sally," I replied, "I want no one to be brought into trouble on my account."

I went forth into the darkness and rain. I ran on till I came to the house of the friend who was to conceal me.

Early the next morning Mr. Flint was at my grandmother's inquiring for me. She told him she had not seen me, and supposed I was at the plantation. He watched her face narrowly, and said, "Don't you know any thing about her running off?" She assured him that she did not. He went on to say, "Last night she ran off without the least provocation. We had treated her very kindly. My wife liked her. She will soon be found and brought back. Are her children with you?" When told that they were, he said, "I am very glad to hear that. If they are here, she cannot be far off. If I find out that any of my niggers have had any thing to do with this damned business, I'll give 'em five hundred lashes." As he started to go to his father's, he turned round and added, persuasively, "Let her be brought back, and she shall have her children to live with her."

The tidings made the old doctor rave and storm at a furious rate. It was a busy day for them. My grandmother's house was searched from top to bottom. As my trunk was empty, they concluded I had taken my clothes with me. Before ten o'clock every vessel northward bound was thoroughly examined, and the law against harboring fugitives was read to all on board. At night a watch was set over the town. Knowing how distressed my grandmother would be, I wanted to send her a message; but it could not be done. Every one who went in or out of her house was closely watched. The doctor said he would take my children, unless she became responsible for them; which of course she willingly did. . . .

XXI.

THE LOOPHOLE OF RETREAT.

A small shed had been added to my grandmother's house years ago. Some boards were laid across the joists at the top, and between these boards and the roof was a very small garret, never occupied by any thing but rats and mice. It was a pent roof, covered with nothing but shingles, according to the southern custom for such buildings. The garret was only nine feet long and seven wide. The highest part was three feet high, and sloped down abruptly to the loose board floor. There was no admission for either light or air. My uncle Phillip, who was a carpenter, had very skilfully made a concealed trap-door, which communicated with the storeroom. He had been doing this while I was waiting in the swamp. The storeroom opened upon a piazza. To this hole I was conveyed as soon as I entered the house. The air was stifling; the darkness total. A bed had been spread on the floor. I could sleep quite comfortably on one side; but the slope was so sudden that I could not turn on the

other without hitting the roof. The rats and mice ran over my
bed; but I was weary, and I slept such sleep as the wretched
may, when a tempest has passed over them. Morning came. I
knew it only by the noises I heard; for in my small den day and
night were all the same. I suffered for air even more than for
light. But I was not comfortless. I heard the voices of my children. There was joy and there was sadness in the sound. It
made my tears flow. How I longed to speak to them! I was
eager to look on their faces; but there was no hole, no crack,
through which I could peep. This continued darkness was op-
pressive. It seemed horrible to sit or lie in a cramped position
day after day, without one gleam of light. Yet I would have
chosen this, rather than my lot as a slave, though white people
considered it an easy one; and it was so compared with the fate
of others. I was never cruelly over-worked; I was never lacerated with the whip from head to foot; I was never so beaten
and bruised that I could not turn from one side to the other; I
never had my heel-strings cut to prevent my running away; I
was never chained to a log and forced to drag it about, while
I toiled in the fields from morning till night; I was never
branded with hot iron, or torn by bloodhounds. On the contrary, I had always been kindly treated, and tenderly cared for,
until I came into the hands of Dr. Flint. I had never wished for
freedom till then. But though my life in slavery was comparatively devoid of hardships, God pity the woman who is compelled to lead such a life!

My food was passed up to me through the trap-door my uncle
had contrived; and my grandmother, my uncle Phillip, and
aunt Nancy would seize such opportunities as they could, to
mount up there and chat with me at the opening. But of course
this was not safe in the daytime. It must all be done in darkness.
It was impossible for me to move in an erect position, but I
crawled about my den for exercise. One day I hit my head
against something, and found it was a gimlet. My uncle had left
it sticking there when he made the trap-door. I was as rejoiced
as Robinson Crusoe could have been at finding such a treasure.
It put a lucky thought into my head. I said to myself, "Now I
will have some light. Now I will see my children." I did not
dare to begin my work during the daytime, for fear of attract-

ing attention. But I groped round; and having found the side
next the street, where I could frequently see my children, I
stuck the gimlet in and waited for evening. I bored three rows
of holes, one above another; then I bored out the interstices between. I thus succeeded in making one hole about an inch long
and an inch broad. I sat by it till late into the night, to enjoy
the little whiff of air that floated in. In the morning I watched
for my children. The first person I saw in the street was Dr.
Flint. I had a shuddering, superstitious feeling that it was a bad
omen. Several familiar faces passed by. At last I heard the
merry laugh of children, and presently two sweet little faces
were looking up at me, as though they knew I was there, and
were conscious of the joy they imparted. How I longed to *tell*
them I was there!

My condition was now a little improved. But for weeks I was
tormented by hundreds of little red insects, fine as a needle's
point, that pierced through my skin, and produced an intolerable burning. The good grandmother gave me herb teas and
cooling medicines, and finally I got rid of them. The heat of
my den was intense, for nothing but thin shingles protected me
from the scorching summer's sun. But I had my consolations.
Through my peeping-hole I could watch the children, and when
they were near enough, I could hear their talk. Aunt Nancy
brought me all the news she could hear at Dr. Flint's. From
her I learned that the doctor had written to New York to a
colored woman, who had been born and raised in our neighborhood, and had breathed his contaminating atmosphere. He offered her a reward if she could find out any thing about me. I
know not what was the nature of her reply; but he soon after
started for New York in haste, saying to his family that he had
business of importance to transact. I peeped at him as he
passed on his way to the steamboat. It was a satisfaction to
have miles of land and water between us, even for a little while;
and it was a still greater satisfaction to know that he believed
me to be in the Free States. My little den seemed less dreary
than it had done. He returned, as he did from his former journey to New York, without obtaining any satisfactory information. When he passed our house next morning, Benny was standing at the gate. He had heard them say that he had gone to find
me, and he called out, "Dr. Flint, did you bring my mother

home? I want to see her." The doctor stamped his foot at him in a rage, and exclaimed, "Get out of the way, you little damned rascal! If you don't, I'll cut off your head."

Benny ran terrified into the house, saying, "You can't put me in jail again. I don't belong to you now." It was well that the wind carried the words away from the doctor's ear. I told my grandmother of it, when we had our next conference at the trapdoor; and begged of her not to allow the children to be impertinent to the irascible old man.

Autumn came, with a pleasant abatement of heat. My eyes had become accustomed to the dim light, and by holding my book or work in a certain position near the aperture I contrived to read and sew. That was a great relief to the tedious monotony of my life. But when winter came, the cold penetrated through the thin shingle roof, and I was dreadfully chilled. The winters there are not so long, or so severe, as in northern latitudes; but the houses are not built to shelter from cold, and my little den was peculiarly comfortless. The kind grandmother brought me bed-clothes and warm drinks. Often I was obliged to lie in bed all day to keep comfortable; but with all my precautions, my shoulders and feet were frostbitten. O, those long, gloomy days, with no object for my eye to rest upon, and no thoughts to occupy my mind, except the dreary past and the uncertain future! I was thankful when there came a day sufficiently mild for me to wrap myself up and sit at the loophole to watch the passers by. Southerners have the habit of stopping and talking in the streets, and I heard many conversations not intended to meet my ears. I heard slave-hunters planning how to catch some poor fugitive. Several times I heard allusions to Dr. Flint, myself, and the history of my children, who, perhaps, were playing near the gate. One would say, "I wouldn't move my little finger to catch her, as old Flint's property." Another would say, "I'll catch *any* nigger for the reward. A man ought to have what belongs to him, if he *is* a damned brute." The opinion was often expressed that I was in the Free States. Very rarely did any one suggest that I might be in the vicinity. Had the least suspicion rested on my grandmother's house, it would have been burned to the ground. But it was the last place they thought of. Yet there was no place, where slavery existed, that could have afforded me so good a place of concealment. . . .

NANCY LUCE

(1820–1890)

Poor Little Hearts. Lines composed by Nancy Luce about poor little Ada Queetie, and poor little Beauty Linna, both deceased. Poor little Ada Queetie died February 25th, Thursday night, at 12 o'clock, 1858, aged most 9 years. Poor little Beauty Linna died January 18th, Tuesday night, most 2 o'clock, 1859, aged over 12 years. She lived 11 months lacking 7 days after poor Sissy's decease. 1860, 1866. 16 pp.

Nancy Luce was a strange and uncommonly interesting poet. She brought intensity to simple things. *Poor Little Hearts,* her masterpiece, is surely the ranking American naïve poem.

Poems and scraps of autobiography, eight items in all, Nancy Luce's little book presents a bibliographic mystery. It is dated 1860 at the top of the second page; the last page says, "Now Aug 1866." Author or printer, or both, moved slowly. Perhaps the printer, who did not put his name to the work, went off to the Civil War.

Island-born and raised, Nancy Luce never set foot on the mainland. Her birthplace, West Tisbury, Massachusetts, on Martha's Vineyard, became, in time, her burial place. Her father, Philip Luce, a small farmer, was forty-nine when she was born; her mother, Anna Manter Luce, was thirty-nine. When Nancy was thirteen, her parents failed in health and could not work. Being the only child, she had to support them. She worked early and late—farming; knitting socks and mittens, which she sold; and also conducting a commission business. She was enterprising, kept her accounts, and wrote a beautiful hand. Riding seems to have been her chief pleasure during her early years. She loved "a good, handsome, lively, cantering horse," and is reputed to have been a fine horsewoman.

But then Nancy, hardly twenty, also became sick. Some have said she expected to marry a young man who left on a whaling voyage and did not return, but evidence is lacking. By the mid-

1840's, Nancy could no longer sit on a horse. "You cannot realize how dreadful hard it is to me," she wrote in one of her tiny hand-stitched journals, "because I cannot ride somewhere. . . . Understand me, it hurts my feelings at such a rate, to see horses cantering. . . . Understand me, the handsomer I see them look, & the smarter I see them, the more it hurts my feelings. . . ."

Illness and debt used up much of her father's property. When he died in 1847, Nancy inherited what was left. Some people thought her peculiar. The selectmen petitioned the court to appoint a guardian for her. They feared she was mentally incompetent, unable to manage by herself, and would become a charge of the town. She was then twenty-eight. The court ruled in Nancy's favor, however, and no guardian was appointed. From 1851, when her mother died, until her own death many years later, Nancy, who never married, lived alone with her animals.

It is hard to say what was actually wrong. The village doctor, William H. Luce, not a relative, was kind. "Dr. W H Luce, has cured many very bad complaints for me, & helpt many more of them, slowly, & patched along many more of them," Nancy Luce wrote. "It seems as if 2 of my worst complaints cannot be cured, only patched along. . . ." There were also those who refused to believe Nancy was not well and who said she only imagined it. She wrote them a poem.

Unbelievers

Walk out, do you good. You go to neighbors.
You do all your work. I glad I found you so comfortable.
I glad I found you so smart. I shall tell I found you well.
I suppose you no courage to do anything.
Put up swing on trees & swing, do you good.
Go south, do you good. Go to campground, do you good.
Take air, do you good. Take my horse & gallop it about.
Take cloth off your head, that is all that ails you.
Eat bread, eat meat, you be well.
Come go out with me or I won't come again. Come ride with me.
You keep your house clean, you do it yourself.
You make lath building yourself. You make butter yourself.
You stick your bean poles yourself.
Take fresh air, do you good.

You go to cattle show. You must come & see me.
You pretty smart. Ride out.
You pretty well. Come down to Edgartown.
You been pretty smart since I saw you last.
I shall tell Dr when I see him, I found you well.

Nancy Luce wrote and painted. None of her pictures survive. Living her life her own way, she shared her roof with her livestock. Hens never had such names as she gave hers: Teedie Leatie, Jantie Jaffy, Kalally Roseike, Teppetee Tappao, Phebea Paedeo, Meleany, Teatolly, Speckekey Lepurlyo, and Levendy Ludandy. Of cows—Nancy owned only one at a time—three got into her verse: Sarah Wilbor, Susannah Allen, and Red Cannon, the last proving worthy of a poem in Nancy's best syncopated style.

Red Cannon's Failings

Loud noise. Keep their noise going.
Won't eat blackgrass hay.
Raven for company
Won't come to be milked.
Go dry half their time when with calf.
Kick. Fluk.
Give little milk. Thin milk.
Rank milk. Hold up her milk.
Milk sour quick. Milk hard.
Horns long forward or turn back.
Horns large. Horns sprawl out to sides.
Hook me. Red cow.
Cream go up top in one night, milk not fit to use.
One part of cow large.
Skittish.
Jump. Hook down fence.
Mash down fence.
Run head through fence.
Meet cattle to fence and hook it down and won't come away.
Can't be governed when she has unclean spirit in her.
Short teats,
Bloody milk.

Nancy Luce struggled hard to make ends meet and avoid, in her eyes, the awful and final disgrace of becoming a pauper and being supported by poor relief. She sold eggs, milk, butter, and poems—her little book, at twenty-five cents a copy—and, later, a photograph of herself holding white bantam hens, also twenty-five cents. These were on sale at her house and also at the Martha's Vineyard Camp Meeting, which, by the 1870's, had become the largest in the world.

After *Poor Little Hearts* came *A Complete Edition of the Works of Nancy Luce, of West Tisbury, Dukes County, Mass.* . . . It was thirty-two pages and was printed in 1871, 1875, 1883, and 1888 by various job printers. In addition to poems, *A Complete Edition* contained a prose treatise, "Hens —Their Diseases and Cure," for Nancy Luce called herself a "doctor of hens." Actually, she knew a great deal about poultry and preached as well as practiced a higher ethic toward animals. "It is as distressing to dumb creatures to undergo sickness and death, as it is for human, and as distressing to be crueled . . ." she wrote.

As she grew older and more peculiar, and summer traffic to Martha's Vineyard increased, Nancy Luce became a legend. Drivers of livery-stable wagons took their fares on rides to see her, her cow, and her graveyard for hens. Some persons, Nancy wrote, "behaved well and bought books of me." Others teased her. "Gross sinners," she called the latter, and "stone hearts." Most regarded her as a harmless, amusing eccentric.

"A Well-Known Person Dead," read the headline to her obituary in the *Vineyard Gazette,* April 18, 1890. Over a period of thirty years, the newspaper said, "hundreds of people" had visited Nancy Luce.

I know of only two copies of *Poor Little Hearts,* one in the Harris Collection of American Poetry at Brown University, the other in the archives of Dukes County Historical Society, Edgartown, Massachusetts. All issues of *A Complete Edition* are scarce. Cheaply printed on poor quality paper, not many copies could have survived. The poem "Unbelievers" was left in manuscript; so far as I know it has not been published before. "Red Cannon's Failings" was not included in either *Poor Little Hearts,* or *A Complete Edition.* Half a dozen pieces have been published about Nancy Luce (see my *Cape Cod and the Offshore Islands,* 1970, p. 253).

POOR LITTLE HEARTS.

———•———

Poor little Ada Queetie has departed this life,
Never to be here no more,
No more to love, no more to speak,
No more to be my friend,
O how I long to see her with me, live and well,
Her heart and mine was united,
Love and feelings deeply rooted for each other,
She and I could never part,
I am left broken hearted.

O my poor deceased little Ada Queetie,
For her to undergo sickness and death,
And the parting of her, is more than I can endure,
She knew such a site, and her love and mine,
So deep in our hearts for each other,
Her sickness and death, and parting of her,
I never can get over, in neither body nor mind,
And it may hasten me to my long home,
My heart is in misery days and nights,
For my poor deceased little Ada Queetie,
Do consider the night I was left,
What I underwent, no tongue can express.

Poor little Ada Queetie's last sickness and death,
Destroyed my health at a unknown rate,
With my heart breaking and weeping,
I kept fire going night after night, to keep poor little dear warm,
Poor little heart, she was sick one week
With froth in her throat,
Then 10 days and grew worse, with dropsy in her stomach,
I keep getting up nights to see how she was,
And see what I could do for her,
I bathed and birthed her stomach,
And then give her medicines, but help was all in vain,

Three her last days and nights
She breathed the breath of life here on earth,
She was taken down very sick,
Then I was up all night long,
The second night I was up till I was going to fall,
When I fixed her in her box warm close by the fire,
Put warm clothes under, over, and around,
And left fire burning and lay down with all my clothes on,
A very little while, and got up and up all the time,
The third night I touched no bed at all,
Poor little heart, she was struck with death at half-past eleven
She died in my arms at twelve o'clock at night,   [o'clock,
O it was heart-rendering,
I could been heard to the road, from that time till daylight,
No tongue could express my misery of mind.

O my heart is consumed in the coffin under ground,
O my heart, my heart, she and I could never part,
Her feelings and mine was so great for each other,
She had more than common love,
And more than common wit,
Her heart was full of love for me,
Now every time I compose a few lines, I have a weeping spell.

O do consider my poor little heart,
She underwent sickness and death,
Deceased and sleeping in her coffin under ground,
O what I undergo for her,
She was my dear, and nearest friend, to love and pity me,
And to believe that I was sick,
She spoke to me, and looked at me most all the time,
And could not go from me.

Poor little heart, she used to jump down to the door to go out.
She would look around, and call me to go with her,
She found I could not go, she would come in again,
She loved her dear friendy so well,
She could not go out and leave me.

O my dear beloved little heart,
She was my own heart within me,   [chair,
When she was well and I was sick, and made out to sit in my

She knew I was sick, because I didn't say but a little to her,
She would stand close to me all the time,
And speak to me, and could not take her eyes off my face,
And looked as grieved, as if her heart must break,
She was so worried for me,
And if I was forced to lay down,
Then she was more worried than ever.

When poor little heart happened be out the room,
And I was forced to lay down,
She would come and speak at me, and take on,
As if her heart must break,
And come straight to me, and lament my case,
And would not go from me,
Her feelings was so deeply rooted,
In her heart for me.

Poor little heart, she has been sick 4 times in her lifetime,
I saved her life 3 times, the 4th time, she was taken away,
I was a doctor, and a nurse for her,
And put a little good porridge, and medicines
In her mouth with a tea spoon.

She was coming 9 years of age, when she was taken away,
By all I found out, very certain true,
Poor Sissy hatched her out her egg in Chilmark,
The reason she was taken away before poor Sissy,
Her constitution was as weak as weak could be.

They were brought from Chilmark to New Town,
And remained there one year,
For me to get able to take care of them,
And then they were brought to me.

No one never can replace my poor little hearts, live and well,
No one never can be company for me again,
No one never can I, have such a heart-aching feeling for again,
No one never can I, set so much by again, as I did by them.

Poor little Ada Queetie,
She used to do everything I told her, let it be what it would,
And knew every word I said to her.

If she was as far off as across the room,
And I made signs to her with my fingers,
She knew what it was, and would spring quick and do it.

If she was far off, and I only spake her name,
She would be sure to run to me at a dreadful swift rate,
Without wanting anything to eat.

She would do 34 wonderful cunning things,
Poor Sissy would do 39,
They would do part of them without telling,
And do all the rest of them with telling.

I used to dream distressing dreams,
About what was coming to pass,
And awoke making a dreadful noise,
And poor little Ada Queetie was making a mournful noise,
She was so worried for me,
Then I would speak to her and say, little dear,
Nothing ails your friendy,
Then she would stop and speak a few pretty words to me.

Now I dream about my poor little hearts,
Ever since they were taken away,
I dream I see them in my arms, then I dream I cant see them,
And keep asking where is my little dears,
No one speaks for a while, then some one speaks and says,
You never will see them again,
Then I awake taking on at a dreadful rate.

Poor little Ada Queetie,
She used to stand and study out things, she wanted to do,
And then she would go and do it.

She was a patient little heart,
And took everything very kind.

She used to turn first one eye, and then the other to look at me,
When I used to nod my head to her, she would come to me.

She used to get up to the glass, and stand and look sober,
And there fix her feathers, and then look again,
To see if she fixed them right.

When I used to go to the glass to put up my hair,
She would be sure and get up and stand close to my face,
Poor little Beauty Linna did the same, most of the times.

Poor little Ada Queetie,
She always used to want to get in my lap
And squeeze me close up, and talk pretty talk to me.

She always used to want I should hug her up close to my face,
And keep still there she loved me so well.

When she used to be in her little box to lay pretty egg,
She would peak up from under the chair,
To see her friendy's face.

When I used to take out account to charge a quart of milk,
She would get up and stand close to me,
And when I told her to shrug up her little shoulders,
She would shrug them up.

She always used to say yesa yesa dear friendy,
I will do just as you say.

She used to do all manner of funny things,
As soon as I told her.

She used to shake my Cape, with all her strength and might,
Every time I told her,
They would both put one foot into my hand,
Every time I told them,
They would both scratch my hand, and pick on my Cape,
Every time I told them.

When some one used to happen to shut them out the room,
They would take on at a dreadful rate,
I let them straight in, and as soon as the person was gone,
Poor little Ada Queetie would not keep out my lap,
Squeezing me close up, talking to me,
Poor little Beauty Linna would not keep off my shoulder,
With her face squeezed close to my face talking to me.
They was so glad they got back in this room with me,
And I wasn't hurt, nor carried away.

Consider those dear little hearts, that loved me so well,
And depended all on me, to be their true friend.

When they was both alive, and I had fire in the kitchen
And it come up too cold for them,
They would both go in the room, and call me to come to them,
They would stand side and side, and look at the fire-place and
Meaning me to make fire there for them,   [look at me,
Then I would make fire there, and they and I set down together,
Now they are gone, and I am left broken-hearted.

Poor little Beauty Linna has departed this life,
My hands was around her by the fire, my heart aching,
I wept steady from that time till next day,
Poor little heart, she underwent sickness, and death,
Is more than I can endure,
I took the best care of her days and nights,
I did everything that could be done
I did the best that I could do,
I sot up with her nights, till it made me very lame,
When I fixed her in her box warm close by the fire,
Put warm clothes under, over, and around,
And left fire burning and lay down with all my clothes on,
And got up very often with her, and sot up as long as I could,
I never took off none of my clothes for 18 days and nights,
And I did everything to help her complaint,
But help was all in vain,
Medicines could not start her complaint,
Away she must be hurled to pay the debt that we all owe,
Which is to nature due,
They had no sin to answer for, human have that.

I found I could not set up all night at a time, with poor little
As I did the year before, with that poor little dear,   [dear,
I wept so much the year before,
It strained me so, I never got over it.

O how I long to see my poor little Beauty Linna live and well,
You know not the company she was for me,
O what a great desire I had for poor little dear to get well,
For she and I to enjoy each others love.

Old age took away poor little Beauty Linna,
Sick over 3 months and grew worse,
With froth in her throat,
Deceased and sleeping in her coffin under ground,
Buried to the south end of poor Sissy's grave,
O how I feel for her,
She was over 12 years of age, when she was taken away,
By all I found out, very certain true.

Poor little heart, never can look at me and laugh,
And speak to me no more.
She did it as long as she was able,
She and I talked together, company for each other,
Poor little heart, never can call me back no more,
When I go out the room,
She did it as long as she was able,
For 8 months after poor Sissy's decease,
She would not let me go out the room,
Called me straight back, as soon as I went out,
When 8 months were at a end,
Her complaint began to make her sick.

I fed her with a tea-spoon in her sickness,
Good milk and nutmeg, and good porridge,
Seldom a time in her sickness,
That she could swallow a little good food,
She would be as wishful,
And try to swallow a little good Cake and Cream.

I made fire days and nights to keep poor little dear warm,
The day before poor little dear was taken away,
She opened her eyes and looked up into my face
For the last time,
O my heart is pierced through days and nights,
For my poor deceased little Beauty Linna.

Poor little dear, she could not have the wind to blow on her,
All her last past summer through,
Hurt her so, she would keep out the wind,
She had a sick turn in June by going out a little,
She got over it again.

Poor little dear, she had a very sick turn in August,
I give her medicines, she got over it again,
She shed some of her feathers in September,
And part of them didn't grow out the full length,
She caught cold in October, without being exposed any,
Then her death complaint began to come in.

Some years ago she had one very dangerous complaint,
I cured her very soon, she got well again,
Her complaint that caused her death,
Was just such a complaint as poor Sissy had,
Only poor Sissy's complaint ended with dropsy in her stomach.

A mournful scene it was to me,
To see their breath depart,
Consider soon my turn will come,
And I must follow on,
How can I be here on earth a great while,
I have met with so much trouble of late years.

O I wish my poor little dears could lived longer
And been well, and when they were taken away,
For me to be able to take care of them.

Anxiety of mind will keep any one up and doing,
If they have a friend sick,
If their own health is very miserable,
No one here on earth can know, but only them that knows,
How hard it is to undergo trouble and sickness.

I never can get over the sickness and death,
Of my two poor little Bantie hearts,
They knew such a site, and loved me so well,
And my feelings so great for them both.

My troubles is so hard, that when it begins to be dark,
I set down by the east window, and have a weeping spell,
Then I go to bed, and catch my breath for hours,
I weep by spells day after day,
And night after night for them,
Heart-rendering days and nights.

My poor little hearts have gone to their long home,
And I want to be better off than to be here,
I undergo so much with sickness, and my trouble is so hard.

O my heart is pierced through,
For my poor little hearts to undergo sickness and death,
And for me to part with them, I feel dreadfully.

When I am taken away,
I want to be buried to the east side
Of my poor little dear's graves,
And a strong yard made around all three of us together,
And always kept in order, fence and graves too.

When the first poor little heart was taken away,
I had the other poor little heart left,
To sympathize with me, and be company for me,
Now I am left all alone,
After they have lived in the room with me about 8 years,
O how I feel, and how I weep, to write those lines about them.
When poor little Beauty Linna and I was left all alone,
She would set in my lap most all the time,
Her mind was so troubled for poor Sissy
When I sot to the end of the bureau,
She would be sure and get up and set herself down
To the corner of the bureau, with her face close to mine,
There she set would set, as long as I sot there,
When I sot to the fire she would be there.

Poor little heart, she remembered poor Sissy,
For 8 months after her decease,
I know it by many things, she sot so much by poor Sissy,
That every time she catched a fly,
She would call with all her strength and might,
For poor Sissy to come and have it,
For Sissy used to do the same by her.

When one got a soft-shell egg broke under her,
She would take hold the tip end of poor Sissy's wing,
And poor poor Sissy knew what she wanted,
And would pick it off for her.

The winter before poor little Beauty Linna was taken away,
Before poor Sissy was taken sick,
She wanted poor Sissy to cover her nights,
She would make a chicken noise,
And run her head in her feathers,
And under poor Sissy's wing.

When I used go out the room,
And left them both together, and come in again,
They would speak to me, they was so glad I came in again,
And if I was gone too long, they would both call me
To come to them.

When they used to be sitting down, and I looked down on them,
They would tip up their little face on one side,
And look at me with one eye, and laugh and speak to me.

They could not stand any dirt, especially poor little Ada Queetie,
She would snap her mouth and go way broadside.

They used to set by the fire close side and side,
Dear little hearts was so tender,
If they meddled with something, I told them you shanty,
They let it alone very willing,
And very seldom they meddled with anything.

If their water happened to be out their little bowl before I knew
They would pick on the lower button of the door,   [it,
And look at me, for me to get them some water.

Their appetite was always very poor,
Must have the best of good cake,
And of good wheat, brought from the west.

If their cake happened to get out their little plate on the floor,
They could not eat it,
They must have their cake out of my hand or plate.

When they used to see some flies up on the window,
They would stand side and side, and look at me, and call me,
To help them to them flies.

When they used to see me in the new buttery,
They would stand side and side to the door,
And look at me till I come out again.

When I used to call them to turn around,
They would turn around,
When I used to tell them to look at anything,
They would look straight at it.

When I used to say pretty babes,
They would both run to me at a dreadful swift rate,
When I used to say make haste, or come here,
They both did it quick. . . .

Poor little Beauty Linna at last,
Had all the appearance of old age,
She pined away for one year,
And could not stand any cold,
And when she departed this life,
She had all the appearance of old age.

God lent me my beloved friends,
Only to remain with me a few years,
And took them home again.

This world is nothing but a place of trouble,
This world is not our home.

I dream every once in a while,
O how I want my poor little dears
Back again, live and well,
Then I dream I have no desire to have them back,
To undergo sickness and death again.

O my dear beloved little friends, they are gone,
Sweetly asleep in their coffins under ground,
No more to wake, no more to speak, no more to love,
No more to have feeling for me,
And I am left here in trouble, broken hearted,
Them that knew me once,
Know—me—no—more.

ANDREW TAYLOR STILL

(1828–1917)

Autobiography of A. T. Still—With a History of the Discovery and Development of the Science of Osteopathy . . . Published by the Author, Kirksville, Missouri, Revised Edition, 1908. 402 pp. Illustrated.

Remarkably full of energy and strength, Andrew Taylor Still was a great original. Studying man "as a machine designed and produced by the mind of the Architect of the Universe," he discovered a system and method of healing, which he called "osteopathy." He based it on the theory that diseases were due chiefly to a loss of structural integrity in the tissues and that this integrity could be restored by manipulation.

After launching osteopathy in Kansas, Andrew Taylor Still moved on to Missouri, where he practiced as an itinerant doctor, preached his medical doctrine, and faced the perils of an innovator. In 1887 he settled in Kirksville, in the northeast part of the state.

"I worked alone with my investigation until about 1892, with such help as my four sons could give," he wrote, "treating many kinds of disease, and hearing much talk, good and bad, for and against the new method of curing the afflicted. Paying no attention to comments, I did the work, which was all I tried to do or thought of doing. The results were far better than I had ever dreamed. . . . People came in great numbers . . . and my practise yielded me quite a little sum. . . . While in Nevada, Missouri, a man asked if his son could go with me and 'ketch on,' as he termed it. I told him it would cost him one hundred dollars to get me to be bored with him or any other person."

The son, a so-called pile doctor, "had been traveling from place to place, treating piles with some kind of ointment. . . . His education was very limited and in fact he was ignorant of the anatomy of the human body," wrote Andrew Taylor Still. For a year, he said, he pounded osteopathy into the young man's head, which was "not quite as hard as a diamond nor near as brilliant"; eventually he became "a fairly good operator." Still's second student, a lightning-rod peddler he had cured of asthma, lived and studied with him on credit, then left without paying.

On May 10, 1892, with three of his sons and a daughter, Andrew Taylor Still founded The American School of Osteopathy in Kirksville, predecessor of the present-day Kirksville College of Osteopathy and Surgery, and the first of all similar institutions. Arthur G. Hildreth, a prospective student, wrote, in *The Lengthening Shadow of Dr. Andrew Taylor Still*, 1938, that Still said, "Arthur, I am looking for one hundred young men who do not drink whiskey, chew tobacco or swear. I want to teach them osteopathy." Hildreth enrolled. Andrew Taylor Still then said to him, "Arthur, if you are coming to me because of the dollars you think you can make out of it, don't come. But if you are wanting a place in life where you can render a real service, then I want you and I need you, and you need not be alarmed about making a living, because the services you will be able to render will take care of your financial needs in a bountiful way."

In 1897 Andrew Taylor Still, almost seventy, put together and published his peculiarly individual book, a miscellany of personal history, lectures, and testimonials. Ten years later, after the plates were lost in a fire, he put out a "revised" edition. "At this point," he wrote, "I shall lay down my trowel as I have finished building the last autobiography of myself and life. Farewell to all. A. T. Still."

The extract that follows comes from the later edition and includes most of the biographical passages.

AUTOBIOGRAPHY OF A. T. STILL

———•———

CHAPTER I.

Early Life—Schoolboy Days, and the Unsparing Rod—A Judge of Dogs—My Flint-Lock Rifle—The First Cook-Stove and Sewing-Machine—End of the World Coming—My First Discovery in Osteopathy.

I suppose I began life as other children, with the animal form, mind, and motion all in running order. I suppose I cried, and filled the bill of nature in the baby life. My mother was as others who had five or six children to yell all night for her comfort. In four or five years I got my first pants; then I was the man of the house. In due time I was sent off to school in a log schoolhouse, taught by an old man by the name of Vandeburgh. He looked wise while he was resting from his duties, which were to thrash the boys and girls, big and little, from 7 A.M. till 6 P.M., with a few lessons in spelling, reading, writing, grammar, and arithmetic. Then the roll-call, with orders to go home and not fight on the road to and from the schoolhouse, and be on time at seven next morning to receive more thrashings, till the boys and girls would not have sense enough left to recite their lessons. Then he made us sit on a horse's skull-bone for our poor spelling, and pardoned our many sins with the "sparing rod," selecting the one suited to the occasion out of twelve which served in the walloping business, until 6 P.M.

In 1834 my father moved from that place of torture, which was at Jonesville, Lee County, Va.,* to Newmarket, Tenn. Then in 1835 I was entered for further schooling with two older brothers, as a student in the "Holston College," which was under the control of the M. E. Church,† and was located at Newmarket, Tenn. The school was conducted by Henry C.

* Andrew Taylor Still was born in Jonesville, Virginia, August 6, 1828.
† Methodist Episcopal Church.

Saffel, a man of high culture, a head full of brains, without any trace of the brute in his work.

In the year of 1827 * my father was appointed by the M. E. conference of Tennessee as a missionary to Missouri. We bade adieu to the fine brick college at Holston, and at the end of seven weeks' journey reached our destination, and found we were in a country where there were neither schools, churches, nor printing-presses, so here schooling ended until 1839. Then my father and six or eight others hired a man by the name of J. D. Halstead to teach us as best he could during the winter of 1839–40. He was very rigid, but not so brutal as Vandeburgh. The spring of 1840 took us from Macon County to Schuyler County, Missouri, and I received no further schooling until 1842. That autumn we felled trees in the woods, and built a log cabin eighteen by twenty feet in size, seven feet high with dirt floor, and one whole log or pole left out of the side wall to admit light, through sheeting tacked over the space so we could see to read and write. This institution of learning was conducted by John Mikel, of Wilkesborough, N. C., for which he was paid at the rate of two dollars per head for ninety days. He was good to his pupils, and they advanced rapidly under his training. The summer of 1843 Mr. John Hindmon, of Virginia, taught a three months' term, during which mental improvement was noted. Then back to the old log-house, for a fall term in Smith's Grammar, under Rev. James N. Calloway. He drilled his class well in the English branches for four months, proving himself to be a great and good man, and departed from our midst with the love and praise of all who knew him.

In the spring of 1845 we returned to Macon County. A school was there taught by G. B. Burkhart, but I did not attend it, as he and I did not agree, so I left home and entered a school at La Plata, Mo., which was conducted by Rev. Samuel Davidson, of the Cumberland Presbyterian church. While attending his school I boarded with John Gilbreath, one of the best men I ever knew. He and his dear wife were as a father and a mother to me, and I cannot say too many kind words of or for them. His grave holds one of the best and dearest friends of my life. They opened their doors, and let myself and a dear friend and

* I think this should be 1837.

schoolmate, John Duvall (long since dead), into their home. Mornings, evenings, and Saturdays my friend and I split rails, milked cows, helped Mrs. Gilbreath tend the babies and do as much of the housework as we could. When we left she wept as a loving mother parting from her children. There are many others of whom I could speak with equal praise, but time and space will not permit. In the summer of 1848 I returned to La Plata, to attend a school given wholly to the science of numbers, under Nicholas Langston, who was a wonderful mathematician. I stayed with him until I had mastered the cube and square root in Ray's third part Arithmetic. Thus ended my school-days in La Plata.

The reader must not suppose that all of my time was spent in acquiring an education at log schoolhouses.

I was like all boys, a little lazy and fond of a gun. I had three dogs,—a spaniel for the water, a hound for the fox, and a bull-dog for bear and panthers. My gun for many years was the old flint-lock, which went chuck, fizz, bang; so you see, to hit where you wanted to, you had to hold still a long time,—and, if the powder was damp in the pan, much longer, for there could be no bang until the fizzing was exhausted, and fire could reach the touch-hole leading to the powder-charge behind the hall. All this required skill and a steady nerve, to hit the spot.

I was called a good judge of dogs, and quoted as authority on the subject. A hound, to be a great dog, must have a flat, broad, and thin tongue, deep-set eyes, thin, long ears, very broad, raised some at the head, and hanging three inches below the under-jaw. The roof of his mouth had to be black, the tail long and very slim, for good coon-dog. Such kind of pups I was supposed to sell for a dollar each, though I usually gave them away. When I went to the woods, armed with my flint-lock and accompanied by my three dogs, they remained with me until I said, "Seize him, Drummer!" which command sent Drummer out on a prospecting trip. When I wanted squirrels I threw a stick up a tree and cried: "Hunt him up, Drummer!" In a short time the faithful beast had treed a squirrel. When I wanted deer I hunted toward the wind, keeping Drummer behind me. When he scented a deer he walked under my gun, which I carried point front. I was always warned by his tail falling that I was about as close as I could get to my game without starting it up from the grass.

This old-fashioned flint-lock hunting was under the Van Buren and Polk's administration; but when Harrison—"old Tip"—came in, I possessed a cap-lock gun. Now I was a "man." "Big Injun me." To pull the trigger was "bang" at once, and I was able to shoot deer "on the run." Shot-guns were not in use at that time, but the frontiersman became very expert with the rifle. I could hit a hawk, wild goose, or any bird that did not fly too high or too fast for my aim. I killed a great number of deer, turkeys, eagles, wildcats, and foxes. My frontier life made me very fleet of foot. Brother Jim and I ran down and caught sixteen foxes in the month of September, 1839. Fearing some one will regard this as a fish story, I will explain that during the summer and fall some kind of disease got among the foxes, and we found them lying in the hot road in the dust, feeble and shaking, as though they had the fever and ague, and were incapable of running away from us. I have never since tried to outrun a fox.

As furs were not worth a cent in September, our sixteen foxes were useless, but during the following winter we caught a mink, and concluded to go to market with its fur as we must have a five-cent bar of lead before we could shoot other game. So I saddled my horse Selim, and went to Bloomington (nine miles) to exchange my mink-skin for lead. The barter was made with my good friend Thomas Sharp (an uncle of Rev. George Sharp, of Kirksville, Mo.), and soon the hide was with his other furs, from coons' and opossums'. Then I mounted Selim and started for home to tell Jim that I had found a permanent market for mink-skins at five cents apiece. In a short time I shot a deer, and had a buck-skin to add to the fur trade, and took my "big" fifty cents in powder, lead, and caps. . . .

My frontier experience varied. I enjoyed advantages which few others had. My father, who was a man educated to do all kinds of work, was a minister, doctor, farmer, and a practical millwright. My mother was a natural mechanic, and made cloth, clothing, and pies to perfection. She believed "to spare the rod would spoil the child," and she did use the rod in a homeopathic way. My father said if you wish to get meal in a bag, hold the mouth open. If you wish to get sense in your head, hold it open. If you wish to ride a horse, get on his back; and if one wished to be a skillful rider, hold on to him. My mother said if you wish to drink milk, put it in your mouth, and not on your clothes; for there was but one way to drink milk. My father, being a farmer, concluded that a little corn-field education would be good with my millwright knowledge, and at an early age I was taught to hold the teams, and do the duties of farm life, until I could manage teams, harrows, plows, and scrapers. When I came from the cornfield for dinner, father told me I could rest myself by carrying slop to the hogs. I did not mind the work; it was the exercise that bothered my mind. When I passed old Dan, the colored man, he would say: "De crown is for de faifful," and many other words of encourage-ment, such as "Go and brung de eggs," "Start a little smoke under de meat," and then he would sing the "Sweet Bye and Bye" for my edification. In due course of time I entered my gawk age, for a long journey. I was awkward, ignorant, and slovenly until I got into my mother's real training-school, in which she used soap and switches freely. After which it seemed I had more spring in my heels and head than ever before. She gave me two buckets and a cup, and told me to go and milk the cows, and be in a hurry about it, so as to help her and Dan'l shear the sheep. By seven o'clock we were in the sheep-pen. Old Dan'l says, "Ketch dat sheep," mother reiterated, "Catch that sheep," and Aunt Becky echoed, "Catch me one." By this time "old black Rachel" came in with her shears, and said: "I wants one too." And right here is where the gawk was knocked out. When I caught a sheep for her, the old ram said, "It is time for music," and sprawled me with his head, causing me to howl, and the others to laugh. This incident taught me to look back-ward and forward, upward and downward, right and left, and never sleep in the enemy's country, but always be on guard.

My instructors, thinking I was well enough trained to be ad-mitted into better society, I was permitted to go with Dan'l to the timber, to be instructed in chopping wood, splitting rails, burning brush, and clearing up the ground for the plow. All went off well except once or twice, when old Dan'l revived my see-ability by playing ram until I could see a limb as big as your finger. He then closed with the proverb, " 'Cleanliness is next to godliness.' I wants all dis trash cleaned up, every moufful of it." At noon he gave the welcome information, "Come on, we's gwine to dinner." When we came near the house, we met Aunt Becky, and she told us the preacher had come to take dinner, and for me to water his horse, take the saddle off, curry him down, then come into the smokehouse and she would give me a piece of pie, but it was not large as my hunger. She said she had something to tell me.

"What is it?" I asked.

"Maybe that man will be your uncle some day. If you will stay in the smokehouse and wait till the second table, I will bring you out the chicken gizzard." I took her at her word and got the gizzard, and she got the preacher, and became the wife of a circuit-rider. Not long after I took a great notion that I would be a circuit-rider, too. I mounted horses, mules, and calves, and tried to look like a preacher. My favorite clerical steed was a calf which had a very stately step. I took him out to the meadow with a halter, mounted him, and began to play preacher. All went well; and I was wondering where my ap-pointment would be, when a snake ran under my calf's nose, and I spread all my preach-ability on the ground before the calf as I sprawled on my back, and it has been there ever since.

I will conclude this chapter of my boyhood experience with an incident which, simple as it was, may be said to be my first discovery in the science of Osteopathy. Early in life I began to hate drugs. One day, when about ten years old, I suffered from a headache. I made a swing of my father's plow-line between two trees; but my head hurt too much to make swinging com-fortable, so I let the rope down to about eight or ten inches of the ground, threw the end of a blanket on it, and I lay down on the ground and used the rope for a swinging pillow. Thus I lay stretched on my back, with my neck across the rope. Soon I became easy and went to sleep, got up in a little while with headache gone. As I knew nothing of anatomy at this time, I took no thought of how a rope could stop headache and the sick stomach which accompanied it. After that discovery I roped my neck whenever I felt one of those spells coming on. . . .

CHAPTER II.

The Wild Game of the Frontier—Mr. Cochran's Deer—The Deer's Foot—Treed by a Buck—I Capture an Eagle—Night Hunting—Brother Jim's Horn—The Philosophy of Skunks and Buzzards—Milking Under Difficulties—Attacked by Panthers.

The lad of the frontier enjoys many thrilling adventures with wild animals, of which the city boy can know nothing save what he reads in books. If he is observing he learns more of the habits and customs of the wild animals he comes in contact with, than he can gain by a course in natural history, for he has the great book of nature constantly spread before him.

Soon after my father moved to Missouri, when I was about eight years old, I was amusing myself in the yard with my younger brothers, three and five years old, when "bang" went a big gun from the back of our house, about a quarter of a mile away. My mother came running to us, and said: "Did you hear that big gun go off over west?" We answered we did. She said: "I expect Judge Cochran has killed a buck. He said he was going out to look for deer at the spring-lick where they came to drink the water that flowed out of the hill, and he promised us venison for supper." By this time we were all wonderfully excited. We climbed on the fence, brother John, Tom, Jim, and Ed, with mother and the little girls standing in the door, all eyes turned expectant toward the deer-lick about half a mile distant. Every nerve in our bodies was on a perfect strain, with our eyes wide open to see who could catch the first glimpse of Judge Cochran. In a very few minutes he walked to an open place in the woods, and we saw him almost at the same instant. I jumped up and down, and brother Jim followed my example. Soon the Judge was in the dooryard; but long before he got there we asked him if he had killed a deer. He answered:

"Yes, I have killed a fine buck, and you can all have some very nice venison, as I promised, for supper." He asked us if we had ever eaten any. We told him no, we had never seen any, much less tasted it.

He said the deer was lying over at the lick, and he would saddle up a horse and bring it in. When he mounted his horse

he asked me if I did not want to go with him after the deer. I
jumped on behind the Judge, and away we went. In a few minutes we were at the lick, and dismounted by the dead deer,
which was the most wonderful thing I had ever seen. It was
about five feet long, from the end of its nose to the tip of its tail,
near four feet high when standing, and its tail was about one
foot long. Its feet and mouth were very much like those of a
sheep, except the feet were very sharp-pointed. Its hair was
about the color of an Irishman's whiskers. Its legs and feet were
very nice and trim, not much larger than a broomstick, but
about three feet long. I thought, Oh! how fast he could run,
before he departed this life, to cheer our table. A deer can jump
as far in one jump as a boy can in six, or about fifty or sixty
feet when running down a hill. He can jump over a man's head
and never touch his hat.

Soon the Judge and I were back to the house with our deer.
We took off his hide and hung him up in a tree to cool off, so
we could have some for breakfast in place of supper. Next
morning we were out of bed bright and early. Mother cooked a
big pot full, put it on a great big dish in the middle of the table.
It was the most palatable food I ever ate. Perhaps the appetite
of the boy and my continual exercise made the meat seem the
sweetest I ever tasted. . . .

My father owned a farm and raised a large amount of corn,
and had a great many horses, mules, cattle, sheep, and hogs to
feed on it, so our crops were consumed at home. We had so
much corn to husk and crib that we were compelled to commence very early, in order to get it stored away before cold
weather. When we were all in our teens, my eldest brother nineteen, the next seventeen, and myself about fifteen, we gathered
corn from early morn till late in the evening, fed the stock, ate
our suppers, and prepared for a good hunt for coons, foxes,
opossums, and skunks. We always took a gun, an ax, a big
butcher-knife, and flint and steel to make fire. We had a pol-
ished cow's horn which we could blow as loud as the horns that
overthrew the walls of Jericho. As brother Jim was a great
talker, we made him chief horn-blower. He went into the yard,
and bracing himself, tooted and tooted and split the air for
miles, while the dogs collected around him and roared and

howled. You never heard such sweet music as brother Jim and the dogs made. Shortly after his melodies began, we were in line of march, front, middle and rear rank, and soon journeyed to the woods to hunt opossums, polecats, coons, wildcats, foxes, and turkeys. Our dogs had a classic education, hunting and killing all classes of "varmints." When on a coon hunt we kept back all the dogs with us but two, Drum and Rouser. The roofs of their mouths were black, their ears long and thin, and their tails very slim. If we wanted coons first, we told Jim to toot for coons, which he could do very nicely. At his sound of music, Drum and Rouser moved off in the darkness, and after some minutes Drum was sure to break the silence by yelping and roaring on the track. The bark of the dog indicated to our trained ear the kind of game he was after. If he barked slow and loud we were pretty sure he had treed a coon; if he barked quick and sharp, we booked him for a fox. If he barked fast and loud we could count on a polecat. In case it was a skunk we ran to the dogs as fast as possible, and ordered Jim at the same time to blow the horn to call them off, for if they ever got the skunk's perfume on them it was so stinking strong that the scent of the animals was destroyed for other game. Sometimes a young untrained dog had the temerity to take hold of a skunk and spoil the hunt, so that all that was left for us was to let the bugle sound the retreat, and go home. The skunk possesses two wonderful powers: he can stink louder and faster than any other known animals; and if you do not kill him, within a few hours he will re-absorb all of his disgusting odors and go away; such is the power and quality placed in him by nature. I would advise you to never kill a skunk, unless you leave his body just where he falls. By so doing the stench will disappear in a very short time. In him you have one of the finest lessons of nature: he gives forth only what he absorbs from his surroundings. . . .

About the year 1852 I killed a great number of deer. I skinned, salted, and dried the meat, supplying not only myself, but my neighbors with all they wanted. One afternoon I killed a very fine young deer, brought him home, and put him in the smokehouse. My clothes, saddle, and horse were badly stained with the blood of the animal. It being late after changing clothes, I took a bucket and **went to** a lot adjoining my stable to milk my cow. In the lot I had about twenty large hogs. I sat down, and was milking the cow, when all at once the hogs jumped up and ran to the further side of the lot, sniffing the air in great terror. I looked to see the cause of their flight, and there in plain view, within thirty feet of me, stood a monster panther not less than nine or ten feet long from the point of his nose to the end of his tail, and fully three feet high. I was milking in a tin bucket, which made a great deal of noise, so he did not molest either myself or the hogs, but jumped out of the pen and ran to the timber. Then he began to roar and scream like a woman in distress. I was very fond of his music, but the farther it was away the sweeter it sounded. I am glad he didn't think enough of me to spend any more time in my company than he did. No doubt it was the blood on the horse and saddle that brought him there. I did not ask him, and only guessed that he came for a haunch of venison.

One day while driving home in my ox-wagon I came upon three panthers in the road,—two old beasts and one young one. I had neither rifle nor knife to defend myself, and had they attacked me they would have killed my oxen and myself. My dogs saw the dangerous brutes, and made a bold charge upon them, and they ran up a tree. No doubt they had seated themselves to feast upon my oxen. Even when they had reached safety in the tree-top, they cast fierce, hungry glances at us. I cracked my whip, which sounded very much like a pistol, and they sprang out of the tree-top and ran off into the thick woods. I drove my oxen home in a hurry, every hair on my head feeling as stiff as a knitting-needle, and I never had any more desire to encounter panthers.

My frontier experience was valuable to me in more ways than I can ever tell. It was invaluable in my scientific researches. Before I had ever studied anatomy from books I had almost perfected the knowledge from the great book of nature. The skinning of squirrels brought me into contact with muscles, nerves, and veins. The bones, the great foundation of the wonderful house we live in, were always a study to me long before I learned the hard names given to them by the scientific world. As the skull of the horse was used at my first school as a seat for the indolent scholar, I have thought it might be typical of the good horse-sense that led me to go to the fountain-head of knowledge and there learn the lesson that drugs are dangerous to the body, and the science of medicine just what some great physicians have declared it to be,—a humbug.

But I am digressing from the purpose of this chapter, which is to give some of my adventures during my early days on the frontier. My adventures were not confined alone to panthers, deers, skunks, and coons. We had an enemy far more subtle and dangerous than either. His fang was poisonous and his bite often meant death. I refer to the snakes of Missouri of an early day. I have killed thousands of them, big and little, long and short, from ten feet in length to six inches, and all colors, red, black, blue, green, copper, spotted,—dangerous and harmless. They were so abundant in the timber and prairie country in the early days that it was necessary to carry a club about the size of a common walking-stick, three or four feet long, as protection. All persons carried something in their hands to kill snakes during the warm weather. Many kinds were very poisonous. I remember a man named Smith Montgomery who was bitten on the foot in the harvest-field, while he was at work barefooted. The snake's tooth penetrated a vein which carries the blood to the heart, and he cried: "I am bitten by a rattlesnake!" walked toward the other men, but after taking about six steps sank to the ground and was instantly dead. The poison of the rattlesnake produces a numb feeling, which runs all through the body, and the lungs and heart cease to move as soon as the blood is conveyed to the heart and the poison gets into the large blood-vessels. . . .

As I was traveling through some timber-land with my friend Jim Jessee, we saw in front of us a very large rattlesnake, six feet in length. I proposed to Jim to have some fun out of the gentleman. I drew my knife from my belt, cut down and trimmed up a bush, left the upper limb, so as to make a fork, with which I straddled his neck, while with other sticks I opened his mouth and filled it with hartshorn (aqua ammonia); then we let him loose and stepped back to see the fun. To our great surprise he never cut a caper. The ammonia had done its work instantaneously. I tied his tail to a bush, thinking he might be only temporarily inactive. At the end of six hours I returned to find him dead and in the possession of the green flies. By that experiment I learned that ammonia would destroy the snake's deadly virus. In all cases of snake-bite, after that, I always used ammonia as an antidote, and if it was not handy I would use soda or some other alkali with equal success, but not equal in activity. I would advise you to always have a little ammonia or soda in your pocket when going among snakes. . . .

CHAPTER III.

My Father—Transferred to Missouri—Long Journey—The First Steamboat—At St. Louis—An Unscrupulous Divine—Hardships in The West—The First Methodist Preacher in Northeast Missouri— Presiding Elder—Trouble in the M. E. Church—Stand Taken by Elder Abram Still—Removal to Kansas.

As I speak of Rev. Abram Still (my father), I will notify the reader that memory alone is my guide, and by it will give my generalized history. . . .

In the spring of 1836, as I now remember, while father was a member of the Holston conference of the M. E. Church of Tennessee, he was transferred by that body to Missouri as a missionary.

We left Tennessee, starting from New Market, Jefferson County, with two wagons, seven horses, and eight in family, and began an overland journey of seven weeks to Macon County, Mo. We had a pleasant time, good roads, and nice traveling until we reached the low land on the Ohio River bottoms opposite Cairo, Ill. Here we began to find some deep mud for a few miles until we reached the river. But long before we reached it, we heard the whistle of a steamboat. We all wanted to see the mouth that could pucker and whistle so squealingly loud. "Oh, my! we could hear it roar just as plain as you could hear a rooster crow if he were on top your head." Just think of that! Meeting a man in the road, father asked how far it was to the river, and he said it was six or seven miles. We whipped up all the teams and pushed on, for we were determined to see that boat,—see it pucker its mouth and whistle. Our ideas of steam were very crude, and we had much company then of the kind who knew but little of steam engines or any other kind of machinery. We drove up to the banks of the river, and there it was, big as life, full of people, cattle, horses, sheep, merchandise, and movers, but they cut no figure with us. The boat was the sight; we saw it, and knew all that could be known. We had seen a real steamboat, and it was a whopper, too. It soon steamed up the river and went out of sight, but we supposed we knew all about steamboats, and this one afforded food for conversation for many days after.

We were now ready to go to North Missouri as missionaries, and educate the heathen, and tell them all about steam. We were taken across the river by a ferry-boat which was run by horse-power, or a treadwheel; the driver whipped his horse shouting: "Water up! water up!" to make them go faster. In about one-half hour we landed in the State of Illinois, and set out through the mud and water from Cairo for St. Louis. We had to hire pilots to guide us through the mud and water of the Illinois bottoms, for by missing the road a few feet we would sink into the mire and never get out.

We crossed the State of Illinois with no bad luck, and drove up to the banks of the Mississippi River in sight of St. Louis, and went on to a steam ferry-boat that landed us on the Missouri side of that muddy stream. We concluded to stay a day or two and hunt up the stationed preacher of the M. E. Church of that place. We found him, and stayed over Sunday, as was father's custom when traveling. I believe his name was Harmon. He borrowed "Brother Still's" money, seven hundred dollars. Father took his note without security, payable in six months, and we left for Macon County, Mo., with Brother Harmon's "God bless you." Mother had a little bag of money ($350), and that was our pile for the wilderness life before us for six months or longer. Brother Harmon did not pay father for eight years, then only paid the principal. By this time father learned that some preachers were not of God, but dirty liars, just the same as some other people are. He was very much disappointed and disgusted to learn that a professed minister would play a confidence game and rob him of the money he had brought with him to support his family while in his missionary work in the wilds of North Missouri. Hard times soon began to close upon us. Money all gone, clothing worn out, and winter on us with all its fury. Our show for shoes was to tan deerskins and make moccasins, or go barefooted—deerskin pants or naked legs. Labor by the day was worth twenty-five cents, so you see money meant much work. . . .

Father worked with us three boys all he could in the spring, and in harvest-time he gave us a start in our work; then mounting his horse, started across the wild prairie to preach the Gospel to the pioneers. His missionary journeys usually lasted six weeks. During his absence, mother had to manage the farm, which she did as well as any one could. She spun, wove, cut and made clothing, butchered hogs or a beef, and managed it just as well as father, or a little better, for she was fully master of the situation.

Father was the first minister of the M. E. Church in North Missouri, and held the fort, preached and established the first churches and classes of Methodists and Methodism in all North Missouri. He stood his ground until 1844, at which time the M. E. Church was divided; those that believed the Bible justified human slavery left the old M. E. organization and organized the church known as the M. E. Church South.

Father did not believe that "human slavery was of Divine origin," and refused to go with the new church. Committees of the M. E. Church South waited on him to induce him to go with them, but without avail. He stayed with the old church, and preached that slavery was a sin, which did not suit his brethren with the pro-slavery sentiments. He attached himself to the Iowa conference of the M. E. Church, and was appointed Presiding Elder (as I now remember) to look after those Missouri Methodists who opposed slavery. His brothers who went with the new organization informed him he must join them or leave Missouri, as his anti-slavery teachings could not be tolerated; but he did not heed their warning, and after a few years' preaching in his old territory, where he had established Methodism, he was appointed as missionary to the Shawnee Indians in Kansas. This ended his fight in Missouri. The latter part of that struggle was full of bitterness, and tar and feathers were strong arguments at that time and were freely used, but not being strong enough, they finally gave place to ropes and bullets.

He was a man of strong convictions, which he maintained at all times and places. He took a bold stand for abolition, which he maintained until he saw human slavery wiped from every foot of North America, whether it was Divine or devilish, and died rejoicing that he had been permitted to live to see all men in his country, whether white or black, free. . . .

CHAPTER IV.

In Which I Take a Wife—The Infair—A Destructive Hail-Storm—At Wakarusa Mission—Bereavement—The Pro-Slavery Trouble—A Dangerous Ride—The Pro-Slavery Men Drilling—My Legislative Experience.

The school boy days, the days of youthful trials and sports, passed like vanishing joys, and I arrived at man's estate. I will omit my later schooling and medical training, and merely state that, like my "Father who are in heaven," I thought it not good to be alone, and began to go on dress parade, to see how the girls would like the looks of a young soldier. Like Bunyan, I shouldered my arms and marked time, until a loving eye was fixed on mine. Behind that eye was the form of Mary M. Vaughn, the daughter of Philamon Vaughn. She was to me beautiful, kind, active, and abounded in love and good sense. She loved God and all His ways. After a few words by Rev. Lorenzo Waugh at her mother's house on January 29th, 1849, her name was changed to Mrs. M. M. Still. The memorable event was followed by a good supper, and the next day we journeyed for an "infair" dinner (as it was then known) at my father's house. After these formalities, so essential to frontier society, I took my wife to our new home, on eighty acres of land one mile from my old home. I was young and stout, worked early and late, put in sixty acres of corn and kept it clean. It was a beauty, all in silk and tassel. I was proud of it. I began to feel that I would soon have a crib filled with many thousand bushels. The morning of the Fourth of July (the day we love to celebrate) came, and I was full of joy and hope. At 3 P.M. a dark cloud arose, which at 4 showered three inches of hail over every acre of my corn, not leaving a single stalk nor a blade of fodder in all my sixty acres. Nor did it leave a bird or

rabbit alive on my farm. All were dead. Some one consoled me
and himself by the following quotation: "The Lord loveth
whom He chasteneth." I had no corn, and he, whose crop was
not torn to shreds like mine, would have some to sell, so after
all, things, as usual, were about evened up. I taught school that
fall and winter at $15 per month, and thus ended my first year
of married life.

In May, 1853, my wife and I moved to the Wakarusa Mission, Kans., which was occupied by the Shawnee tribe. It was
all Indian there. English was not spoken much outside the mission school. My wife taught the pappooses that summer, while I
with six yoke of oxen in a string, fastened to a twenty-inch
plow, turned ninety acres of land, closing the job the last of
July. Some days I broke four acres of sod. Then during the fall
with my father I doctored the Indians. Erysipelas, fever, flux,
pneumonia, and cholera prevailed among them. The Indians'
treatment for cholera was not much more ridiculous than are
some of the treatments used by some of the so-called scientific
doctors of medicine. The Indians dug two holes in the ground,
about twenty inches apart. The patient lay stretched over the
two,—vomiting in one hole and purging in the other, and died
stretched out in this manner with a blanket thrown over him.
Here I witnessed the cramps which go with cholera and which
dislocate hips and turn legs out from the body. I sometimes had
to force the hips back to get the corpse into the coffin. As cura-
tives they gave teas made of black-root, ladies' thumb, sagatee,
muck-quaw, chenee olachee. Thus they doctored and died, and
went to Illinoywa Tapamalaqua, "the house of God."

I soon learned to speak their tongue, and gave them such
drugs as white men used, cured most of the cases that I met,
and was well received by the Shawnees. I was at the Shawnee
mission of the M. E. Church, located forty miles west of Kansas
City on the Wakarusa, east of Lawrence, Kansas, about six
miles. A treaty was made in 1854 with the Shawnees and other
tribes of Indians, in which the Government purchased much of
the Indian lands which were then declared open to white settlement. In 1855 the country was alive with home hunters, though
some squatters came into the territory in 1854. After the treaty
was made, people began to settle up the country. Then my wife,

who had shared my misfortunes, trials, and sorrows, and had lived with me until September 29th, 1859, (at which time the thread of life was cut, and she soared to that world of love and glory for which she had lived all her life), left me to care for her three children. Two of them have since gone to join her. The eldest, Rusha H., at the age of eighteen, married John W. Cowgill, of Ottawa, Kansas, and at the present time is living on a farm near that place. Since our friends by legions have become celestial beings, to be with them any more in this life is hopeless, we are to make the best of the few years left us in this world, and seek the company of the terrestial beings. Some are angels of mercy, love, wisdom and kindness, and say, "Come unto me and I will help you bear the burden of life," which has been proven to be true by one Mary E. Turner, who on November 20th, 1860, became Mrs. Mary E. Still. She is now the mother of four children living,—three boys and one girl. . . .

During the bloody days of the Kansas war in the fifties, the man who loved freedom was hated upon the face of the earth, and the enemies of freedom thought he had no right to live, so he was hunted with shot-guns and revolvers. It was dangerous for a free-state man to be found alone, and as I was one of the freedom-loving men of the Territory of Kansas, and was practicing medicine all over the country, I usually traveled roads I knew to be safe, especially during the periods of the highest excitement, at which time the pro-slavery element of the country was assembled together for the purpose of war, and the free-state men collected together at one common headquarters for defense. Both armies armed and equipped—on the one side to extend slavery, on the other to prohibit it. During the year 1855 the territory was in a condition of civil war. Partisan bands were arrayed against each other, and skirmishes and assassinations were of daily occurrence.

During this period I once found myself in a dangerous position. On returning home from one of my professional visits I suddenly found myself cut off by a creek which had steep banks. The only means of crossing this stream was by a log hewn on the upper side to a face of fourteen inches, with the ends imbedded in the banks. The log was a cottonwood about twenty feet long, thirty inches in diameter. The two ends were made fast in the banks on both sides of the creek. This log was used for a foot log for the people of the neighborhood. I must cross the stream at this point to reach home or take a four mile circuit, with many chances of being killed by the pro-slavery party, who hated me with the gall of political bitterness, which had long ceased to be a joke. Thus I took the choice with my life in my hands and my body upon the back of a trusty mule that had just been roughly shod. She pressed her nose down to the log, which was ten feet above the surface of the ice covered water. The ice was not over an inch thick, then two feet of water, with two feet more of mud under it, while the distance from bank to bank was sixteen feet. My mule placed first one foot and then another upon the log and boldly undertook with firm and cautious feet, and nose to the log, to transfer me to the adjacent bank. She succeeded, and in one minute's time the log and all dangers were left behind me. I was soon in the camp of my friends, about a half mile on my way home.

When I told my mule and log story in camp there were many unbelievers. Having a great admiration for the truth, and not relishing the accusation of false statements, I requested the Captain to give me a committee of three, and I would prove that the mule had crossed on the log. As the log was less than a half mile off, the Captain said: "We will resolve ourselves into a committee of a whole," and then all went with me, saying that if they found I had told a lie they would put me in the creek. On reaching the place the Captain said: "Here are marks of horse shoes all over the log, and as they correspond with the shoes on the mule's feet, Still has told the truth, and the shoe marks are his witnesses."

A few months after the mule and foot-log adventure I was called to visit a sick lady named Jones, about ten miles from my home, and in order to make the trip to and from short as possible I took cross cuts, some of which led through the woods. On this particular occasion, by going through a thick body of timber I could save about two miles. Entering the timber, I followed a path at full gallop. All at once my mule began to slack up and threw her ears forward, walked carefully and very reluctantly, by which I knew that men were close. Knowing that the blood of the opposition was up to a fever heat, I brought my revolvers front in my belt, unslung my sharpshooter, and prepared for any emergency. Not knowing the exact position or the number of the enemy, I concluded the best plan to be safe, was to prepare to be dangerous. In a minute's time I was in an open space of about one acre in the timber, in presence of a company of fifty or more pro-slavery men, my deadly enemies in politics, who had assembled in this secluded and secret place to drill for the purpose of fighting anti-slavery men within a very few days. I cannot say that my hair stood on end. Under the circumstances, I didn't consider there was any time to fool with hair, and knowing that the bulge counts much in all engagements, I spoke with a loud, firm, and commanding voice:

"What in the d—l are you fellows up to?" I was answered by the Captain in command:

"Where in the h—l are you going?" I saw in a moment that my firmness had produced good effect, and there was no further danger.

I rode up and stopped in front of the company, shook hands with the Captain, told him to give the command to me and I would drill his men, and show him how Jim Lane and John Brown did it, concluding with: "If you don't have your men better trained, and Jim Lane ever meets you, he will shake you up."

The Captain turned his men over to me, and I drew them up in line, put them through all the cavalry movements, tangled them up, straightened them out, and told the Captain he must drill better, so they could get out of tight places when they met us. Then I turned the company over to the original Captain Owens, who said: "Attention, company; this is Dr. Still, the d—dest abolitionist out of h—l, who is not afraid of h—l or high water. When you are sick, go for him; he saved my wife's life from an attack of cholera, and I know him to be successful in any place you are a mind to put him. In politics he is our enemy, in sickness he has proven to be our friend." And closed by saying: "Doc, go home to dinner with me, and I will go with you to see Mrs. Jones." I went with the Captain to dinner, and he made his word good by going with me. From that time until the close of the pro-slavery question in 1857 I met, passed, and repassed his men without fear of molestation.

I was chosen by the people to represent Douglas County, Kansas, in the Legislature. Among my colleagues were such men as John Speer, George Ditzler, and Hiram Appleman, all ardent "free-state men," who loved to hate slavery, in all its forms, believing it to be opposed to all progress of men and nations. . . .

At the close of our deliberations, March, 1858, we had a territorial law that was all new (except that referring to the records of deeds and marriages), which was thankfully received, and peace followed.

I went home to follow the practice of medicine and saw lumber, which I did until 1860, except the time spent in the Legislature. During the fall of 1860 we elected "Abraham Lincoln" to champion the coming conflict between Slavery and Freedom —not of Kansas alone, but of all North America. Then the struggle began, and lasted until he dipped his pen and wrote the golden words: "Forever free, without regard to race or color." I will add—or sex. When the war of the Rebellion was declared against the laws and authorities of the United States, I saw at once another move, the object of which was to extend slavery and illiteracy by a division of the Territory, which could only be an example for other States to imitate when any political party was unsuccessful in an election, and divide the country up into a "North and South" and East, Middle and West, Southern Confederacy. Then the East, Middle, and West, Northern Confederacy, and thus have six empires of quareling fools, who would ruin all our forefathers had given us under a sworn pledge to keep inviolate to the end of time. Lincoln said: "I will keep that pledge. Who will help me?"

With a roar the loyal legions from all over the nation answered "I!" War was on us, in all its diabolical fury, and ran rivers of blood and death until over a million fell to rise no more.

CHAPTER V.

I Enlist in Company F, Ninth Cavalry Volunteers—Our Mission—At Kansas City—Pursuit of Price—The Army at Springfield—Summary Vengeance on Guerrillas—Captain Company D of the Eighteenth Kansas Militia—Major of the Twenty-First Kansas Militia—On the Missouri Frontier—Fighting Joe Shelby—Osteopathy in Danger—Burying Dead Under a Flag of Truce—The Regiment Treated to a Surprise.

In September, 1861, at Fort Leavenworth, I enlisted in the Ninth Kansas Cavalry, in Company F, T. J. Mewhinne, captain. The regiment was composed mainly of Kansas men who had been christened in the baptism of fire during the proslavery contest. . . .

About the 1st of April, 1862, the Third Battalion of the Ninth Kansas was disbanded, which let me out of the service. . . .

A few months later there came another order to consolidate with some other battalions, by which I was transferred, and commissioned major of the Twenty-first Kansas militia. I did service in this capacity in Kansas until the autumn of 1864, when on the 10th of October General Curtis ordered us to the borderline between Missouri and Kansas to fight General Price, who was expected at Kansas City or Independence at an early day. . . .

During the hottest period of the fight a musket-ball passed through the lapels of my vest, carrying away a pair of gloves I had stuck in the bosom of it. Another minie-ball passed through the back of my coat just above the buttons, making an entry and exit about six inches apart. Had the rebels known how close they were to shooting Osteopathy, perhaps they would not have been quite so careless.

During this engagement I was mounted on the same mule which had walked the log with me back in Kansas. The antics of this creature when the leaden balls came whizzing thickest about her were amusing. She seemed under the impression that they were nit-flies, while I was thoroughly convinced they were bullets.

Many amusing incidents occurred during our conflict. Some of our boys fell to praying for the Lord to save them. Under the circumstances I deemed it best to suspend devotional services, and get into line to fight the rebels who were spattering us with lead, so I leaped from my mule, and planting my foot close behind some of them, I broke the spell. They closed up the front and made good soldiers throughout the remainder of the fight.

We held the field until Price's forces withdrew, leaving fifty-two dead on the ground, and one hundred and twenty-seven horses which fell into our hands. Shortly after the departure of the enemy night spread her friendly mantle over the scene, shutting out from our sight the horrors of war. Our regiment marched west two miles, then north six, east one, and went into camp near Shawneetown. About six o'clock next morning the artillery under General Totten opened fire east of Westport and south for six or eight miles—twenty-eight pieces joining in the chorus, with a spattering of small arms, which made a sullen roar, rolling along the entire line. The fighting was severe until about eight o'clock, when General Price began his retreat south. We followed him, skirmishing all the way, until we had pursued him a distance of ninety miles, had captured twenty-eight cannon, and were only a mile or two east of Fort Scott.

At this point we decided not to escort General Price any farther, but leave him to take care of himself. Finding the Confederate General Marmaduke in bad company, we invited him to go home with us; and as we were prepared to enforce the invitation, he consented with some reluctance, for the general had a "hankering after the stars and bars."

After Price's forces began their retreat the firing ceased for a while, and they had gone fully twenty miles before it was again resumed.

The privilege was given the enemy to bury their dead, and soon a company of one hundred and forty of our brave foes came to my headquarters under a flag of truce, which we always respected. I ordered the captain and his men to dismount and stack their arms, which they did. I then instructed the officer in command to form his men in line before me, and stationed a guard over their arms. Addressing the captain, I asked:

"How are you off for grub?"

"Almost out, major!" he answered.

Then in a tone and manner as serious as I could assume, I said:

"I want you to listen to what I have to say for about five minutes, and not move a muscle until I get through."

Then I went on to picture the horrors of war and the extreme measures sometimes necessary. I wound up by saying the rebels had been in the habit of shooting many of our men, and notwithstanding they had come in under a flag of truce, I intended to shoot the captain and every man with him. At this every cheek blanched and their breath came quick. Some were about to interpose, when I broke in with:

"I mean I will shoot you all in the mouth with food and coffee, as I want to convert all your sorrows into joy. Break ranks, go to the commissary, and get enough to fill up."

The captain and officers gave me a friendly grasp, and regretted that war made us (who should be by all laws of nature friends), enemies, and hoped that the angel of peace might soon spread her white wings over our beloved land. Those rebels certainly enjoyed that meal, and it was no doubt the first good meal the poor fellows had had for many days.

After chasing Price for ninety miles, as stated, we went into Kansas at De Soto, and on Tuesday morning, October 27th, 1864, I received orders to disband the Twenty-first Regiment and go home. I kept the order to myself, determined to try the grit of the boys and have a little fun at their expense.

Ordering the whole regiment to be drawn up in line, I made them a speech in which I said we had a very long march before us and a desperate battle at the end of it. I stated that I did not wish any one to undertake this arduous march or to engage in the terrible conflict who was not fully equal to the emergency. If any felt too sick, faint, or weak to accompany us, or for any cause felt they could not endure the hardship and danger, they would not be forced to go. All who would volunteer to go with me through any trial or danger were requested to step six paces to the front.

About one-third of the command stepped out six paces and thus declared their willingness to follow anywhere. Then in a tone loud enough to be heard by all I read the order for the disbanding of the regiment, told those who did not feel well enough to accompany us, to go to the hospital under the doctor's care, and to the others said: "Boys, we will go home!"

Shouts and roars of laughter drowned any further utterance, and in ten minutes we had not a sick man in the regiment. The regiment was disbanded, we all went home, and that ended my experience as a soldier.

CHAPTER VI.

The End of the War—Rejoicing at the Dawn of Peace—New Dangers —The Evil of Drugs—Terrible Visions—A Picture Drawn—Digging in Indian Graves for Subjects—Studying from the Great Book of Nature—The Ravages of That Terrible Disease Meningitis—Prayers and Medicine—Death of Four Members of My Family—Is Medicine a Failure?

The war ended as every thinking person must have reasoned it would end. Hate, passion, and avarice might prevail for a while, but in the end the spunky little South which fought so gallantly was compelled to yield to the determined North.

On the one side, men and money became too scarce to continue the struggle longer. A surrender, and peace was proclaimed, and human slavery ceased to be a part of the institutions of America. All gladly quit the conflict and resumed the life of the peaceful citizen. I gladly left the field of bloody contention, with all of the others, to resume the duties of a private citizen. I was not long in discovering that we had habits, customs, and traditions no better than slavery in its worst days, and far more tyrannical. My sleep was well nigh ruined; by day and night I saw legions of men and women staggering to and fro, all over the land, crying for freedom from habits of drugs and drink. My heart trembled, my brain rested not by day nor by night, to see man made in the image of his Creator treated with such little respect and sense by men who should know better. I saw men and women dosed with drugs whose poisonous fangs showed the serpent of habit, that was as sure to eat its victim as a stone was sure to return to the earth when cast into the air. I dreamed of the dead and dying who were and had been slaves of habit. I sought to know the cause of so much death, bondage,

and distress among my race. I found the cause to be the ignorance of our "Schools of Medicine." I found that he who gave
the first persuasive dose was also an example of the same habit
of dosing and drinking himself, and was a staggering form of
humanity, wound hopelessly tight in the serpent's coil. In vain
he cried: "Who can free me from this serpent who has enslaved
all my liberties and the joys of myself and loved ones?" In the
anguish of his soul he said:

"I wish I was as free as the negro for whose freedom I faced
the deadly cannon three long years."

"Oh!" says one, who is cultivating this habit of drugs and
drink, "I can quit my master any time I choose, but the nigger
could not, because the law held him in slavery with rawhide
whips, bloodhounds, and shot-guns, to torture him to obedience; and I am free to use drugs or quit just when I want to."

If you will chalk his back and watch him, you will soon find
him about a drug-store complaining of not feeling well. He has
taken a cold, and says:

"My wife belongs to church, and the meetings are held so
late, and the rooms are so hot, that I catch cold going home,
and I think I ought to take something."

The druggist says: "Professor, I think a little Jamaica gin-
ger and about an ounce of old rye is just what will fix you
up."

"Well, I will try some, I believe; still I hate to go to church
stinking of whisky."

"Chew a few cloves and cardamon seeds and they will dis-
guise the whisky smell," says the druggist. Soon church ends
its night sessions, but the Professor continues to come with
pains in his back and says: "I was out all last night after a fox,
and caught more cold," and winks at the druggist and says:
"Fix me the same you did before, and give me half a pint to
take to granny."

Such hypocritical pretension became more and more disgusting to me. I who had had some experience in alleviating
pain found medicine a failure. Since early life I had been a
student of nature's book. In my early days in windswept Kansas I had devoted my attention to the study of anatomy. I became a robber in the name of science. Indian graves were dese-

crated and the bodies of the sleeping dead exhumed in the name of science. Yes, I grew to be one of those vultures with the scalpel, and studied the dead that the living might be benefited.

I had printed books, but went back to the great book of nature as my chief study. The poet has said that, "The greatest study of man is man." I believed this, and would have believed it if he had said nothing about it. The best way to study man is to dissect a few bodies.

My subjects were the bodies exhumed from the Indian graves. Day and night, I roamed about the country, often at moonlight and often in the day-time with shovel disinterred the dead Indian and utilized his body for the good of science. Some one says the end justifies the means, and I adopted this theory to satisfy the qualms of conscience. The dead Indians never objected to being object-lessons for the development of science. Their relatives knew nothing about it; and as, "where ignorance is bliss it is folly to be wise," and as the knowledge which I gained by this research has aided me to relieve countless thousands of suffering human beings, and snatch many from the grave, I shall not allow my equanimity of mind to be disturbed by the thoughts that I once sought knowledge from Indian bones.

My science or discovery was born in Kansas under many trying circumstances. On the frontier while fighting the pro-slavery sentiment and snakes and badgers, then later on through the Civil War, and after the Civil War, until on June 22nd, 1874, like a burst of sunshine the whole truth dawned on my mind, that I was gradually approaching a science by study, research, and observation that would be a great benefit to the world.

Is the frontier a place to study science? our college-bred gentleman may ask. Henry Ward Beecher once remarked that it made very little difference how one acquired an education, whether it be in the classic shades and frescoed halls of old Oxford or Harvard, or by the fireside in the lonely cabin on the frontier. The frontier is a good place to get the truth. There is no one there to bother you. Beecher was then in mature years, and knew whereof he spoke. He had by the experience of a lifetime come to realize that a college education would not put good sense in a head where no brains existed. . . .

In the quiet of the frontier, surrounded by nature, I continued my study of anatomy with more zeal and more satisfactory results than I had at college. With no teacher but the facts of nature, and no classmates save the badger, coyote, and my mule, I sat down to my desk on the prairie to study over what I had learned at medical schools. With the theory firmly fixed in my mind that the "greatest study of man is man," I began with the skeleton. I improved my store in anatomical knowledge until I was quite familiar with every bone in the human body. The study of these bodies of ours has ever been fascinating to me. I love the study and have always pursued it with zeal. Indian after Indian was exhumed and dissected, and still I was not satisfied. A thousand experiments were made with bones, until I became quite familiar with the bony structure.

I might have advanced more rapidly in Osteopathy had not our Civil War interfered with the progress of my studies. We cannot say how a thing will appear until it is developed, and then we often find that the greatest good follows the greatest grief and woe, as you all know fire is the greatest test of the purity of gold. It may be good for the metal, but it is hard on the gold. Not until I had been tried by fire did I cut loose from the stupidity of drugs. Not until my heart had been torn and lacerated with grief and affliction could I fully realize the inefficacy of drugs. Some may say that it was necessary that I should suffer in order that good might come, but I feel that my grief came through gross ignorance on the part of the medical profession.

It was in the spring of 1864; the distant thunders of the retreating war could be easily heard; but now a new enemy appeared. War had been very merciful to me compared with this foe. War had left my family unharmed; but when the dark wings of spinal meningitis hovered over the land, it seemed to select my loved ones for its prey. The doctors came and were faithful in their attendance. Day and night they nursed and cared for my sick, and administered their most trustworthy remedies, but all to no purpose. The loved ones sank lower and lower. The minister came and consoled us. Surely with the men of God to invoke divine aid, and men skilled in scientific research, my loved ones would be saved. Any one might hope that between prayers and pills, the angel of death would be driven from our door. But he is a stubborn enemy, and when he has set his seal on a victim, prayers and pills will not avail. I had great faith in the honesty of my preacher and doctors then, and I have not lost that faith. God knows I believe they did what they thought was for the best. They never neglected their patients and they dosed, and added to and changed doses, hoping to hit upon that which would defeat the enemy; but it was of no avail.

It was when I stood gazing upon three members of my family,—two of my own children and one an adopted child,—all dead from the disease, spinal meningitis, that I propounded to myself the serious questions "In sickness has God left man in a world of guessing? Guess what is the matter? What to give, and guess the result? And when dead, guess where he goes?" I decided then that God was not a guessing God, but a God of truth. And all His works, spiritual and material, are harmonious. His law of animal life is absolute. So wise a God had certainly placed the remedy within the material house in which the spirit of life dwells.

With this thought I trimmed my sail and launched my craft as an explorer. Like Columbus I found driftwood upon the surface. I noticed the course of the wind, whence they came, and steered my vessel accordingly. Soon I saw the green islands of health all over the sea of reason. Ever since then I have watched for the driftwood and course of the wind, and I have never failed to find the source whence the drift came.

Believing that a loving, intelligent Maker of man had deposited in his body in some place or throughout the whole system drugs in abundance to cure all infirmities, on every voyage of exploration I have been able to bring back a cargo of indisputable truths, that all the remedies necessary to health exist in the human body. They can be administered by adjusting the body in such a manner that the remedies may naturally associate themselves together, hear the cries, and relieve the afflicted. I have never failed to find all remedies in plain view on the front shelves and in the store house of the Infinite—the human body.

When I first started out as an explorer, I discovered that

there were some remedies in bottles and jars high up and low down on the shelves, and not so visible as those in general demand. But by a close study, I found they would blend with all the other drugs, and give the wanted relief.

Thus I have prosecuted the voyage from sea to sea, until I have discovered that nature is never without all necessary remedies. I am better prepared today, after a twenty years' voyage and close observation, to say that God or nature is the only doctor whom man should respect. Man should study and use the drugs compounded in his own body.

CHAPTER VII.

As an Inventor—The Tired Arm—The Reaper and Mower—The Rake —The Steel Fingers—An Invention Lost—On a Farm—A Smart Wife—Churning—The Philosophy of Butter—Another Invention— Studying the Drive-Wheels of Nature—The Science of Osteopathy Developed.

As Osteopathy is a science built upon the principle that man is a machine, I will have to draw your attention to the fact that I began the study of machinery in 1855 and continued it, on to 1870. We had millions of broad acres of wheat, oats, and rye, growing, ripening, and being harvested; and the feeble right arm of man was the only servant on whom the nations could depend for their bread. That year I began to study the question, How shall this arm be made to enjoy the benefits, if possible, of those great and glorious words, "Forever free, without regard to race or color?"

From a boy of fourteen my arm was a willing, though a tired and sore servant at my side. My father, brothers, and the hired help, together with the harvest men all over the land, seemed to send up their hopeless groans for relief; each succeeding year seemed to bring news to the arm that it and its posterity shall ever be servants and swing the side cradle from morning until night, or go to bed hungry, also those dependent upon it.

At this time the skilled arts had thought out and manufactured a mowing-machine, with a blade or sickle about four feet long, so attached that it extended out at right angles four to six feet farther than the right wheel of the machine. It had a bar

and many sections called blades, so adjusted as to fit slots made
in fingers attached to the sickle for the purpose of cutting hay,
native, or wild.

At about this time there was something like a reel placed
upon the machine which would push the grass backward as it
was falling after being cut. Then by a rake some one would
throw it off in bunches on the ground.

I saw that by this invention there was much relief coming to
the arm, but the labor was just as hard for the man who threw
the grain off as the one who swung the scythe and cradle. It was
profitable, inasmuch as one man could push the grain off as fast
as two horses could travel in a swath of six feet. So I began to
reason on the mowing-machine, and thought out a plan where I
could make two long steel fingers that would stay in place and
catch the falling grain. They were made strong enough to hold
fifty pounds without sagging. When a sufficient quantity fell
upon these fingers to make a bundle, I would bear upon the
lever and instantly jerk those steel fingers from under the grain
and let it fall upon the ground in a bunch for the binder.

During the progress of the development of my invention I
was, as I now remember, visited by a representative from the
Wood Mowing Machine Co., which was located in Illinois.
During the next season the Wood Company sent out reapers
with fingers to catch the falling grain, which was held up by machinery until grain enough accumulated to make a bundle.
Then the driver let the fingers fall to the ground and pass out
from under the wheat. Wood had the benefit of my idea in dollars and cents, and I had the experience. The world was at the
beginning of a reaping revolution. No more swinging of the old
cradles and scythes. Reapers and mowers took their place. So
much for the study of the machinery of the harvest-field.

Soon after the aching arm had been set at liberty through
improved machinery, I proceeded to purchase a farm, and
stock it with horses, cattle, hogs, chickens, and the necessary
rigging to run it. We had a number of cows and a great deal of
milk. My family was small, my wife was busy, and I had to
churn. I churned and banged away for hours. I would raise the
lid and lick the dasher, go through all the maneuvers of churning and pounding milk by the hour. I would churn and churn

and churn, and rub my arm and churn, until I concluded that churning was as hard work as harvesting with the old cradle. But the churning brought me into the study of the chemistry of milk, cream, casein, margarine, and butyric acid, until I found that each atom of butter was incased in a covering of casein, similar in form to a hen egg. Now the question was how to break the egg and get the butter out. I constructed a drive-wheel eight inches in diameter to match the end of a pinion attached to the upper end of a half-inch rod, which extended from the top to the bottom of the churn. On this rod I had an adjustable arm, with a hole through it, and a set-screw to fasten it to a rod so as to raise or lower to suit the quantity of milk in the churn. Tin tubes were fastened to the outer ends of the arm in holes, so as to dip up the milk. These tubes were inclined down for that purpose. The receiving end through which the milk passed was one inch in diameter, coming out through a half-inch hole. Thus you see the tube was made tapering from receipt to exit of the milk. With this drive-wheel, pinion, and rod that crossed into an iron socket at the end of the churn, I could easily get a motion of the cups equal to five hundred or more revolutions per minute. This would throw the milk and cream against the resisting wall of the churn with the velocity of three to five miles a minute.

I succeeded in breaking the egg that contained all the elements found in butter, and give the hungry children butter from this new churn in one minute and a quarter from the word go, temperature and all being favorable. Three to ten minutes was the average time spent in churning by this new invention.

This was the first time that I had cause to rejoice that I made one of my worst enemies (the churn), the footstool of amusement. I spent some time in introducing my new invention, until the summer of 1874. This year I began an extended study of the drive-wheels, pinions, cups, arms, and shafts of human life, with their forces, supplies, framework, attachments by ligaments, muscles, their origin, and insertion; nerves, their origin and supply; blood supply from and to the heart; how and where the motor-nerves received their power and motion; how the sensory nerves acted in their functions, voluntary and involuntary nerves in performing their duties, the source of their supply, and the work done in health, in the obstructing parts, in the places, through which they passed to perform their part in the economy of life; all this study awoke a new interest within me. I believed that something abnormal could be found in some of the nerve divisions which would tolerate a temporary or permanent suspension of the blood either in arteries or veins, and cause disease.

With this thought in view I began to ask myself, What is fever? Is it an effect, or is it a being, as commonly described by medical authors? I concluded it was only an effect, and on that line I have experimented and proven the position I then took to be a truth, wonderfully sustained by nature responding every time in the affirmative. I have concluded after twenty-five years of close observation and experimenting that there is no such disease as fever, flux, diphtheria, typhus, typhoid, lung-fever, or any other fever classed under the common head of fever or rheumatism, sciatica, gout, colic, liver disease, nettle-rash, or croup, on to the end of the list, they do not exist as diseases. All these separate and combined are only effects. The cause can be found and does exist in the limited or excited action of the nerves which control the fluids of part or the whole of the body. It appears perfectly reasonable to any person born above the condition of an idiot, who has familiarized himself with anatomy and its working with the machinery of life, that all diseases are mere effects, the cause being a partial or complete failure of the nerves to properly conduct the fluids of life. . . .

CHAPTER VIII.

An Effort to Draw the Attention of the People to Osteopathy—Failure at Baldwin, Kans.—History of Baker University—Prayers for the Man Possessed—Brother Jim's Scepticism—Faith of My Good Wife —A Wandering Osteopath.

Having finally solved the great problem of Osteopathy, and having established the science in my own mind, I determined to try my luck in the introduction of what I had proven to be a new discovery and a remedy for human ills. My first effort was to draw to it the attention of the thinking people of my home town, Baldwin, Kansas. Baldwin is the home of the Baldwin and Baker University, which had been located there by three commissioners, appointed by the general conference of the M. E. Church between 1854 and 1856. My father, Abram Still, L. B. Dennis, and Elder Hood were the commissioners to purchase a site. They advertised for offers from towns, villages, and other places, where might be wanted a great university, backed by and under the auspices of the M. E. Church. Palmyra (afterward named Baldwin) made the offer, which was accepted by the locating committee.

I lived in Palmyra at that time, took an active part in rushing the scheme on, and was appointed by the commissioners of the general conference as agent with my brother Thomas, J. B. Abbott, Dan'l Fry, James Blood, and others, to select and locate a spot for the university building. We gave the church six-hundred and forty acres of land, all in one body. Myself and two brothers donated four hundred and eighty acres of land for the town site of Baldwin to assist in the establishment of Baker University. We—myself, brother, and two men named Barricklow—purchased and erected a forty horse-power steam-sawmill, and sawed all the lumber for the university and the other buildings at Baldwin (as Palmyra was called after the founding of the college), and all the country for twenty miles around. I was ground agent of the work, and was five years engaged in sawing, building, and doctoring the sick through small-pox, cholera, and other diseases, and representing the people of Douglas County in the Kansas legislature, during which time we washed and ironed the last wrinkle of human slavery out of the State, as I have told in former chapters. I was called a good doctor, a faithful legislator, a sober, sound, and loyal man, abounding with truth and justice, and a heart full of love to all. But, alas! when I said, "God has no use for drugs in disease, and I can prove it by his works;" when I said "I could twist a man one way and cure flux, fever, colds, and the diseases of the climate; shake a child and stop scarlet fever, croup, diphtheria, and cure whooping-cough in three days by a wring of the child's neck, and so on," all my good character was at once gone. You would have been ashamed of man or any other animal with two legs, if you had heard the prayers that were sent up by men and women to save my soul from hell. When I asked the privilege of explaining Osteopathy in the Baldwin University the doors of the structure I had helped build were closed against me.

I stayed in Kansas, and listened and laughed, until ready to go to Missouri, where I stopped with my brother, E. C. Still. He had been poor in health for a number of years, and was so reduced he could scarcely walk, and had been led up to and turned loose in the pastures of hell by "allopathy," and was using seventy-five bottles of morphine annually. I realized that bad could be worse. I stayed three months with him, got him free from opium, and started on to Kirksville, which I supposed would be the next cussing-post. I stayed three months, then sent for my wife and four babies, who came to me in May, 1875. My wife was a Methodist, and could stand cussing pretty well. She said: "I will stand by you; we'll be cussed together; maybe we can get it done cheaper." She studied economy, and was as gritty as an eagle, who loves to fight for her young ones. I did not tell her that when I came to Missouri I found a letter addressed to my brother Edward, from brother Rev. James M. Still, of Eudora, Kans., stating that I was crazy, had lost my mind and supply of truth-loving manhood. I read it and thought, as the eagle stirreth up her nest, so stir away, Jim, till your head lets down some of the milk of reason into some of the starved lobes of your brain. I believed Jim's brain would ripen in time, so I let him pray, until at the end of eighteen years he said:

"Hallelujah, Drew, you are right; there is money in it, and I want to study 'Osteopathy'." At this time Jim is a member in good standing, and doing much good in the cause. When he happens to think of it, he says:

"Osteopathy is the greatest scientific gift of God to man," and he regrets that his mind was so far below high-water mark, that he could not see its perfection as a healing art, when it was held up to his view that he might have a mental feast, far back in the seventies. I have told much that I would have held out of this history, but for the reason that I took my pen to write the whole truth of my journey with my son and child, "Osteopathy." . . .

ANONYMOUS

(1 8 4 0 ? – ?)

Six Hundred Dollars a Year: A Wife's Effort at Low Living, Under High Prices. Ticknor and Fields, Boston, 1867. 183 pp.

Even after a considerable amount of sleuthing I am still unable to discover who wrote *Six Hundred Dollars a Year*. Knowing nothing about the author, I cannot be sure it is the work of a naïve genius, rather than a professional writer, but I give it the benefit of the doubt.

The first federal income tax was imposed in 1862 to help finance the Civil War. It allowed a $600 exemption. When peace returned, inflation came, and the cost of living soared. *Six Hundred Dollars a Year* is a lively account of making ends meet on that sum, and thus avoiding taxes. Kitty tells how she managed and ran her household with genteel respectability for her husband, Arthur, a Union Army veteran and salaried white-collar worker, and their child, Percy. In spite of her limited budget, she was able to keep a servant girl, her equivalent of today's laundry machine and dishwasher.

There is no meaningful way to relate the dollar of 1867 to present-day purchasing power. The changes in monetary values have been qualitative even more than quantitative. Everyone knows the dollar buys less today; at the same time, many more ways of spending it are available. So the dollar has suffered a double diminution. The real worth of money and what it can do for the individual are not measured simply by how much it buys, but by how much of the kinds of things wanted and felt to be necessary can be bought.

Records of the publisher, Ticknor and Fields, preserved in the Houghton Reading Room, Harvard University, show they ordered three printings of *Six Hundred Dollars a Year*, 2,000 copies in November 1866, 1,000 in February 1867, and 1,180 in March 1867, at a cost of $1,781.57. The book sold for two dollars. If the author received a 10-per-cent royalty, she would have netted $836, a nice addition to her allotted $600.

203

SIX HUNDRED DOLLARS
A YEAR

CHAPTER I.

The Tax-gatherer.—Comforts of a small Income—High Rents and Rising Prices.—Everybody but us becoming Rich.

"Next week, Madam.—Please fill the blanks in this paper, and have it ready for me when I shall call next week."

Such was the salutation which greeted me as, in response to a ring at the bell, I opened the street door one morning, the speaker at the same time handing me a large printed document. He was a small, dapper-looking fellow, quite civil in his address, but moving and talking like one who had a world of business to get through with. It is probable he had his full share, as I noticed that he had in his hand a large bundle of documents exactly similar in appearance to that which he had given to me, while his coatpockets were almost bursting with bundles of similar papers. The circumstance, and the man, struck me as being novelties; so as he left the door and went down the street, I leaned forward and watched his motions.

He knocked or rung at every door upon the street, said something in a hurried way,—no doubt the very words he had used to me,—and delivered one of the mysterious papers to whoever responded to his summons. Nobody refused it, for it was not a quack almanac, the reading of which alone is enough to make one sick, nor a cure for some terrible species of human infirmity. I wondered at thus seeing all my neighbors so generously supplied, and felt quite sure that, whatever the good news might be, the whole town was in a fair way of speedily learning all about it.

My curiosity at what was going on in the street being thus gratified, I felt somewhat desirous of ascertaining what the document contained, and, closing the door, retired to my little sitting-room, where I had been busily employed with needle and thread during the greater part of the morning, endeavoring, as best I might, to mend up the tattered garments that had come from the weekly wash. I opened the mysterious, legal-looking parcel, to see what it might contain of interest to myself. It was a printed schedule of searching questions, of an intensely personal nature,—so personal that they must have been considered downright impertinent and offensive, but for the official authority which was announced (perhaps by way of apology) at the very top of the page.

As I had observed that the man had given a similar paper to each of my neighbors, I consoled myself by thinking that, instead of the insult being limited to ourselves, all the town was to be similarly outraged. Thus in some degree smoothing down my half-ruffled temper, I looked further into the contents of the inquisitorial document.

At the head of the page were the words, "Internal Revenue," "Income Tax," &c., and farther down came the before-mentioned interrogatories, beginning with such items as these:—

"What was your income last year?"

"Have you any Real Estate?"

"Have you any Stocks?"

"Has your wife any income?" &c., &c.

What, thought I, ask *me* if I have any corner lots, or stocks, or any income! I knew that Arthur had an eight-by-ten in the "Sylvan Cemetery," in which all of us will probably be some day buried, and that beyond this investment he was no more richly endowed than myself. All the stock that I possessed consisted of clothing and furniture, such as my own limited means had supplied when I was married. The considerate official who had prepared this schedule had left a space at every query, in which the party addressed was expected to write out a minute reply, solemnly and truly, under heavy penalties in case of delinquency or evasion. Nay, it must be sworn to, if required. Such inquisition, thought I, may be formidable to the wealthy, or to those who, without being rich, assume to be so; but why need it have any terrors for us?

After this came a list of taxable articles contained in almost every house, such as watches, musical instruments, silver plate, &c., of which we were also to give a strict account, and then submit to the prescribed taxation.

Well, in looking it all over, it did seem as if they had remembered even the minutest possession one might be supposed to have; and I must own to a certain feeling of satisfaction even in the consciousness of our poverty, for the idea of taxation is not a pleasant one, even for loyal citizens such as we have always been.

As to silver, the schedule allowed us to have forty ounces, free of tax. But that item occasioned me no alarm. What had we but the little cup which my father had given to baby when he found his name perpetuated in his grandson, and one or two dozen spoons of various sizes? Our tea service and forks were merely plated ware, genteel and handsome though, for all that, and looking quite as well as the most pretentious silver. There were no very costly presents at *my* wedding, such as one hears of in fashionable life. Hence, as we had no profusion of plate, so we had none to be taxed. It may be sometimes inconvenient to do without the one, but it is surprisingly consolatory to be able to escape the other.

When my husband came home from his daily duties, I confess I did really dislike to show him this irritating and unwelcome paper; so I postponed it until we had finished our evening meal, and then drew it forth cautiously and laid it before him, saying, as I did so,—

"See, Arthur, what a blessed thing it is to be poor."

He glanced rapidly down the list, and, although it was the first year the income tax had been levied, yet he took in the whole sum and substance of its contents. I, not so well informed as he, watched his countenance anxiously, to read his feelings. I knew how very hard he labored for the little income we enjoyed, and how close was the economy practised in our household; and now to think of having new and greater taxes to pay seemed too bad for consideration, and altogether impossible to be borne. But, though closely watching his calm face as he read the document aloud, commenting upon every item as he went on, I discovered no indication of anxiety or distress. He laughed repeatedly at the idea of *his* owning pleasure yachts or carriages,—the idea of *his* being in receipt of rents, dividends, or interest. In fact, he made so merry over the affair as to quite reassure me, and make me satisfied that I had not entirely understood the matter. But the fact is, that anything like a legal document is apt to confuse and even to alarm a woman. Why, I can distinctly remember how my heart fluttered when I first saw my own marriage certificate.

Laying the schedule on the table, he turned to me, and, in a voice so cheerful that I remember its inspiriting tones even now, he said,—

"Well, little wife, *we* need not distress ourselves, for our income is exempt; six hundred dollars are allowed us, you will observe, besides our house-rent, and that is all we have, you know. True, there is your piano, but that will take only two dollars a year; a single performance on it by you, especially when you add the song, is worth that,—at least to me. Then our watches are silver, so they are exempt. I reckon we shall manage our taxes well enough, without cheating Uncle Sam."

I cannot describe what a relief it was to hear him speak so, for I had dwelt upon the alarming document during the entire day, and, strangely enough, had quite overlooked the exemption clause; so, for the first time realizing the questionable comforts of poverty, I grew contented, and thereby *rich*, on the small sum of six hundred a year. Of course it was but a moment's work to write in the appointed place, $2, for a piano. The paper was then folded up and put in a safe place, to await the Assessor's promised call.

It was a fine October evening, not cool enough for a fire, but sufficiently comfortable to be seated around the lamp; with my husband stretching himself lazily in his easy-chair, to read the paper, while I undressed the baby, and prepared him for his night's repose.

Occasionally Arthur would read aloud, when any interesting item came in his way; and when the infant had been disposed of in his crib, he was ready to lay the sheet aside altogether, for a quiet chat, in which, as it was Saturday night, we reviewed the week's experience, and discussed those little domestic arrangements on which so much of the future was to depend.

Happily, I was able to produce a clear and fair account of

the household expenditure for the week; I had it down in black and white. We had not gone beyond our allowance, small though it was,—to some too small to live upon respectably. Even to us, who were accustomed to the closest calculations and to constant self-denials, it was quite too limited to be entirely agreeable.

Humble as was our position in the great world, we had a certain status to maintain. We must live in a respectable house, we must dress genteelly at least, and keep a servant too. To do all these, was now a heavy tax. Prices for everything were steadily rising, thus constantly encroaching on the fixed income which my husband received.

Provisions and clothing were thus so high that, notwithstanding the recent addition of two hundred dollars to our former income, we still had but the old sum of six hundred a year to live upon. The landlord had doubled our rent, and from the scarcity of dwellings we had been forced to remain where we were, or give up housekeeping altogether. A host of applicants stood waiting to secure our pleasant little home, if we should decide to give it up. But a careful calculation had convinced us that it was really cheaper to live as we were doing, than to board, besides being so much more comfortable in our own home, than we could possibly be if cramped up in one or two rooms of a boarding-house.

Our residence was in a thriving manufacturing town, where my husband was employed in superintending the machinery in one of the factories. His salary of eight hundred a year was very small, but he hoped to win promotion by a close attention to his employer's interests. We had seen among our friends so many lamentable instances of trying to become suddenly rich, many times by speculation, that we had wisely determined to be satisfied for the present with a bare competency, rather than come to grief through extravagance, or business ventures on a false capital. . . .

CHAPTER III.

The Tax-gatherer Again.—House and Furniture.—Our Garden.—Its Pleasures and Its Profits.—Making Wine.

In a few days, punctual to his word, the dapper little Internal Revenue man called for his paper, and found it all ready. I think he was rather surprised to find there was so little due from us, for he looked inquiringly around the parlor, and remarked how comfortably we were fixed.

"Have you no more than six hundred a year, madam?" he asked, incredulously.

"Only six hundred besides house-rent, which is two hundred more," I answered, thinking him very impertinent.

"I do not mean to doubt your word at all," he said, apologetically. "You have a pleasant situation here."

I said, "Yes," mechanically, for I was afraid he had some designs upon our house,—perhaps was looking for one himself; and so nervous did the idea make me that I was much relieved when he had taken his departure.

As soon as Arthur came home in the evening, I told him my fears, and we discussed the propriety of at once forestalling the man, in case such was his object, by applying for a five years' lease on our little house. My husband approved of the plan, so before bedtime he had called on the landlord, and secured our right for the above-mentioned term.

Our house was a pleasant, snug little affair, with a cosey parlor and dining-room back, a large kitchen, and a shed for wash-house and summer cooking. Up stairs were three good chambers in the second story, with bath, and two attics above.

The house was comfortably furnished, for I had bought the furniture myself at the time of my marriage, with a legacy of seven hundred dollars left me by the aunt in whose honor I was named. But for that, we should have been poorly off; for Arthur had little to spare when we began life, and my own father had too large a family depending on him to give much to set out his oldest daughter. A good supply of clothing was therefore the most I could expect from him; and the generous good-will with which he gave me that was as much as many dollars given grudgingly. Fortunately, at the time of our going to housekeeping the prices of such things were moderate, and I furnished my house entirely with the sum I have named. My piano, I should mention, had been used for a short time before I bought it, and was really worth much more than it cost me.

I have only to refer to my bills to tell just what were the items.

PARLOR FURNITURE.

Forty yards Tapestry Carpet, at $1.00	$40.00
Walnut Hair-Cloth Sofa	30.00
Four Walnut Chairs, at $3.00	12.00
Walnut Centre-Table	5.00
Cloth Cover	2.00
Small Pier Table with Marble Top	8.00
Piano and Stool	200.00
Two Window-Shades of White Linen	2.00
Total, .	$299.00

FURNITURE FOR THREE CHAMBERS.

Seventy yards Ingrain Carpet, at $0.75 . . .	$52.50
Three Cottage-Sets, at $40 each	120.00
Beds and Bedding	50.00
Crockery Ware	6.00
Muslin Curtains	3.00
Total, .	$231.50

DINING-ROOM

Twenty yards Carpet, at $0.75	$15.00
A Good Second-Hand Table	5.00
Six Cane-Seat Chairs, at $1.50	9.00
Cutlery	10.00
Stone-China Dinner Set	10.00
Tea Set, white French China	5.00
Window-Shades	1.00
Total, .	$55.00

Kitchen Furniture, and Cooking Utensils . . .	$30.00
Hall Furniture, and Stair Carpet	30.00
	$60.00

Total cost of House Furniture   .   . $685.50

This left me just $41.50 for table-linen, sheets, pillow-cases, and towels; which was little enough, it is true, but as muslin was cheap then, it bought me a dozen sheets, a dozen pillow-cases, five table-cloths, a dozen napkins, a dozen fine hucka-back towels, a dozen crash ones for kitchen use, and left me some twelve dollars for sundry knicknacks, such as brushes and combs, waiters, dust-brushes, and lamps. So, when everything was arranged in its proper place, our house was indeed a model of comfort and convenience.

Then there was the garden outside, which, if it added some-what to our labor, contributed very materially to our comfort also. It was not large,—certainly not more than an eighth of an acre,—yet we managed to cultivate it without a dollar's hiring. All but the few shillings' worth of seed, and an occasional bar-row-load of manure, was therefore clear gain.

Down on each side, and quite around the lot, was a row of currant-bushes, which after the first season, produced splen-didly. The few original plants that we found there were large, spreading ones, with much dead wood, and the majority of new stalks were without fruit. They had grown undisturbed for years, and contained enough to plant around the entire margin. Early in the spring, before the leaf-buds had opened, my hus-band dug them up, one at a time, undertaking only so much as he could finish up each day, in the hour before breakfast that he had determined to devote to this work. The ground next the fence had first been well spaded up and levelled, and each large bush when taken up was separated into ten or fifteen pieces, every one having good and healthy fibrous roots. These were at once set out at a distance of three feet apart, before they had had time to wither. Thus, after a few mornings' work, we had our whole garden hedged around with currant-bushes, which seemed to occupy no room at all, and soon blossomed forth with great luxuriance. That year's crop was not so large, be-cause the smaller plants did not bear at all; but by the second season they were very full, and hung in long crimson clusters from every stalk.

The remainder of the ground we planted with vegetables, as follows: an onion-bed, which, from three quarts of sets, costing twenty-one cents, produced us over a bushel of fine onions;

string-beans, and Lima beans; a few tomato-plants which I purchased from a gardener at three cents each, and which came
into bearing very early. The first six tomatoes produced me
thirty cents, and the green-grocer gladly took them in exchange
for other things of that value. The next six brought twenty-five
cents, and the next twenty-five cents the quarter peck. All together, we sold a dollar and thirty cents' worth, which more
than paid the whole cost of our seeds, plants, and bean-poles,
and after that we enjoyed the rest of them ourselves, having
them for breakfast, dinner, or tea every day during the season.
All this was from ten plants. Besides these, we had a few egg-
plants, which produced well; two or three cucumber-vines,
which furnished us pickles, almost enough to last during the
year, having at hand in the cellar a tub of brine, into which
they were put every day as they were gathered. Our nice beds
of salad, parsley, thyme, sweet majoram, summer-savory, and
sage, especially the herbs, were a great source of comfort during the entire year. At the proper season we cut and dried them
for winter use, and I was thus not only provided myself with
the means of making many savory dishes, but was often able to
accommodate my less fortunate and provident neighbors.

When the currants were ripe, I made enough jelly to answer
our requirements, and then from the rest I made both wine and
shrub,—the latter a cooling and refreshing beverage for the hot
weather, and, indeed, for any season. . . .

Around the door and all about the house were nice grass-
plots and flower-beds, these last being my own especial charge.
During the first two years after my marriage I spent much time
in sowing, transplanting, and weeding my pretty *parterres*, and
was richly repaid for all my pains in their gay appearance, and
the never-failing bouquet they furnished for my parlor. Even in
later years, when my hands were busy with nursing baby, I still
found a little time to use my garden tools; and in the morning I
had but to take the little fellow out in his coach, and place him
under the shade of a tree close at hand, where he could watch
me pull up the weeds, and crow his approbation, until the task
was accomplished.

I think I have clearly demonstrated that a house with even
such a strip of garden room as ours is worth far more than one

without it. Yet considerable management is necessary in order to prevent it from becoming a positive expense rather than a profit. My husband loved the care of a garden, and those early morning hours which he gave to the work were positively the pleasantest of the day.

It was wonderful to see how his appetite for breakfast increased by the healthful exercise they gave him. His regular business was of a very different kind, so this variety was therefore the more agreeable; besides, as the plants grew and flourished, and bore fruit, only those who have done as he did can understand how well he was repaid for all his toil. That the vegetables tasted better than those we bought was no mere conceit, for they were ripe and fresh, and therefore good and wholesome.

But if, on the other hand, we had hired our garden cultivated, and paid for the work by the day, the cost would have far exceeded the profit, and one of the chief pleasures of our humble home would have been lost to us.

CHAPTER IV.

Beginning to keep House.—Good Management.—Cost of Living.— Clothing.—Buying Bargains.

. . . we had at least $125 per annum for our clothing; and with careful management we were able to dress ourselves very genteelly on that amount. For myself, a few good dresses were better than many poor ones, and I have always found it the cheapest to buy good material, even if the first cost is rather greater, than to get a coarse or thin article, which will last but a single season. I do not mean by this, however, that I bought expensive or extravagant dresses, or showy or costly shawls and cloaks. One dress of a season, of alpaca, cashmere, or all-wool delaine, cost about $12, including making and trimming; for I could sew it entirely myself, merely paying a dressmaker to cut and fit it for me, at a cost of twenty-five cents.

For summer, a nice barége, or some similar material, could be had for about $6, and a calico for $2 more. Cloaks and shawls were heavier articles, and therefore but one such item could be indulged in each year. But even for a winter cloak I could buy the materials, of fine, good cloth, for $10, and with a paper pattern by which to cut it out, I could make it and trim it as well as a regular cloakmaker, although I had never learned the trade. Then if the fashions changed, I was able to alter or refit it so as to insure its looking well for at least five years.

Another year I would spend about the same sum for a shawl or mantilla, and, once in two or three years, a new silk dress. As for bonnets, on which so many ladies expend such large sums, I was able myself to manufacture as pretty a one as I cared to wear. The materials for a bonnet cost but a trifle compared with the price asked in the milliners' shops for the manufactured articles; so when the season came round for a new bonnet, I generally paid a visit to the city and took a survey of the various styles on exhibition in the windows and glass cases at the shop doors, made my selection, and then purchased my frame, ribbons, flowers, &c., accordingly. A few seasons' experience had enabled me to judge pretty accurately of the quantity required for any particular shape or style, and I could always work up my old material, and make over the last season's bonnet so as to look as well as new. Very often a handsome silk or velvet bonnet was produced in this way, for three or four dollars, which could not have been bought for less than twenty at the stores. I had a large box into which I always put the odds and ends of bonnet materials, so, as the fashion was continually varying, I was constantly able to bring out of my treasure-house new combinations of silk and lace and velvet, which the world at large would have supposed were altogether new. To me, the consciousness that I had done well, and with so little outlay, added greatly to the satisfaction I felt in wearing my new bonnets. . . .

One day I attended an auction sale of furniture, held in the neighborhood, with the intention of procuring one or two trifling articles of kitchen ware that were needed. Many of my friends were there also,—it was quite fashionable to go to auctions in our town,—and I walked through the house to see what was to be sold. In one of the upper rooms hung a large mirror, with a very shabby gilt frame,—not broken at all,—but only discolored, and almost bare of gilding. It had evidently been exposed to flies, as well as to careless management, for many years. I saw at a glance that it was a valuable glass, but it did not enter my mind to bid on it for myself until I heard the auctioneer crying it off at the paltry sum of one dollar and ninety-five cents. Waiting just a second, to hear some one bid higher before it was sacrificed at that price, his eye suddenly rested on my face, and almost without a thought of obtaining the prize, I gave him a nod which indeed secured it for me at the low rate of two dollars. I was as much surprised as any one there, for when I left home, I had not dreamed of making such a purchase.

Well, it required but a few moments to have it removed to our own house; but before I had been at home ten minutes, a friend who had heard of my bargain called to offer me double the price, if I were disposed to sell. I did not decline the offer then, but promised to let her know the next day, as I had some experiments to be tried first, which I was in haste to begin. On receiving the glass at home I had had it carried into the parlor, where it was to remain until dinner was over, and Arthur had gone back to the factory. I especially desired that he should not see it until I had exercised my ingenuity upon its time-worn frame. As usual, he did not go into the parlor at all, but went out again immediately after dinner; and for that once, at least, I was glad to see him depart.

Then began my work of renovating the shabby frame. It was indeed beautifully ornamented with scroll-work, and other designs, only that the whole was changed by careless washings to a general whitey-black appearance, which was anything but handsome.

It was but a few moments' work to wash and wipe carefully the dust from every part of it. Then with a brush I laid on the brown varnish paint, such as cabinet-makers use for staining wood in imitation of walnut or rosewood. Working it well into all the cracks and corners of the frame, I soon covered up all the shabby gilding, and changed the whole appearance of the thing. I know it did not look handsomer, even in the days of its primeval grandeur, than it did when I had finished those simple artistic touches.

I kept the parlor door closely shut in order to prevent the odor of paint from escaping to tell my secret, for I had determined, if possible, to surprise my husband with a first sight of the new mirror after it had been hung. I knew that it would look so much handsomer when it should be in its place between the parlor windows. As it was summertime, and flies were plenty, I had a good excuse for proposing that we should sit on the pleasant piazza, instead of opening the parlor, and in the evening we went out to make a few visits, which occupied the hours until bedtime. Thus my secret was unsuspected that night.

Next morning, with the assistance of my girl, and a borrowed step-ladder, I managed to hang up my new mirror with its carved rosewood frame, and I could not have imagined the good effect of such an addition to our parlor furniture. It not only looked well itself, but everything else looked better in its company. In a word, I was delighted with my bargain, and was now as impatient to let Arthur see it as I had been to prevent his doing so.

I was singing one of his favorite songs, when I heard his latch-key in the street door, and I knew he would be sure to come at once into the parlor, so I only turned around to see him enter. He was in the act of crossing the room, when he caught a glimpse of his own image reflected in the glass, and turning around almost involuntarily, he saw the new mirror, and stopped in amazement before it.

"Why, what have we here?" he exclaimed, looking into my conscious face. "How did this come about?"

"*I* bought it, my dear. Don't you think it handsome?" I answered, cautiously, for I knew what he would say next.

"Very handsome indeed; but, Kitty, do you think it was right to buy anything like this until we can afford it better?"

He said this reproachfully, but I knew how to answer him, so rejoined, "Why, how much do you suppose it cost?"

"I cannot well guess; but some twenty-five or thirty dollars I suppose: these rosewood frames are quite expensive."

"Well, my dear Arthur, it only cost *us* two dollars and twenty-five cents all together, and I am offered double that already if we choose to sell it. But it shall be just as you decide."

He looked incredulously at me, but there was the auctioneer's bill and receipt for the two dollars. The other twenty-five cents were for the paint and porterage.

"Well, little wife, you are a rare hand for bargains; but I guess we'll keep this one ourselves, and not let Mrs. L. have it."

I had privately resolved to save the cost of my purchase by doing without some equivalent item of my own wardrobe, and so I did; but I took far more satisfaction in my looking-glass than I could have derived from the articles dispensed with. After this, whenever my husband would laugh at my propensity for "bargains," I had only to quote this case to turn the joke on the other side.

It must not be supposed, however, that I often indulged in such episodes, nor had I the means to launch out into those expensive and attractive items which more favored housekeepers might have secured. I knew that, not only was our income limited, but that our house was small and plain also, and I would have considered it quite out of taste to have in my little parlor anything too costly or pretentious to correspond with my other furniture.

I was, however, very fond of fancy-work, and took great delight in making various little articles that came under this name, all of which tended to beautify our little home, and render it still more charming in our partial eyes.

CHAPTER VI.

Cousin Lucy's Visit.—Working for the Soldiers.—Making Wax-Flowers.—A New Idea.—Earning Money.—A New Visitor.—About Servants.—Bill of Fare.—A Tea-Party.

It was during the period of which I am now writing—the second year after my marriage—that my cousin Lucy Graham came to pay me a little visit. She had promised to come for a long time; but being one of the useful sort, always employed in good works, and never consulting her pleasure before her duty, this expected treat had been very long deferred. Indeed, when I heard of her many engagements, and of her prominence in all the public movements of the day in which women may take part, I despaired of ever seeing her at all. But one morning she came with her little trunk to pay that memorable visit. I say *memorable;* and in the course of my story I will explain why I may justly call it so.

Lucy was much older than myself. She was probably at this time over thirty, and I only two-and-twenty. Ever since I could remember, I had looked up to her as a very lovely and superior person, expert in many beautiful arts, intelligent and literary, —in a word, she was a sort of beau-ideal to me, whose good qualities I continually endeavored to imitate. This was her first visit to me, and I received her with the warmest and most affectionate welcome. I felt both pride and pleasure in showing her my house and its arrangements, and she entered so cordially into all my plans and contrivances, and approved so much of my system of household expenditures, that I loved to talk over my affairs with her, asking her advice on divers little matters in which I was in doubt.

Like ourselves, she was an early riser, so in the morning, as soon as breakfast was over, and my little domestic duties attended to, we sat down together, to our several employments, she in turn telling me of the work in which she was then most interested. It was just at this time that the war was occupying everybody's attention, and patriotic women were beginning to work for the soldiers who had gone to battle for the Union. In every city and town, and even in every village of the North, the "Ladies' Aid" Societies were being organized, and little bands of women were busy making shirts and drawers, or scraping lint, and rolling bandages for the hospitals. The great "Sanitary Commission," too, with its vast machinery, into whose storehouses, as to a huge reservoir, all those little streams flowed, was beginning its work of humanity.

I had lived, as it were, out of the world, and needed to be told of these things, and have the grand movements of the day explained to me. No one then could do it better than my cousin Lucy, who was one of those foremost in the work. She had devoted almost her whole time to it, and already held a responsible position as a member of the "Commission." "For," as she remarked, "what else can we women do, at such a time as this? We cannot fight ourselves, but we can help those who can, and comfort those who have fallen, from wounds or sickness, by our sympathy, our prayers, and our offerings."

Indeed, as I listened I grew so much interested, and my patriotism became so lively, that I wished very much for the means to begin some such work in our own town. I told Lucy how gladly I would do what I could, but my hands were tied because of my slender purse; and she knew that I spoke truly.

"But there are many others who could do liberally, and would, no doubt," she said, "if the thing could only be started."

"Certainly, Lucy," I answered, "but who will take the lead?"

"If there is no one else, then why not yourself?" she asked, emphatically. "These are not the times for any to lack courage when duty calls us. Come, I will go with you, and let us see what can be done now, this very day."

If I had stopped to think it all over, and had realized how large a matter I was undertaking, I might have shrunk from the task; but not so: Lucy gave me no time to hesitate. The text she quoted to me was this one,—"Whatsoever thy hand findeth to do, do it with thy might," and, acting in this mind, we set out on our errand.

I will not here recount the particulars of our expedition, in which we called on many of the wealthiest people of the town, but will only state that enough were interested to constitute the nucleus of a "Ladies' Aid Society," whose operations continued during the whole period of the war. As the existence of the organization became more widely known by means of its published reports and acknowledgments, contributions began to flow in, and additional workers were enrolled, until it came to be a most valuable auxiliary of the Sanitary Commission. Many boxes and barrels of supplies were sent to the sick and wounded men who languished in hospitals so far away from home and friends, to whom those jellies and cordials, and clean clothes seemed like a reminder of the absent, while it was so cheering to them to feel that the country that had called them to defend her did not forget her brave champions, nor leave them uncared for in their times of trouble and sickness.

So this was the way our society started, and hence my own warm personal interest in its success. We met one evening in a week in each others' houses, and while a few older ones cut out and fixed the work, the others sewed the seams and finished off the garments. We sent them off whenever we had enough to fill a box, and this was quite often, so that by the time the war was over, and our society closed its operations, we were able to show a report of some ten or twelve thousand garments which we had given to the soldiers, besides a large quantity of wines, cordials, jellies, etc.

But to return to Lucy's visit, which had only just begun. While we sat together during those pleasant mornings that passed so swiftly, I became much interested in watching her work. She was making wax-flowers,—and *such* wax-flowers as they were!

I had often seen ordinary wax-work in the shop windows, but never such exquisite things as hers. They seemed to rival nature itself, so lifelike and natural were the shapes and tints, and so delicate were the groupings of her sprays. I had never cared to learn the art until I saw Lucy's manipulations, but now I was seized with a strong desire to do so, and she generously promised to teach me all she could. So the lessons began forthwith, and every day I gained some fresh knowledge, until by the time her visit was done I had made more than one bouquet, and felt myself almost mistress of the art. My wax-flowers began to be the wonder and admiration of all my friends, even more than my leather-work had been. Indeed, I confessed secretly to myself how beautiful they were, and how well I had improved my opportunity.

Lucy's wax-flowers were all given to help the funds of the Sanitary Commission. I think by the time her labors for the cause were completed, she must have given, in this way, many hundreds of dollars. When she told me of the ready sale they met with, I began to think of doing the same with some of mine,—a few at least. I would gladly have given more, had I felt able to do so, but the materials were expensive, and every one I made cost me something.

The first bouquet Arthur insisted upon having placed on our own parlor mantel, and the next I gave very freely to the fair we were just about starting for the benefit of the "Aid Society." When the fair did take place, I was surprised and delighted to find how quickly it was sold, and I really believe I could have sold twenty more if they had been there.

One day, while Lucy was teaching me, she told me of several of her friends who had made large sums of money, and were still doing so, simply from the sale of fancy-work. Some did this for their own support, and some in order that they might have the means to give to others. Her information made a great impression on my mind. I began to think how acceptable, just now, would be a little accession to my own income, and how pleasantly I might thus provide myself with a fund on which I could draw at discretion. This idea took such firm hold on me that I confided it to Lucy, and asked her advice and assistance in the matter. After all that I have said of her generosity and kindness, I need scarcely tell how willingly she gave me both, and volunteered to introduce me to one who would either purchase my flowers or sell them for me on commission.

The Holidays were approaching, and this I knew was my time to begin; so, as soon as I could prepare a few, I sent them as specimens to the place she had designated, and in a few days afterward came an order for more. I can scarcely describe my sensations as I read the letter, I was so overjoyed at my success; and the idea that I was really able to earn a little money was so pleasing that I could hardly contain myself; yet I set busily about the bouquets, and in a few days was able to forward the second lot to the large establishment in the city.

Dear Cousin Lucy,—her visit was so short; and yet, when I look back to it now, and think of all that it did for me, I bless her more and more, and feel that the value of those lessons of independence and self-reliance she taught me then can never be estimated. I did not see her again for two years afterward, but I heard of her often, as one of the Florence Nightingales of our own land, who watched beside the sick and dying in the hospitals and on the battle-fields. Many a last message she carried to the absent friends of the dying soldier and many a prayer she offered for the departing spirits, who but for this, would have had no holy words to comfort them in that solemn hour.

When New Year was past, and I received my pay, I had over a hundred dollars coming to me, which was pretty well for my first season.

Here my wax-work ceased for many months, for other business came before long, which crowded everything else out of the way. Before spring another most important and engrossing individual was added to our family in the person of our precious baby, who, if he brought with him a world of care and anxiety, and a most weighty sense of responsibility, brought also a love which overbalanced all, and made these new labors seem very light. My little hoard of money, which was doubly valuable because it was all my own, was indeed a windfall,—at this time, especially, when so much was to be provided for the new-comer. Every article for an infant's wardrobe was so expensive that many dollars were needed to procure the necessary amount of flannel and cambric, not to speak of cradle, crib, and little coach. This last article saved me almost the expense of hiring another girl, as I was able to take the child out myself; indeed, after this, I was seldom able to go out in the daytime without taking him with me.

Jane* was fortunately very fond of children, and this was to me another source of great thankfulness, for, inasmuch as nursing baby was not her legitimate business, I could not demand her services in this new department of our daily work.

I was often asked by my friends and neighbors to explain how I managed to keep my girl so long, when they were so constantly changing theirs. The only way I could do this was by inquiring a little into our several modes of management. Mrs. Travis, our opposite neighbor, could never keep a servant more than six weeks, and paid by the year at the intelligence office, they engaging to supply her with as many of the kind as she might need. I felt sure there must be some mismanagement about it, and that there was probably a little fault on the side of the mistress, as well as the maid. One day, when calling there, the subject was brought up for discussion,—the "irrepressible conflict" between housekeepers and servants.

"I quite envy you," she began,—"you, who never change; but where you managed to secure such a prize, and how you manage to keep her, too, are perfect problems to me."

"Jane is a very good girl," I answered, "and I own myself fortunate in having her; but perhaps she might not suit you as well, if you had her. She is not faultless, I assure you."

"But her faults cannot be bad ones," she insisted, "or you could not keep her at all."

"Well, Mrs. Travis," I said, "she has many good qualities,

* The servant.

which, in my estimation, overbalance her faults; but I know that in some families she could not stay a month."

"Why, how do *you* manage her then?" asked my friend.

"Well, you see, Jane is a respectable girl, and deserves to be treated as such. She is quite above the common run of servants, who depend on intelligence offices for places, and change them so often as never to become attached to either place or people. She has been with us more than two years, and I think really loves us, and would do almost anything to serve us. If I am sick, she is kindness itself, and would be ready to lose her sleep, or give up any of her own privileges, at such times. Now these are matters which go far towards outweighing those minor faults that all servants have. She is sometimes quite heedless, and forgets my directions, but then I know it is unintentional, and so I do not censure her too severely. If I did I might lose her, and not be able to suit myself again as well."

"Heedlessness is a bad fault," remarked my auditor. "Wastefulness is another, and I have had experience in both; but save me from your 'respectable' servants who think they must eat just the same as you do yourself, and indeed act as if they were quite on a level with their employers. I always expect to have the servants' stores separate from my own, and give them their allowance every week, which, unless they are wasteful, is ample for all their wants."

"I see that we differ a little in our views," I said earnestly. "I do not mean an impudent or presuming servant, when I say 'respectable,' but one who has right views of her duties and responsibilities, and knows how to value a good home. Besides, it has been my plan to give Jane the same food that we eat ourselves."

"What! the same butter, coffee, desserts, etc., that you have on your own table, and as much of them as she chooses to take?" asked Mrs. Travis in amazement. "Why, I have always heard you praised as such a good manager and economical housekeeper."

"As to that, I may have been credited with more than I deserve," I answered; "but I certainly think it would have been poor economy to have a different set of provisions laid for Jane, when there is always enough left after we are done to feed her

well. It would be poor economy to waste that surplus, merely
because she was a servant and required servants' fare. You will
now understand what I mean by having a *respectable* servant.
Our Jane is too conscientious to waste anything and eats and
behaves with as much propriety as most people in different circumstances."

"Well, I always thought that all ladies pursued the same plan
in regard to servants' supplies. You surely do not allow them
sweetmeats and desserts?" she said.

"Our Jane, as I said before, is honest and decent, and she
always sits down after our meal is over, and partakes of whatever we have left. If there are sweetmeats, I have always observed that she helped herself to a small quantity, and then put
the rest away as carefully as I would have done myself. I could
not think of telling her she could not have any."

"How different are our ideas on this point, or else how
different are the servants we have to deal with," she remarked.

"I think you are right in both cases," I answered. "Perhaps
you would find my Jane a nuisance, and I suppose that under
your system she would soon become quite a different girl."

But there was little use in reasoning with my neighbor; for
her views were so totally different from mine that it was better
for us to differ amicably without continuing the discussion. I
am sure, however, that the price which she annually paid to the
intelligence office more than equalled the cost of all the desserts
and sweetmeats eaten by Jane. She continued to discourse constantly of servants and their faults, and changed hers as often
as ever.

In the mean time Jane did our work as usual, and after the
housework was over, she, of her own accord, would hold the
baby, or sit by the cradle while I rested or went out. She felt at
home with us, and had become interested in our affairs. She
knew and understood how limited our means were, and she did
her best to economize. There are few houses in which there is
less waste than in ours, for Jane was both ready and willing to
turn everything to good account. When we had scraps of meat
left from dinner, she would save them carefully and prepared a
nice dish of hash or croquets for the next day, which were
really better than fresh meat would have been. In our house I

can truly say that there was nothing wasted. The bread, however stale, was used for puddings, sauces, and dressings; cold potatoes were always fried and browned nicely for breakfast, and even sour milk was used to mix those delicious griddle-cakes which Arthur liked so well. My cookery-book had in it receipts of all kinds. There were rich cakes, expensive pastry, and extravagant bills of fare, but it was the plainer ones that we chose.

Our table was plentiful, but plain. For breakfast we always had good bread or rolls in summer, and in winter griddle-cakes of buckwheat, wheat, or Indian meal, with fried potatoes, broiled mackerel, or fresh fish, an omelette, boiled eggs, or a meat stew, made of the remains of yesterday's dinner; but only one of those items at a time. For dinner we rarely dispensed with meat or fish, because Arthur needed strong food to sustain him under such close application of the duties of his position. But we bought only the necessary quantity, and seldom indulged in large joints, and fine poultry. A turkey for Christmas, and a goose or ducks for New Year, with a chicken now and then throughout the year, was the extent of our experience in the poultry line. But then every day there were nicely cooked vegetables, frequently of our own raising, and a plain good pudding or pie for dessert. Then for our evening meal we needed little more than tea and toast, with a dish of chipped beef, sliced tomatoes, or ripe fruit.

If a friend came to take a meal with us, our rule was to make no deviation from our usual fare. I might, it is true, set the table with greater care, and display my nicest dishes and finest table-linen, because this cost me nothing but a little trouble. But, on principle, we refrained from useless profusion. We could not afford to make feasts or to give parties, and while we endeavored to "use hospitality without grudging," we also remembered, that to live beyond one's means is not consistent either with reason or religion. In my own visiting experience, however, I always found that a warm welcome, and a cordial spirit, was a surer source of gratification to the guest, than a table loaded with costly viands. . . .

CHAPTER IX.

Glimpses of our Neighbors . . . The Ardleys . . . Spring Employment . . .

. . . In looking around further among our friends, what different ideas I find prevailing,—ideas of enjoyment, of expediency, of economy and household management. After Mr. Travis moved away from the house across the street, a family named Ardley came into it. We had some knowledge of them before they came, and so of course went to call on them as soon as they were fixed. The parlor was not only elegantly, but gorgeously furnished, with a grand display of lace curtains, rosewood and brocatelle sofas, mirrors, and mantel ornaments of the most costly description. There was a pretentious style about the whole establishment that impressed one exceedingly, and the white-aproned colored boy who opened the front door would have answered the same purpose in a millionaire's mansion, so well had he been trained to the business. Mrs. Ardley entered the room with her oldest daughter, a pretty but idealess girl of twenty, and received us with great ease and affability. Their conversation was commonplace, though there was always something about the whole family which pleased me, in spite of the difference in our views and styles of living. We had exchanged several calls before I left home, and now that we were once more settled, the acquaintance was renewed, and we grew quite sociable, occasionally comparing notes in housekeeping.

I then discovered how differently we two families lived, on about the same income. Mrs. Ardley's thoughts were all on show, while mine were on comfort. She kept no servant but the black boy I had seen, whom she had taken to bring up, thus securing his services with no further cost than his food and clothing. She and her daughters did the rest of the work, and lived on as little as possible. I have heard that often they had only mush and potatoes, or some such thing for dinner, and bought the cheapest meat in the market, drinking also the cheapest substitutes for coffee, and the poorest tea. This was when they were alone, of course; but when company came, it was quite different, and a temporary cook was employed, who served up the most sumptuous meals in the highest French style. Once when Mrs. Ardley was ill, I was sent for to see her, and went up into her chamber,—a poorly furnished room, with the commonest wooden-bottomed chairs, a coarse straw bed, and no carpet on the cold floor. I was surprised to see it, for the grand appearance of everything down stairs did not correspond with the poverty displayed above. I caught a glimpse of the large front bedroom, however, and there saw that things were in quite different style. A large and massive walnut bedstead, with carved headboard, a handsome dressing-table to match, with all the other belongings of an elegant chamber, a rich carpet also covering the floor. This was the state chamber into which company were shown; but it was kept shut up on all other occasions, as too good to use. The money, moreover, that had been expended on the furniture of that one room would have furnished all the others in neat and comfortable style; but this would not have comported with Mrs. Ardley's notions. She had been seized with a sudden illness, and was alarmed, or she would not have had me see her bare and uncomfortable-looking room, and but for that accident I probably never should have been allowed to enter it. . . .

In cleaning our house my rule has always been, to undertake only one room a day, and to finish it before night; then if sickness or company should come,—for at such a time one is nearly as unwelcome as the other,—or if one has even an evening call, you are not found in confusion, and tired almost to death, in the bargain. I know some housekeepers, and good ones too, who are so anxious to get the dirt all out of the house at once that they begin this annual nuisance by taking up every carpet at once; thus leaving the family without a single comfortable place to live in. Then, of course, the upper rooms are first finished by degrees, and afterwards the lower ones; but the operation lasts for more than a week, during all which the men of the household are so incommoded as to be in a perpetual ill-humor. I have known families in which this domestic chaos has been kept up so many days as to compel the male portion to dine out until order has been restored. It is this ill-judged method of cleaning the house that makes the operation a sort of periodical horror to all concerned. If there is sickness or death,

or if visitors come for a night's lodging, under such management, no place in the house is in order. This mode of upsetting
things may be satisfactory to some people, but I prefer my own
plan; hence there is always a comfortable place, both for sitting
and sleeping, during the whole period we are at work. When
the carpets were to be put down, I examined them well, to discover if there were any worn places or moth-holes, and wherever I perceived any evidence of the same, they were turned
round so as to bring the worn portion into another part of the
room, first neatly darning the holes. By using these precautions
my carpets will last three times as long as if I omitted them,
and these times of high prices are not such as to encourage
waste, or to wear out carpets needlessly. . . .

CHAPTER XI.

Changed Times.—The Shoddyites.—Scarcity of Horses.—Disasters and
    Struggles.—The Twins.—Contrasts.

The reader may have been surprised to learn that the comparatively moderate house we occupied had commanded so
high a rent as a thousand dollars a year. But the war had
broken up the old order of prices, and changed the lowest into
what in former times would have been the highest. I presume it
must have been the abundance of paper money that produced
this change,—at least, this is a reasonable inference. These new
thousands of millions of paper dollars, which were scattered
over the country by the necessities of the war, fell to the share
of numerous government contractors, who thus became suddenly rich. The government, as we have before said, was a huge
customer for every description of manufactured goods, and
bought its supplies by contract. Judging by what the newspapers said, it appeared to me that whoever was lucky enough to
secure a large contract was equally sure of a large fortune. No
matter how poor a man might be, if he only obtained a contract, we might expect to witness his speedy transformation
from absolute poverty to abundant wealth.

Some of these instances were really wonderful. There was a
very ingenious middle-aged man within our knowledge, whose
dissipation had reduced him to the condition of a pauper in the

almshouse. While thus domiciled, he invented a little conven-
ience for the soldiers in their tents. I think it was a light, port-
able cooking apparatus. By help of an acquaintance he had it
patented, and then that acquaintance, who had a friend at
headquarters, managed to secure a contract for the supply of an
immense number for the army. The profit was so great that all
three became rich. Two of them had previously been living on
their wits, while the other had lived on the public. As might
have been expected, the sudden change from poverty to wealth
tempted them all into lavish expenditures,—their money had
come easily and it must needs go in the same easy way. The
pauper came out of the almshouse and forthwith set up as a
gentleman.

This description of people were known as "shoddyites." The
origin of the word is easily traced to the worthless imitations
palmed off by unprincipled manufacturers for genuine cloth.
Perhaps it is quite as easy to detect the "shoddy" in society as
in goods; time, at least, will prove them both. Every city was
full of this class. As all had abundance of money, so all spent it
with a sort of reckless extravagance that astonished such plain
people as ourselves. If they wanted any luxury, the price was no
discouragement. It was not the men only that were thus foolish:
the wives and daughters of the "shoddyites" were carried away
by the same mania for spending money. Never having had any
until now, they appeared to have no just conception of its
value, and became impatient to part with it. I think that
women's dresses were never so extravagant; and it was curious
to think how we had all accustomed ourselves to the high prices
of material. Though silks and laces were two or three times as
high as formerly, yet those who wanted them bought them just
as readily. Indeed, the high price of an article really seemed to
promote its sales, and common things fell into comparative dis-
use.

It was well ascertained that more trinkets and jewelry, gold
watches and precious stones, found buyers in one year of these
times than in three preceding ones. Then, at the watering-
places there was an unprecedented crowd of *parvenus*, who
really seemed to enjoy themselves in proportion to the unheard-
of prices charged by the landlords. This general rise must nec-

essarily extend to house and furniture. Apart from the bewildering abundance of paper money, there were two other causes operating to produce a rise in them. There were fewer houses being built than formerly, owing to the advance in wages and materials. Then there was a large influx of refugees from the South, who crowded the cities and villages of the North, having been driven from home by the discomforts existing there. A demand was thus created for houses, which could not be supplied except at an advanced price. The newspapers contained multitudes of advertisements from persons offering large premiums to any one who would procure them a house. Several of our neighbors were tempted by even higher prices than we obtained to give up house and furniture and take to boarding with their friends. Thus it was that I found the unsettled condition of public affairs, and the hazards to which my husband had been exposed in the army, had some slight show of compensation. . . .

But the times were out of joint in many other particulars. While one set of people were thus easily acquiring and spending fortunes, others sank into comparative destitution. I know that to such the former gave abundant charities; for when our cup runs over, we sometimes permit others to drink the drops that fall,—but too rarely a drop from within the rim,—and call it charity. When the war closed, and the soldiers were discharged, our town had its full share of stragglers of various descriptions. Some of these were wounded soldiers, some mere camp-followers, others were impostors; but all knocked at our doors, and demanded help of some sort, either of food or clothing or money, to help them homeward. I never could find it in my heart to turn away the sick or crippled hero of the loyal army without giving him whatever he solicited. A moderate contribution was rarely too much for my limited means, and while thus relieving their wants, how could I fail to return thanks to God that he had given me both the ability and the will to do so? I found, even in the closest of times, that, when the heart was all right, a trifle could be spared for such purposes, from even six hundred a year.

Then, besides these, there were wives whose husbands had been reported as "missing," some of whom may return, but many will never again be heard of; and widows, from whose stricken hearts even this faint hope had wholly gone out. All were to be sympathized with, and most of them to be relieved. Hundreds of them, however, were nobly endeavoring to help themselves; hence there were daily calls at the door from somebody who wanted to sell the little necessaries which another class of pedlers had formerly brought,—song-books, stories of the war, portraits of the great generals, pictures of the dreadful battles, soap, combs, and shoelaces, and all such simple articles of trade. Little children sometimes came on these errands, all seeking to do something better than to beg. Poor orphans! the legacy of heroic fathers to a nation which can never repay the debt it owes them! Many of these I have taken in, and treated to the remaining cakes and coffee of the breakfast, or the fragmentary residuum of a dinner; and I never thus took one in without feeling amply repaid by his grateful looks and words.

There is one Scripture passage which cannot surely be intended to command a literal obedience. Else how can people with our limited means ever hope to be faithful, or win the promise?

"Never turn thy face from any poor man, and then the face of the Lord shall not be turned away from thee."

How often I had heard it read in church, and meditated upon the subject; for with only six hundred a year we could not well feed every one who asked an alms. The residuum of our table or wardrobes we could spare, but there was certainly a limit to our giving much besides. Now that we had a little more to dispense, I had set apart a certain sum, which was sacred to the cause of benevolence and humanity. I could enjoy giving now, and surely it was but right that I should lend the Lord a portion of the plenty he had bestowed on me, by thus giving to his poor.

One bitterly cold morning, soon after we returned home, when the frost lay thick and crisp on every chamber window, while getting up from the breakfast-table, a faint movement of the bell overhead gave notice that some one was at the street door. I knew by the feebleness of the ring that it must be the effort of a child. Sure enough, on opening the door, I discovered a girl of apparently ten years, who stood shivering in the snow upon the marble step, her little arms and shoulders covered with a thin and faded shawl. A common cotton sunbonnet protected her head; but it was clean if not very warm, and from underneath it

> "Her sunny locks
> Hung down her temples like a golden fleece."

I think I never saw a child whose appearance so immediately secured my sympathy as this one, and I was about telling her to come in out of the cold, when a boy, apparently about the same age, ran up on the steps, and, touching his hat politely, said,—

"Clean off the snow, ma'am?—only a dime."

Just then my husband came to the door, and hearing the boy's question, told him to go to work, whereupon I brought the little girl in.

"I'll wait for you, sister," said the boy to her, as he saw her entering the door.

"What," I inquired, as we traversed the hall on our way to the dining-room, "is he your brother?"

"Yes, ma'am. Henry and me are twins," was the reply. "O," she continued, as I led her up to the stove, "how good it feels to be so warm!" and she put down her little basket, rubbed her benumbed hands together, and drew closer to the stove. Looking up to me as she said this, and the light falling directly on her face, I saw the two most beautiful hazel eyes that ever were set in human countenance, soft, gentle, and confiding.

"Am I to give this one her breakfast too?" asked Jane in a low voice.

I nodded assent, and, turning to the child, I inquired if she had breakfasted.

"We never get breakfast till we've made a quarter, ma'am," she replied.

"But how long are you in making a quarter?" I rejoined.

"Sometimes not for several hours, sometimes not till noon, ma'am, but we've got a shilling already, this morning, and brother will get a dime from you, and that is nearly a quarter," and a smile of satisfaction came over her young face as she counted up their collected earnings on that inclement morning.

Then, as if alive to the fact of being still deficient, she lifted her basket from the floor, uncovered it, and, holding it up to me, inquired,—

"Wouldn't you like to buy some cuffs and collars, ma'am?"

I took the basket from her hand in order to examine its contents, just as Jane looked in from the kitchen and said that breakfast was ready for the child; so, setting it down again, I directed the little one to go out first, and invite her brother to come in also. She looked at me in momentary surprise, and then bounded off to the door, where I could hear her call out in gleeful tones,—

"Come, brother, the good lady is going to give us our breakfast. Come, brother."

The boy came in, cold indeed, for it was the bitterest morning of the winter, but well-bred and respectful. He was a bluff, robust, and honest-looking lad. We set before them a plentiful meal, but as I sat by, apparently attending only to Percy, and his morning ablutions, I could not help noticing the strong affection which these two children manifested towards each other. The butter on the table had dwindled to a mere trifle, and Jane had forgotten to replenish it, so that a modicum only was left on the plate, when, not at the moment understanding what was referred to, I heard the boy whisper,—

"Take it, Nancy," and, looking up, saw him handing her the plate.

"Dear Harry, I won't have it; you take it yourself," was the reply.

"And you say that you are twins?" I remarked to Henry, when they had concluded a meal which both had eaten with evident relish. "And how old are you?"

"Nine and a half, ma'am."

"What is your father's name?" I inquired.

"Father's dead, ma'am; he went to the war, and got killed at Gettysburg, and mother's never been right since," replied the boy.

Alas! I thought, how often I have heard that terrible story. It sometimes seemed as if I only had escaped the common grief.

"How does your mother live?" I inquired, addressing Nancy.

"O, we help to keep her," she answered with great sprightliness. "Brother John works in a factory; and grandfather stays home, and cooks, and watches mother; and I sell collars that I buy at the factory where John works; and Henry, he does any jobs that folks give him to do."

"But do you not go to school, Nancy?" I rejoined.

"O yes, ma'am, two days in the week, and twice on Sunday; and we can both read and write."

She told me her mother's name and residence, and then, dismissing Harry to finish his job at the front door, I bargained with Nancy for enough collars to last me a year, and prevailed on Jane to become a purchaser also. Paying Nancy her money, and advancing Harry from a dime to a shilling, I let them go. They left the door, thanking me gratefully, and walked away hand-in-hand, he to shovel off the snow for some one else, and she to find other customers for cuffs and collars.

Next day, I took time to call upon the mother. All that the children had said was true. The father had indeed fallen in battle, and to the delicate wife the shock had brought a lingering death. She was sinking under a weight of grief from which, thus far, she had found no alleviation.

But this is only one of a thousand unwritten domestic histories of the day. The tremendous consequences of the great war were manifestly operating almost as powerfully on the generation of mere children as upon their parents. The necessities of the latter were sending them into the streets to supply by premature effort the wants created by the havoc of the conflict. If its vast expenditures made thousands rich, there were still more impoverished.

One of our neighbors, on returning from a trip to the West, encountered, in the cars, a boy twelve years old, who had with him an infant sister that had not been weaned. The father, who had been living in Minnesota when the war broke out, joined the army, and was killed in battle. The very day after the news of his death came, the mother died, leaving the two children with none to take care of them. The boy, as if nerved by the crisis, set off immediately with his little sister, intending to take her to an aunt, who resided in Pennsylvania.

Our neighbor travelled with them several days. It was a great charge for so young a nurse, and he a boy. But when the passengers became apprised of the circumstances of the case, the manifestations of sympathy were so general that there was no scarcity of nurses. The lady passengers relieved him of his charge, and occasionally one who had a baby of her own, permitted this little waif to drink at the same natural fountain, while the men contributed in money. But here was a small boy laying aside childish things, and developing traits of manliness that would do honor to maturer years. It will be remembered by many how numerous were the anecdotes of boyish heroism in actual battle which the army correspondence brought to us in the newspapers. Thus the juvenile spirit rose, like that of the adult portion of the community, with the magnitude of the national crisis.

It appeared to me that there were strange contrasts and incongruities about those times. Some of them, it is true, have since disappeared under the regulating influence of peace, but the reader cannot have forgotten them all. At the same time that those poor little twins, with perhaps hundreds of other children, were tramping over the cold streets, endeavoring to gain a scanty livelihood, the brilliant displays in those very streets presented striking contrasts to the condition of such as sought them out on similar errands. The shop windows were surpassingly gay and tempting to the crowds which thronged the pavements. All appeared to have money wherewith to indulge their various tastes. Trinkets and precious stones, in unprecedented profusion, glistened in the plate-glass windows of the fashionable jewellers. In the countercase of a single establishment a dozen fortunes were displayed. Costly silks and shawls hung gracefully in other equally elaborate windows, unfolding tints and patterns which would draw thousands from the delighted multitude who stopped to admire them. All that art and taste and ingenuity could combine, to please the fancy and exhaust the purse, was concentrated on the shelves and counters. Surely the people had forgotten that there had just been a bloody war in the land, and that the nation was now struggling with a heavy debt, which would require many years of taxation to discharge.

These contrasts are visible everywhere. While humble homes, like that of the orphan twins, are scantily supplied with even the commonest food, the market-houses are overloaded with every possible luxury of the land. I see this for myself, as I mostly do the marketing, and often think it would be impossible to collect in one place a greater profusion of good things for human consumption. Nothing that the appetite can crave seems wanting to the well-filled and open purse.

But the nation has come out safely from its long and perilous travail, and it is perhaps natural that public joy should succeed to public sorrow. It is equally natural that these contrasts and discrepancies should happen. Human life, I find with its diversities of trials and compensations, is a mystery which my poor philosophy must vainly seek to unravel. How manifold are our allotments! how checkered our destinies! We live in vanity and grossness, as well as in greatness. The Divine Intelligence alone can lift the curtain which hides from us the profound mysteries of our existence. . . .

LUCY P. VINCENT SMITH

(1842–1933)

"Journal Written on Bark Nautilus 1869–1874." Unpublished manuscript, The Nicholson Collection, Providence (Rhode Island) Public Library.

Even though steam and speed were the coming thing in the latter part of the nineteenth century, sailing ships still characterized the tempo of life for many. Among the scores of logs and journals written on voyages under sail, Lucy P. Vincent Smith's record of a whaling expedition made with her husband is notable.

Born in Edgartown, Massachusetts, on a farm between the village and the sea, Lucy Vincent came from a family of fishermen and farmers. She must have excelled in the country school she attended, for at age fourteen she became a teacher. She was seventeen when she married George A. Smith, a thirty-one-year-old whaler, who, in due course, rose to the rank of captain. Ten years later, when he set out in command of the whaling bark *Nautilus,* Lucy and their three-and-one-half-year-old son, Freddie, sailed with him.

Wives seldom went on whaling voyages, though captains were privileged to take them along. Few women could face the rigors, the tedium, and the isolation of being the only woman on board. In spite of such hardships, Lucy Smith preferred going to sea to staying at home, which would have meant separation from her husband for the duration of the trip—three to five years.

When she wrote her journal, Lucy Smith did not describe the layout of the captain's quarters; she took for granted that people knew what a whaling ship was like. She could not foresee that a hundred years later a whole way of life would have disappeared, not only the whalers and the ships, but also the whales.

Like other whalers, the *Nautilus* had three masts, was probably between 250 and 400 tons, and was a little over 100 feet
long and 25 feet wide. This may sound sizable, but actually a
whaleship was crowded and cramped. She carried virtually all
the supplies for a lengthy voyage for a ship's company of about
twenty-six, as well as the small boats and gear used in hunting,
capturing, and slaughtering whales. The tryworks in which the
whale's flesh was rendered into oil took up considerable space
on deck, and the barrels the oil was stored in required much of
the space below.

The captain's cabin, which Lucy and Freddie shared with
George, could hardly have been commodious, and may have
been little more than a cell with slitlike ports through the ship's
heavy timbers. Very likely there was a skylight with bars to
protect the glass. Most ceilings were so low that a tall person
could not stand erect except between the overhead framing.
Standard for a captain's cabin was a horsehair sofa long
enough to sleep on, fitted across-ships at the stern of the vessel,
with cupboards built into the space above. The captain's writing table and chair usually stood against the forward partition
convenient to an overhead compass. Sometimes a wife found
room for a rocking chair brought from home, potted plants,
even a parlor organ. Music must have been a welcome diversion.

Adjoining the captain's cabin on the starboard side was the
captain's stateroom, with a double bed set in gimbals. Though
the bed remained level when the ship rolled, the gimbals could
not counteract pitching or wallowing in a quartering sea. There
was little space to move in, only two or three feet between the
bed and the cabin partition. On some ships the washroom occupied a separate compartment; on others, the washstand stood at
the foot of the bed. The privy was scarcely more than a narrow
box.

The dining room, small and bare, lay immediately forward
of the captain's cabin. Day after day, Lucy and Freddie ate
with George, the mates, and two or three boatsteerers around a
built-in table with a railing to keep the dishes from sliding off
in rough weather. The food was served from an adjacent pan-
try after having been prepared in the galley on deck.

The captain's cabin, stateroom, and dining room were the limits for a wife belowdecks. She was permitted to use the galley to do her own cooking, or bake a pie, only when the ship's cook was off duty. On deck, she could venture forward to about the middle of the ship, where a place might be improvised for her to sew or read. Probably it was there or at the captain's table that Lucy did her writing.

Under such conditions and in such quarters, Lucy made a home for her husband and child. Her journal must have been her outlet and solace during the long months at sea, and also during those times she was left ashore, in Honolulu and San Francisco. When the *Nautilus* hunted for whales in the Arctic, Lucy was not allowed to go.

Little is known of her later life; but it is certain she made at least one more trip with George, who died in 1891. Freddie grew up to become a newspaperman, selectman, and county commissioner, and Lucy lived with him during her last years. She died on December 22, 1933, almost ninety-two. I am indebted to *Whaling Wives*, by Emma Mayhew Whiting and Henry Beetle Hough, 1953, for these details.

Lucy P. Vincent Smith's "Journal" comprises two large bound volumes, eight by thirteen inches. Volume One, on white pages, a brand-new book when she began writing in it, is quite legible. Volume Two, on blue pages, is a different story. It had been previously used to catalog a coin collection. Lucy Smith wrote in whatever space she could find, and overwrote some pages. The second volume seems to have been harder going, and certainly makes harder reading. Though unpublished in its entirety, portions of Lucy Smith's "Journal" appeared in the Edgartown, Massachusetts, newspaper, the *Vineyard Gazette*, May 1, 1964.

JOURNAL WRITTEN ON
BARK NAUTILUS 1869–1874

————•————

On board bark Nautilus Oct. 20, 1869. Two weeks this morn since we left New Bedford and for the first time I now write in my journal. Old Neptune has proved an exacting master and demanded daily tribute for more than a week. He is now beginning to free me from his power and I hope soon to say that I am entirely free. Freddie has got along nicely, has been sick two or three times for a short time but soon recovered, and is very happy. Although I have been seasick I have not yet been homesick, nor have I even for a moment thought I would wish my husband to be here without me. We have had rough weather the most of the time since we left. Light winds and not favorable, with a heavy swell. We are now in Lat 31–46 N Lon 46–52. Everything has gone along peaceably so far and I hope will continue to do so. Have not taken any oil yet but hope to soon. Have written one letter to Lydia Ann and shall write to Father this afternoon.

Thursday, Oct 21st. With George's assistance I have done quite a large washing. It is a pleasant day but calm so we are not getting along much. Yesterday about four P.M. the boats were lowered to try the crew at rowing. Some are green hands in every sense of the word while others did nicely. George did not go but the 4th mate, Mr. Lisbond, went with his boat. It was quite amusing to me to watch them darting the iron and from the noise they made we ought to have as much as a hundred barrels of oil, but killing whales in imagination and reality are quite different affairs, so we are still clean. I have finished a shaded lamp mat and commenced a ring tidy. . . .

Friday, Oct. 22nd. Another beautiful day; with very little wind and that is directly ahead so we are getting along the backward way. This morn I ironed the clothes I washed yesterday and this afternoon have used my sewing machine for the first time since I left home, have been making a signal for the ship. It is now five o'clock and while I write the men are washing down decks. Mr. Boyer stands at the wheel. . . .

Sunday, Oct. 24th . . . I would dearly love to hear the sound of the church-going bell. . . . Yet God is upon the water the same as on the land. . . . We had for dinner Green Corn, mutton pie, Apple pudding, boiled beef and pork. . . .

Sunday, Oct, 31st . . . This morn one of my canarys flew away, the cage door being accidentally left open. I could not at first help shedding a few tears but soon came to the conclusion that it was useless to cry for spilt milk. . . .

Nov. 25, Thanksgiving. No observation. . . . Far from the old homestead. . . .

Tuesday, Dec. 14. It is just one week since I last opened my journal and in that time I have seen the ocean when it has looked as if it were all ready to receive us and cover us forever from the sight of man. We have had a very squally rough time and been obliged to run before the wind many miles out of our track. Today is the first pleasant day we have had in a week and we are now trying to work our way back on to the whaling ground. During the week I have knit Freddie a pair of mittens, made him a cap, crocheted a scarf for a Christmas present, finished my tidy, knit some on my stockings, and today commenced a pair for Freddie. I have the rheumatism in my right arm quite badly, it is hard work to write. During one of the squalls hundreds of birds from the land were blown off and came around the ship, two came on board.

Dec. 17. I gladly record the events of this day. At about eight ½ o'clock this morn I was standing on deck beside George when he exclaimed "There Blows," and looking where he directed me I very soon saw it. There were men at the masthead that did not discover it until the Capt. called to them. At ten minutes of nine lowered the mate and second mate's boats and at fifteen minutes past nine the mate had got fast but thinking that three boats could do better than two, George started with his boat and he, was soon fast to him, also the second mate's boat. They were but a short distance from the ship so I could watch them all the time. The whale died under water and if the three boats had not been fast they would have lost him but the three were fortunate enough to raise him and before one o'clock had him alongside. I watched the boats with an anxious eye, I was so afraid of an accident. I was on deck all day, for Freddie was so excited I could not keep him below nor trust him on deck unless I was with him, as everyone had enough to do without taking care of him. I have got my face badly sunburned. Mr. Fisher came on board and went to bed as soon as the whale was alongside. Capt., officers and men worked until eight o'clock but could not finish cutting. Had a rough time to cut. . . .

Wednesday, Dec. 22nd. We have had a beautiful day and I have improved it in washing a large wash. About six o'clock tonight a man at masthead raised whales but they proved to be humpbacks. I have made a ball today for Freddie but Santa Claus will get credit for it. My teeth are troublesome yet.

Sat 25th. Christmas is nearly gone and it has not been a very merry one to me, for I have felt unusually sad this afternoon. As I look forward there seems to be so little on earth to live for. I can hardly say that I desire long life except when I look on my little child. I then feel that I do have a strong desire to live to take care of him and may God give me grace and patience to train him in the way he should go. I would love dearly to hear from home, but I will try to be patient. We have had pleasant weather during the day, with a head wind. Have seen nothing.

Dec. 30. George did not go to bed but laid down on the sofa an hour or two and then all got up and went to cutting in,* finished about six this morn and today have been getting it ready to try out.† I have cut my flannel sack and basted it. . . .

Jan. 1st 1870. We have had a pleasant day with a head wind. I was sick all day yesterday but feel better today. Yesterday it was very rough all day so did not commence boiling the humpback until this morn. I have finished my stockings commenced so long ago. I would love dearly to know how the folks at home are prospering.

Sun Jan 9. Since last Tuesday we have had a severe storm.

---

* The process of cutting the blubber from the carcass of a whale. The *Nautilus* got one the day before.

† To melt, to render the oil from the blubber.

For two nights I scarcely slept at all. Some part of the time I was fearful we should be wrecked but our kind Heavenly Father has watched over us and spared us to behold another beautiful Sabbath. It is very pleasant. Thursday night it was so very rough about one o'clock my trunk and George's chest both tipped over although we thought them properly secured. My trunk caught under our bed but George got it up without much difficulty. In the chest were several bottles, one of brandy, of liniment and a jar of pickles but fortunately nothing was broken. Freddie slept quietly through the night. We are all well except Mr. Fisher who is quite sick again. I expect he will leave for home the first opportunity. George is feeling discouraged because we have taken no more oil, but I am hoping we will soon have more. During the week have been working at odd jobs and have knit a pair of mittens for George.

Jan. 15, 1870. Four years this morn since Freddie first saw the light, four long weary years. How many changes since then. Little did I then think that four years from that day would find us on the wide ocean but so it is. We know not what a day may bring forth. We have a beautiful day. The coast of Patagonia in sight about eight miles distant. Mr. Holmes with his boats crew have gone on shore fishing and gunning. George has just killed a bird from the deck. Some of the foremast hands have cleaned it and cook is now roasting it for them. I opened a can of plain cake this afternoon. It had moulded on the outside but the center is good. The weather today is very warm for this latitude, the warmest day for a long time. Mr. Fisher is some better today. I have been fitting pieces on Freddie's plaid pants, to make them large enough for him. He has learned fourteen letters. I am now going to write to Lydia Ann.

January 16th. The Sabbath dawned bright and beautiful and has continued so during the day. It has not seemed much like Sunday. About noon there was a large school of Porpoise came round the ship and played around for several hours. We caught eight. Last night after tea there were the most birds around the ship that I ever saw, there were thousands of them, the water was covered as far as the eye could reach. . . .

Mon. 17th . . . I have taken the sun twice today, made the Lat. the same as George and Longitude within two miles and

George says that is as near alike as two persons usually get the altitudes. . . .

Tues Jan. 18th . . . I have taken the sun twice today and made the Lat & Lon exactly the same as George did, to a second, without any help from him, or knowing what his altitudes were until mine was worked out. . . .

Sat. 29th . . . I wish I could say we were getting along pleasantly but some, or at least one of our officers is the most disagreeable man I ever met with and he makes it very unpleasant for me here. Were he as agreeable as he ought to be I should enjoy myself nicely but he seems inclined to make it as unpleasant as he can for me. . . .

Feb. 4. Have been ironing and mending this afternoon, have covered the cushion to the seat of sitting room. Nothing in sight, this is a lonely place. I wish we were where we could see something occasionally.

Feb. 10. Have the same old story to record, of head wind and nothing in sight. We are near good whaling ground, but with this head wind cannot get there.

Feb. 16. My health is some better than it was when I last wrote in this but it is not now as good as I could wish, but I try to keep up good courage. . . . Nothing in sight.

March 4. It is the 42 anniversary of George's birth and I wish it could have been celebrated by taking a sperm whale, but there is none to be found today. Have seen four sails. Have been on different tacks.

March 11. Have had another rough day with occasional showers, George still continues to have diarrhea. I have felt sick all day so I have set up but little. Nothing in sight. . . .

Saturday 12. George is no better, last night had showers with lightning. This morn it is better weather but . . . there is a heavy swell, oh how I wish we could see something, it is so discouraging day after day passing and are getting nothing. We shall soon have to go into Port. I do hope we may get a little more oil before we go.

Sunday 13. Another Sabbath is numbered with those gone before, one the less to spend on Earth, one day nearer our Eternal home. . . .

Tues 15. This morn while I was dressing Capt. came down and informed me there was a whaler quite near. It proved to be the A. R. Tucker, Barstow, and about eight o'clock we hailed and soon after the Capt. came on board with a boat's crew and Mr. Holmes with his crew went on board the Tucker. The Capt. is very pleasant. He belongs in Wareham, he has passed the day and went back about six o'clock. He was at St. Catharines* a few weeks before we were there and has taken a hundred barrels of sperm since then. He is now sixteen months out with 320 of sperm. This is my first experience at gamming and I find it pleasant although with a stranger. Their long. and ours differs about ten miles. We are now with short sail on the wind heading the most of the day SE, now at seven o'clock S.

Wedns 16th. Another day is drawing to a close and no more oil. The A. R. Tucker was in sight this morn but we have left her astern, out of sight. About noon a large merchant ship passed quite near. Then after dinner we saw a large shark. I have been washing today. George has just taken the clothes down from the line for me. When Mr. Holmes returned to the ship last night he brought quite a large bundle of books and papers but I shall not probably be any the wiser for what they contain as he has not offered me any and probably will not, and I shall not ask him. . . .

Thurs 17th. Another day is closing and the record must again be nothing in sight. This morn passed signals and Long. with an English merchant ship. He was about as far to the East as Capt. Barstow was to the West of us. As ours is midway between the two I hope it is correct. I have been ironing and mending. Beside my usual ironing have starched and ironed a bosom shirt, twelve collars, five pair of cuffs, and now feel quite tired. . . .

Monday 28th. Last night was an almost sleepless one to me. We did not retire until after nine and it was a long time before I could get to sleep. At one o'clock Sylvia called the Capt. saying that Mr. Lisbond wanted to see him. I heard loud talk and knew there was trouble. Capt. went immediately up and found one of the men, George Gilbert by name, had refused to take the wheel when it was his turn. Capt. ordered him to go. He said he would not but would jump overboard first. Capt. then told him he should have to tie him up to the rigging. He still refused duty so he tied his hands to the rigging. He remained

* Maritime state in southern Brazil.

very quietly until the morn watch was called, about an hour and a half, then wanted to be released but was not allowed so in about half an hour we were startled with the cry lower away the boat, man overboard. All rushed on deck. Mr. Holmes went down and in a few minutes picked him up, he had slipped his hands out and jumped overboard. Capt. then told him he should put him in irons and they were got out, and when they were putting them on he cried, said he was sorry he had refused duty, and would never do it again but would obey every officer in future. So he was forgiven and sent forward. I was frightened when he was in the water for I feared he would drown. The excitement has made me almost sick. I am glad that he was released as it was his first offense and I hope will be his last. We have always considered him one of our best men. I expect he will try to run away when we get to St. Catharine's as his ship's bill is quite heavy, he will like to get clear. . . .

Thurs 31st . . . saw Wave lower for whales. Capt. Briggs was fast but lost both his lines; he came on board Nautilus . . . so we mated with Capt. Briggs and together lowered five boats, and if it had not been so near night they would probably have got one or more, but darkness overtook us, and the boats have come on board. Capt. Briggs is here too. They are just eating. The whales are very large. Saw five in all.

April 8. This morn saw a bark about ten o'clock that we soon afterwards found to be the Awashonks, Capt. Ariel Norton, spoke them. About twelve o'clock Capt. N. came on board and took dinner and supper with us. I enjoyed his visit very much. He was homeward bound and promised to call and see our dear ones when he arrives. . . .

April 17 . . . Have had a very pleasant day, but it has not seemed much like the Sabbath.* The people are Catholics and today is what they call Easter. Last night the bells were ringing, firecrackers and rockets . . . and music all night long. . . .

April 18. This morn Capt. was roused from his slumbers by a rap at the door, it proved to be a boatsteerer from our Ship, he said that four men from the ship had deserted and they had three others in irons. . . . They were put in irons for selling all their clothes and reported as going to run away.

* The *Nautilus* had arrived at Santa Catarina, Brazil, five days earlier.

April 21 . . . five more men deserted . . . rumors of yellow fever.

April 22 . . . shipped three men to replace deserters.

April 26. Good news! Good news! We passed the day at the consul's. Just before we left a gentleman from Montevideo called there and brought me five letters, two from Lydia, two from Pameloa, and one from Katie Mellen, oh how glad I was to get them and know that up to the 17th of January our friends were all living and well. . . .

Thurs 28 . . . I saw for the first time a cotton tree. I never before had much idea how it grew, also saw coffee, Mummy apples, sweet lemons, oranges, etc. We now have 6,000 oranges, 57 bunches of bananas on board. Capt. Braley and son dined with us. The customs house officer came on board the first of the afternoon and brought me a beautiful bouquet. He stopped to tea. Frank Briggs was also here to tea. We had quite a concert which was highly complimented by the listeners. Capt. Braley stopped the evening.

Fri 29 . . . one man deserted. . . . We hope to get out to sea tomorrow and I shall be glad to go for there is so much care and confusion, and men running away all the time and we can get none to replace them. . . .

Monday 2nd . . . could not wash today on account of my washroom being nearly filled with onions.

Sat 7th rough weather . . . illness on board: Capt. Smith has cold, Mr. Lisbond fever, Mr. Holmes hurt his hand and caught cold in it. . . . I have been putting up some bananas as they were ripe and would not keep . . . rough weather. . . .

Tues, 10th . . . Capt. has been selling off the chests, clothes etc. of deserters . . . has sold all but four chests.

Wed, 18 . . . about twelve o'clock the weather was so bad I feared we might not behold again the light of the sun but our kind Heavenly Father watched over us and we still live, spared monuments of his mercy . . . did not sleep until four when the wind abated. . . .

Tues 24th . . . have finished washing but my ironing will take some time as I have ten bosom shirts, two starched dresses, besides several doz collars and cuffs. . . .

May 25 . . . began ironing at eight A.M. and ironed until

three this afternoon. My hands are almost blistered holding on
to the iron. I feel very tired. We crossed the meridian of Green-
wich last night, are now in East Longitude. . . .

June 4, 1870 . . . near land but foggy, near enough to see
breakers. . . .

Monday June 6 . . . saw first humpback since reaching
coast, but he was going like lightning to windward.

June 7. This morn the fog cleared up, saw a school of blackfish near the ship and lowered for them but did not take any.
Two of the boats got away from the ship so we had a fog horn
blowed many times before they found the ship, the fog was so
dense. It cleared away about ten and at eleven lowered again
for a very large school of blackfish. The larboard boat, Mr.
Holmes, got three, Mr. Thaxter with the waist boat, took two,
and Mr. Lisbond with the bow boat took one, so we have six.
Capt. thinks they will make three or four bbls. While looking
over the stem of the ship watching the fish and the boats that
were there, near the ship, towing fish, I saw the mate's agreeable
countenance turned towards me and heard the beautiful expression, Damn you look if you want to. It makes my life far more
unpleasant than it would otherwise be to hear such language
used. . . . There is not much to be seen and when the boats are
chasing fish I like to watch them and think there is no harm in
doing so but I never can do so without Mr. Holmes cursing me.
If I do not hear him do so I hear of it afterwards. Without exception I think him nearest to a savage of anyone I ever met. He
possesses a very quick ungovernable temper, is also very jealous,
and is very ignorant of the rules of good breeding, and yet has
a very high opinion of himself. At times he is very social and at
other times will not answer when spoken to. If we only had
decently civil officers I should enjoy life. As it is there is but
little enjoyment. All that induces me to endure it is my husband's society. I live hoping for better days when we shall go
where we can get some officers. Capt. is sadly tried with them
but tries very hard to be patient.

Wed 8. About noon the larboard and bow boats went fishing
along the coast. Mr. Thaxter did not go for some time, in fact
ever since we left St. Catharine's he has acted as if he was mad
about something, so today George has had some talk with him.
I hope it will result in good, oh dear, how hard it is to know

what to do right but God can see our hearts and knows whether we want to do right or not. . . .

Fri 10 . . . off Little Fish Bay. Capt. is going ashore to try to get some men as we are six short of full crew.

Sat June 11 . . . Capt. could not get men without anchoring his ship and that he would not do . . . brought off a quarter of beef and sweet potatoes. Brought two birds, one jet black with very white bill . . . the lady wished me to call him Silver Bill. The other is a very beautiful brown with a dove colored head and bright red bill. He changes the color of his plumage every six months. . . .

Sunday 12 . . . I neglected to write last night of Mr. Holmes kindness while my husband was ashore. He was very social and gentlemanly. He is a good man to take care of a ship, took excellent care of it yesterday and made himself very agreeable. . . .

June 15, 1870 . . . Freddie has not been well today and about five o'clock seemed worse so I was very much afraid he was going into a fit. I put him in warm water and gave him a dose of Ayers Pills and he seemed better. Went to sleep and breathed easily. Capt. is almost sick with a severe cold and sore throat but is not yet off duty.

June 16. Freddie was very restless last night. I have given him a dose of oil. Exchanged signals with a Portuguese gunboat. . . . Freddie's oil has operated and he seems better. I think his sickness was occasioned by his being in the sun so much when the boats were chasing fish he wanted to watch them. I have cut and made a suit of denim today. Have not used my machine before for a long time. It still works well. I made the whole suit with the exception of button holes. . . .

June 17 . . . had to break out barrels from bottom tier from which humpback oil had been taken at St. Catharine's . . . filled with salt water . . . had bilged. . . .

June 20 anchored off harbor of St. Paul de Loando; large fleet of vessels in harbor. . . Capt. bought three large fish from a canoe . . . chowdered for all hands. They were very nice. . . . The natives were very black and naked except for a strip of cloth tied around the waist that came about to their knees. . . .

June 21. Capt., Mr. Thaxter, and picked crew went ashore,

met shore boat coming out, and returned; Capt. told no one could land unless ship anchored in inner harbor, and that could get no men unless entered and cleared. As there was no certainty of getting men, Capt. concluded to heave up anchor and leave. . . .

June 21, 1870. For the few days past I have been thinking of the years that have passed and in imagination have lived over again some of these pleasant days that are gone never to return. It is eleven years last Sunday since I was introduced to him whom I now call by the endearing name of husband and eleven years ago this afternoon he called on me at my father's and carried me to ride. We went to the Camp Ground and on our homeward passage he asked the privilege of paying me his addresses. I did not then think I should ever call him my own, but so it has proved. How little I thought that the eleventh anniversary would find me on the ocean with him. As I glance at the years that have passed since then I can see many sad hours and I have passed through scenes of trial and affliction. A darling child and mother have been lain to rest in the grave and although I have shed many bitter tears when thinking of my loss, yet I would not recall them if I could for they are in heaven where pain can never reach them more, and I feel they are angels beckoning us who are left to those brighter, fairer shores. . . .

Thursday, June 23, 1870. This morn I cut two suits of clothes for Freddie and have made one pair of the pants with the exception of buttonholes. They are of brown linen that we purchased in St. Cath. Immediately after dinner the larboard boat was lowered, to go fishing, and just as he was leaving the ship the Capt. raised two humpbacks and lowered the Waist and Bow boats and all three started in pursuit. Mr. Holmes was soon fast and at dark was still being towed away from the ship and the other boats were rowing trying to get up to him. It is now seven o'clock and dark and neither of the Boats have come on board. Signal lanterns are hung out, and we are trying hard to go towards where we saw them last but the wind has died away so we move slowly. I hope they will soon get back. We were at noon about ten miles from land in latitude 6 40 but have since been working off shore and Capt. was watching the boats so closely that he forgot to get the sun until it was too late. I hope the boats may be fortunate enough to secure the whale but fear they will not as only one boat had got fast when we last saw them and Mr. Holmes will probably have to cut his line or be towed far out to sea alone. The whale he fastened to was a large one.

Friday, 24th. The boats got to the ship about eight o'clock without the whale. Mr. Holmes had to cut from him, after firing seven bomb lances and three hand lances, rather a poor beginning but we hope the season will end well. Immediately after dinner saw two humpbacks and lowered two boats but did not succeed in taking anything as they would spout but once at a rising the boats had no chance to get to them. We saw but two whales from the ship but the boats saw four. I hope we may get one tomorrow. About ten this morn we were off the mouth of the Congo River. The water that flows from the river is a different color and does not seem to mingle with the water of the ocean. You could see a long distance the difference in color in a strait line and it seemed to be but a few feet deep and the ship's rudder would stir up the green water underneath. The current is very strong. We have been heading on the land and have drifted off from it. We shall try to get nearer the shore in the morning and drop anchor. . . .

Sunday, July 3rd. This morn the officers and crew took breakfast at half past three and immediately after all four boats started from the ship to go to the south, so at daylight to be several miles south and hope to meet whales. Capt. has gone with one man short but those he has are good ones. He takes one of the crew for boatsteerer and has the cook for one of the crew so there is only the steward, cooper, and a sick boatsteerer left aboard. I do not approve of whaling Sundays, but that makes no difference, they go just the same. I hope they may be successful. This afternoon the church at home gathers around. . . . Nine months today since I last met with them yet my Heavenly Father has been ever near me and preserved us until the present time. May he still be with us and the dear ones at home, watch over and keep us all, and permit us to meet again on Earth, but if we meet not on Earth may we be an unbroken band in Heaven. The boats returned without anything.

Had seen two whales but there was no wind so they could not strike them. I have written two letters, one to father, the other to Pameloa.

Tuesday, 5th . . . It is one year today since my beloved husband returned from a four years' voyage. Oh! how glad I am that I can be with him this voyage instead of being left at home, and hope he will never go another voyage without me. One year ago today my darling boy was hurt while I was visiting dear sister Annie, of the agony I felt as I looked on him and thought he could not live, but God in His mercy spared his life and I earnestly pray he may be spared to grow to manhood and be the means of doing much good in the world. The boats have returned, got here about seven. Have seen ten whales but could not get near enough to strike as there was no wind and the whales would hear the paddles and go down. Coming on board tonight Mr. Thaxter ran into the Capt.'s boat and had not the Capt. held water, there would have been damage done. Mr. T did it because he was ugly. . . .

July 13. Our vessel is the dirtiest place I ever saw as there has been no chance to clean up as there is the blubber of one whale on deck besides casks of oil and the oil has run out of the blubber so it is frequently scooped up off the deck. They have now nearly finished trying the stinking blubber and got the blubber room nearly cleared. The blubber on deck will not smell so.

July 14 . . . I have done no work for two days past except a little mending, the ship is so dirty that I do not like to get out any work. Freddie is in the midst of everything, as dirty as a little pig, then rubbing around me, together with what I get from the ship, my clothes are too dirty to take any work on.

Aug. 24 1870. Mr. Holmes has been very pleasant today. I think the liquor he drank last night on board the Triton might have had something to do with it. He really insisted on changing parrots with us this afternoon. I was unwilling to do so as his bird was the best and he paid a great price for it. He had given Freddie a very nice one some time ago, but he said he wanted me to have the best as he should probably give away or sell it if he kept it, so he brought it aft and put it in my cage and took mine. . . .

Sunday, Aug. 28, 1870. All the boats down all day, chasing whales. They were very shy so a boat could not get near them except a cow and calf that Mr. Holmes went alongside and his boatsteerer missed again. It is strange for he has been one of the best boatsteerers we have and has struck the most of our whales. We have been having very hard luck but hope it will soon change. Oh for a quiet Sabbath. Freddie is very troublesome when the boats are all down and I have no time to read or meditate. When all the boats are down there is only the steward, cooper, and a sick man left.

Jan. 1, 1872 . . . We are now past Straits of Magellan and nearing Straits of Le Maire. Geo. thinks he will go through them on Wednesday if pleasant unless we see whales tomorrow. Our New Years dinner consisted of a "Whole Pig" stuffed and roasted, Potatoes, Bread and Butter, Pumpkin Pie.

Jan. 11 . . . saw a large ship carrying double topsails and topgallant sails, jib and flying jib. We had double-reefed topsails and were pitching about dreadfully. George says he never saw so much sail on a ship in such weather. They were reaching directly into land. Geo. says they must have either been drunk or crazy or both.

Sunday, Feb 4, 1872. My thirtieth birthday. I cannot realize I am so old. . . .

April 22nd . . . Oh what a long lonely day this has been, George has gone and I am so lonely but not so lonely as he must be far out at sea. As I think of him and his lonely situation my heart seems breaking. Oh how I wish I were with him today. Gladly would I brave all the hardships and dangers could I only be with him but all I can do is pray that God's blessing may rest upon him. . . . Freddie has tried hard to comfort me today, he has come to my room every few minutes and begged me not to cry for he would be my good little boy all the time papa was gone. . . .*

June 3, 1872. I must now say good-bye old journal, your pages are filled and I must find another. . . .

Thursday, Dec. 31. On this the last night of the year 1872 I am seated to write a few lines. The old year with its joys and

* George had gone to the Arctic. The owners of the *Nautilus* would not permit Lucy and Freddie to accompany him north.

sorrows will soon have passed away and we are all one year nearer our eternal resting place. As I look backward I see much to regret, many duties neglected and much that should have been neglected that has been done, and my heart rises to God in prayer for grace and patience to enable me to do far better in the future. . . .

Feb 4 . . . thirty-first birthday and the fourth since I left home. . . . Though so far out at sea have received a present from my beloved husband of a silver pencil case and gold pen.

April 2 . . . sighted Maui.* . . . Now off Molokai . . . one year today I saw Hon for the first time. . . .

Feb. 4, 1874. My thirty-second birthday. . . . I have finished my quilts tonight. It contains 1452 pieces and 1034 different pieces. My head and teeth are still very painful.

May 21 . . . sighted Long Island about three. . . . Chronometer about 60 miles out, had expected to make east end but made near the west. Geo. was up most of night and will not sleep much tonight.

This will probably be our last night on board the Nautilus and although many times life on board has not been particularly pleasant, I have spent many happy hours on board the little bark, hours that I shall love to think of in future life, and it is with feelings of pleasure not unmingled with pain that I shall bid her adieu. She has borne us safely thousands of miles and for more than four and a half years has been our home. That our Heavenly Father watch over us in the future as He has in the past, and also bless those who next occupy the rooms that we have so long occupied, is my prayer. Farewell to journal writing on board the Nautilus. This will probably be the end of my Log.

* Hawaiian Islands.

JOSHUA SLOCUM

(1844–1909)

Voyage of the "Destroyer" from New York to Brazil. By Captain Joshua Slocum. Press of Robinson Printing Company, Boston, 1894. 37 pp.

Having just returned from an utterly frustrating voyage, and without a penny to show for it, Joshua Slocum dashed off *Voyage of the "Destroyer" from New York to Brazil*. Written in fury, it echoes with sardonic laughter. He called it a footnote to history; it was also a fragment of autobiography.

A naturalized Yankee, born in Nova Scotia, Slocum was raised to seafaring. By the early 1880's, in command of one of the finest American sailing ships afloat, he had reached the zenith of a merchant captain's career. The age of sail, however, was rapidly passing; wind-driven ships were already outmoded. Many sailing masters were switching to steam, but Slocum chose to stick with a dying profession.

Then, in a space of five years, disaster following disaster, he lost his wife, his ship, his wealth, and, finally, his occupation, for there was no longer a place for a master in sail.

In 1892, unemployed and broke, he began rebuilding an ancient oyster sloop named *Spray*. He had hardly completed what was, in effect, a new boat when, unexpectedly, he got an offer of a job.

Civil war had erupted in Brazil, a country whose ports were well known to him; in earlier years he had sailed the Brazilian coast as freighter and trader. Rebel officers had seized control of naval forces at Rio de Janeiro and demanded the resignation of the president. The president replied by buying whatever warships his agents could find abroad; in the United States he acquired the 130-foot *Destroyer*. Untried and untested, it had been lying idle since the death of its builder, John Ericsson (1803–1889), four years earlier.

255

A seagoing tug was engaged to tow the *Destroyer* to Brazil, and Slocum was hired as "navigator in command." He was known to be daring, and daring would be required. The *Destroyer* had never put to sea; both her seaworthiness and her destructive abilities were entirely unknown. It was a dubious sort of job, but Slocum had reasons for taking it. He needed the money, and he wanted to get to Brazil, where he hoped to settle a long-standing feud with government officials.

After delivering the warship, Slocum returned north by steamer in March 1894 and went to Fairhaven, Massachusetts, where he had left the *Spray*. A year and a half later, in November 1895, as he was sailing the *Spray* singlehanded around the world, Slocum put in to Rio de Janeiro and called on government officials to ask again for wages due him for bringing the *Destroyer* from New York. Political fortunes, however, had changed. In 1893 the legal government had hired him; by 1895 the former rebels were in power and, as Slocum said, felt under less obligation to him than he could have wished.

His subsequent circumnavigation and his book *Sailing Alone Around the World* won him fame and money enough to buy a farm on the island of Martha's Vineyard. But instead of farming, he kept on sailing. In 1909, at age sixty-five, still alone on the *Spray*, he left Vineyard Haven, Massachusetts, and was never heard from again.

Many have read *Sailing Alone Around the World* in American or English editions or in foreign translation. Few know *Voyage of the "Destroyer."* It is said that Slocum had 500 copies printed. In years of searching I have seen only three: one in the State Library, State House, Boston; one that belonged to Slocum's oldest son; and the copy I bought in 1953. In 1958, in an omnibus edition of Slocum's books and letters, *The Voyages of Joshua Slocum,* published by Rutgers University Press, I included the complete text of *Voyage of the "Destroyer" from New York to Brazil.*

VOYAGE OF THE "DESTROYER" FROM NEW YORK TO BRAZIL

---•---

INTRODUCTION.

From the quiet cabin of my home on the *Spray*, the reminiscence of a war.

Frankly it was with a thrill of delight that I joined the service of Brazil to lend a hand to the legal government of a people in whose country I had spent happy days; and where moreover I found lasting friends who will join me now in a grin over peacock sailors playing man-o'-war.

Brazil has indeed sailors of her own, but to find them one must go down to the *barcassa* and the *jangada* where the born son of Neptune lives. In his unassuming and lowly condition, a true child of the sea.

To these friends let me tell now, who have come from the war, the story of the voyage of the famous *Destroyer*, the first ship of the strong right arm of future Brazil.

VOYAGE OF THE "DESTROYER."

To sail the *Destroyer* from New York to Brazil in the northern winter months was not promising of great ease or comfort —but what of that! I, for one, undertook the contract of the novel adventure myself, with its boding hardships and risks which soon were met face to face. Twelve brave fellows—better sailors I shall never see—casting their lot with me in the voyage were willing also to accept whatever fate might have in store for them, hoping,—always, for the best. Curiously enough the fatalistic number of the crew (thirteen) was not thought of before sailing. Every one was looking for good omen. Some of the older sailors made a search for rats, but not even the sign of a mouse could be found. Still no one backed out—times were hard ashore!

A young man to fight the ship, in case of being "attacked by pirates" on the coast of Brazil, came from a recent class of Naval Cadets of Annapolis. With sufficient confidence in his theory, this young man came early, bringing plans of the fight along with him, if there should be any, for he was bound to begin right.

Also a nobleman, who came principally as Count, engaged himself to be with us. The position of "specialist" was spoken of as his, but that was by the way. The Count was a good judge of an hotel.

There came, too, I should not forget it, a young officer of the British Royal Marine Artillery, who became in time a feature of the crew. This young man had accumulated handsome gold bands for his caps, which he frequently lost in the sea, upon the voyage,—caps and all. The sword, which by merit he had won, was of enormous size. This sword and a heavy Colt's revolver, which he wore night and day, gave my young officer, I must say—for a little man—a formidable appearance. The prodigious sword, I recall, "won by valor at the Soudan," and "presented by Her Gracious Majesty, the Queen," had the American eagle stamped upon its blade. This was the famous sword, which buckled on over a dashing red coat, secured for him the position of third gunner's mate to the Count, Mr. W——, a gentleman of influence procuring him the place upon first sight of this rig and the cut of his sails, for it must be borne in mind that we are to make a strong warlike appearance when we come to Brazil, if not before.

Of all these awe inspiring weapons, my old sailors made due note. Well, this young man came also, but taking passage along with the fighting Captain and the Count on the steamer that towed us he was always three hundred fathoms ahead, except in the ports we touched on the voyage, and again came together to recount deeds of valor and trophies won; my sailors always standing in awe of sword or gun; being, too, always touched at the sight of the unmistakable bird spreading its wings over the Queen's gift.

My own position on the ship: of "navigator in command," was hardly less important than those above mentioned. Being a man of a peaceful turn of mind, however, no fighting was expected of me, except in the battle with the elements, which should begin at Sandy Hook. So on the 7th of December, 1893, after devious adventures in the getting ready, we sailed for Brazil, in tow of the *Santuit*, of Boston, and began our fight early in the voyage.

The most noteworthy of the adventures spoken of in "the getting ready" was the destruction of a stout projecting pier, which apparently stood in the *Destroyer*'s way, on leaving the Erie basin. It was plain to be seen then that she could do the work well for which she was designed and named: A destroyer not of piers however. But, shades of Ericsson,—ship or pier! She could evidently knock them *all* down!

I was not in command at the time: *better* than that, the fighting captain was— But didn't the splinters fly! I thought of the poor "pirates" on the coast of Brazil and pitied them if, by their misguiding star, they should fall athwart the *Destroyer*, in her fighting mood.

It was six in the morning when we tripped anchor from Robins' reef, stowed all and proceeded down the bay.

The clear breath of heaven came free to every sailor on board and a voice that I knew hailed: "The ship is all your own." We were free unshackled from the land.

The *Destroyer* towed smoothly and steadily enough; and gliding along by the channel buoys she marked a fair rate of speed.

Off Sandy Hook, and clear of the shoals, the tow was stopped, that we might readjust the thimble in the towline, a sharp point having pressed against the rope threatened to cut it off. This thing, though small in itself, was the beginning of a series of mishaps that came soon enough. My sailors on the beak of the bow with tackle, crowbar and sledge-hammer fixed up the defective thimble, as far as a job of the kind could be remedied. The sailors wondering what longshoremen would do, if they hadn't old tars to finish their work at sea! I mention these things now for the guidance of sailors hereafter.

The propellor at this point was disconnected, it having been decided to use steam only for the pumps and the whistle. A code of signals was arranged between the two vessels: Rockets and lights for the night: the Universal Code of Flags for the day, and the steam whistle for day or night, making a complete arrangement in all. Nothing was left undone by the agents in New York, looking to the safety of the ship and the completion of the voyage. Having been many years out of commission she got a great overhauling—on paper.

Her lockers bespoke in that department, the highest class of a seaworthy condition.

Long after when we were all under water and could get no fire to burn, one of the stokers, cloyed of good things, damned his fate that he should ever have to breakfast on cold roast turkey and cold chicken. I shall come upon this low wretch again on the voyage.

The crazy thimble being repaired, all seemed well and the *Destroyer* was again headed on her course.

The wind was from West to Nor'west, blowing a moderate breeze. The sea was smooth. The ship making good headway, skirted the coast with the land close aboard as far South as Winter Quarter Shoal; whence taking her departure she headed boldly away for the Gulf Stream.

At 6 A.M., Dec. 8th, the light on the shoal was visible a-beam.

The latitude at noon was 37° 03′ N.

Longitude at noon was 75° 05′ W.

Distance run in 28 hours 220 miles.

The wind has veered to the N.N.E. The sea is not so smooth as it was. The ship behaves well, however, all things considered, though occasionally now she rolls down low in the water and takes short cuts clean through the waves. Steam is up, it has been kept up since we left New York.

The steam pumps are at work—the vessel is making water. A calamity has overtaken us. The ship's top seams are opening and one of the new sponsons, the starboard one, is already waterlogged.

All hands are pumping and bailing to keep the ship afloat, but the water gains steadily, and by midnight, it is washing the fires and putting them out. Steam *must* be kept up, else we go down.

The sea is rough! What can we do?

Rounds of fat pork are heaped upon the struggling fires.

Hard bread smeared with fish oil is hurled into the furnace by the barrel, and all available light stuff, as well, that will burn on the top of dead coals, such as tables and chairs, is thrown on the fire. There is no longer any draft, the rising water has cut the draft off. But the pork, and the bread and oil, and our furniture after a while—a long while it seems—makes a joyful fire that sends steam flying into the tubes and pipes to lend us its giant strength. Danger signals of rockets and blue-lights have been shown through the night.

The *Santuit* responded promptly to all of our signals, and handled the *Destroyer* with great care, on her part, in the rough sea. The storm continued through the 9th. But with energy taxed to the utmost, we gain mastery over the sea, and the water in the hold is so reduced by daylight, that coals may burn again on the grates. A number of holes and leaks have been found through which the water has been streaming all night. We caulk some of them with cotton waste, and plug others with pine wood.

We signal the tug boat to go ahead, that we are "all right." We are out of the first danger!

A stout canvas bag is made now, one that will hold a barrel of water. A derrick at the hatch is also rigged for a hoisting purchase. Hardly is this done, when sorely needed. All night long (Saturday), this bag is hoisted and emptied by eight pairs of strong arms. The rest of the people on board are driving the steam pumps, and repairing defective valves and making new ones, all as fast as they can. The cook, throughout the storm, prepares warm coffee for all hands. There are no idlers around these days of storm and toil. The steam pumps after a while are working again all right; then a long pull and a strong pull at the big canvas bucket along with the pump for a matter of four hours more, without a rest, and the ship has free bilges once more.

December 10th, 11th, 12th and 13th are days like those just gone, and ones to come of incessant care, anxiety and toil. The sea runs more regularly, though, as we proceed southward, nearing the regions of the trade winds, which is at least some respite. And although destined to disappointment when we shall actually meet them, the all expected fine weather of the "trades" stands before all on board as a beacon of hope. No energy is spared to "reach the trades."

The water in the hold is kept down from one to three feet. Occasionally a rolling suck is gained, which in our joy of it, we call free bilge. Great quantities of water go over the ship. She washes heavily, still, going often under the seas, like a great duck, fond of diving. Everything is wet. There is not a dry place in the entire ship! We are most literally sailing under the sea.

The *Destroyer* comes out of the storm today (13th), decked from the top of smokestack to bottom of the lifelines in Saragossa weeds or flowers. All along the man-ropes fore and aft, are hanging in clusters, these flowers of the sea: a rare and beautiful sight!

The good Swede, Ericsson, whom we all know, conceived the *Destroyer,* a ship to turn navies topsy turvy. This, the first one of the kind, was intended for harbor defense and to remain on the coast at home. It was a Yankee, so I believe, who guessed that she could be taken to another hemisphere: and here we are well on the way with her, already "across the Gulf," the great bugbear of the voyage. All of her seagoing qualities are tested, we know what they are. The *Destroyer* laughs at the storm, but her sailors cry "shame, shame" on some folk now snug ashore. The solvent sea leaves nothing undone in its work, and Neptune abhors a skim. Putty and paint put in the seams I don't know when, or by whom, washes out like clay, and poor clay at that.

December 13th comes in with storm and cross sea.

We suffer!

The fires are threatened by water again up to the bars. Pumping and bailing go on together again all night. The tug upon our signal slows down and heads to the sea, that we may again free the ship of water and plug up more leaks, which we search for now as keenly as one would look for precious gems.

Later in the day, the sea goes down somewhat. The tropical storm was short. Coal and water, under great difficulties, were procured from the *Santuit* to-day. Also some carbolic acid is procured, with which to wash a dangerous wound. Assistant Engineer Hamilton, an oldish man, becoming exhausted in the storm last night, fell backwards down the engine room hatch, receiving a fearful gash clean across his bald pate which had to be herring-boned together. The wound was dressed, and Hamilton, made easy, was stowed away till further comforts could be given.

One Thomas Brennan, the stoker, who complained of roast turkey in the storm, mentioned before, showing frequent signs of mutiny, refused to mind the fires, as directed by Hamilton, his watch officer, before the accident. Brennan kicked Hamilton, when no one was by to interfere, then jumping upon the old man, bit him on the face like a wild beast. My sailors are exceptionally good seamen; up to the standard of manliness in many ways. If the sea could be rid of all such brutes as this Brennan, good sailors would be happy. His case will be attended to later on.

December 14th, the ship is heading for Mona Passage, no great distance away.

The trade winds are very strong and a heavy cross sea is encountered as we near the Windward Capes of Tahita. Twenty miles N.W. of Mona Passage, the rudder is disabled. We can put it but two spokes to port, and but half of its proper angle to starboard. With this much, however, she is kept fairly in the wake of the tow-boat; both ships steering excellently well.

December 15th, early in the forenoon, the *Destroyer* has entered and is passing through Mona Passage. In the afternoon, she hauled to under the lee of the S.W. point of Puerto Rico, to receive more coal and water from our supply ship, the *Santuit*. Thence proceeding instantly to sea, she headed direct for Martinique. Now, if the trade winds were strong outside, they are fierce in the Caribbean Sea. The waves are sharp and fierce in here, where times out of mind, we have all seen it so smooth.

Wet to the bone before, our *hope* is dampened now! body and soul is soaked in the sea! But there's no help for it, we all know—for nearly all on board are sailors—and if the *Destroyer* won't go over the seas, go under them she may. All hands will pump her out and hold on, for go to Brazil she shall; nearly all have decided on that, so far as human skill can decide. To encourage this sentiment, and see that the tow-line is always well fast and secure is largely the duty of the "navigating officer" of the good ship *Destroyer*.

A pump brake more often than the sextant is in his hand, and instead of taking lunar and stellar observations in the higher art of nautical astronomy, he has to acknowledge that the more important part in this case, is of searching out leaks and repairing the defects. To work a lunar distance is one thing, but to free a leaky ship and keep her so in a gale of wind, is quite another thing—it is well at times to have a knowledge of all these fine sciences and arts.

This night, the sea is rough and dangerous. The storm is wild and bad. The port sponson, as well as the starboard one, is now waterlogged. He was a clever man who designed those sponsons and saw them constructed in such a manner that both of them didn't fill up together.

The crew have all they can do to keep the ship afloat to-night. The water puts our fires out. All we can do, we can't keep the water down; all hands bailing for life.

The main hull of the *Destroyer* is already a foot under water, and going on down. The crew have not seen the thing as I have looked upon it to-night, all they have seen is hard work and salt water. Not like driven cattle, do they work either, but as stout, loyal men. The owner of the *Destroyer*, seeing that she would not insure, will reward these men handsomely (?) for their excessive exertions in keeping her afloat at all. She could not be insured for the voyage; nor would any company insure a life on board.

Well, I left her going down, a foot under water. Believe me, the *Destroyer*, to-night, was just about ready to make her last dive under the sea, to go down deeper than ever before. The tank that we lived in on deck, was all that buoyed her up; the base of this, too, was well submerged when "Big Alec" of Salem said, "Captain, steam in the man is going down, too; we can't keep up much longer." But the storm was breaking away, and the first streaks of dawn appeared to cheer every soul aboard. With a wild yell the men flew to their work, with re-doubled energy and wrought like demons.

This saved the *Destroyer*, and probably our own lives, too, for it is doubtful if a small boat could have lived in the storm, for it was still raging high.

The *Santuit* has seen our signals of distress, and is standing by as near as it is prudent to come in the gale. Twice in the night, I was washed from the wheel, and I usually hold a pretty good grip. Dizziness, from a constant pelting sea, made me reel sometimes for a moment. To clear my senses and make sure that the voyage was a fact, and that the iron tank on which we were driving through the waves had in reality a bottom to it somewhere under the sea, was all that I could do and reason out.

The storm goes down by daylight, as suddenly as it came up in the night. And we get in under the lee of a small island for shelter and rest—Ye Gods—a rest!

It was the Island of Caja de Muerties, adjacent to Puerto Rico, which gave us this comfort. Here we cast anchor at 9 A.M. and lay till 8 P.M. of the same day (December 16th), when propitious appearances in the heavens, we sailed again on the, now, somewhat irksome voyage. But "the Windward Islands will soon be gained," we all said, and "to the south of them, the trades we *know,* will be fine." And so the expedition went on, heading now for Martinique.

At Caja de Muerties, the *Santuit*'s crew lent a liberal hand to straighten things up on board after the hard pumping and bailing. Colonel Burt, himself, on the *Santuit,* in command of the expedition, gave ample signs of his appreciation of the merits of a good crew. The ship had free bilges before she cast anchor at the island.

There is but little to say of the rest of the voyage through the Caribbean Sea. The ship is taking a circuitous route, the sooner to gain the lee of the islands. Proceeding under low speed, and changing her course from time to time, to accommodate the ship to the run of the sea, she goes hopefully on.

December 18th, the best steam pump is broken beyond the possibility of repair on board. Nothing, except new, will take the place of the broken parts. But happily enough, the sea has gone down and we suffer but little now from leakage. The kind influence of the islands is with us this time in our need, and we'll soon be in smoother water still. So the ship goes now full speed ahead, with no rough sea to hinder.

December 19th, at daylight in the morning, the islands of Guadaloupe Maria Galante—(God preserve the name), and

Dominique, are all in sight. The sea is smooth and the trades regular. The *Destroyer* is heading direct for Martinique, she raises the island soon, and at 4 P.M. of this day, came to anchor at port St. Pierre—in a leaky condition!

Here at St. Pierre, we met the *America,* as was anticipated. The stoker, Brennan, the kicker and biter, was transferred to that ship, where his mutinous conduct could be conveniently restrained in a "brig," which she rated. I own, here, that I was ugly enough to ask it as a favor: that instead of a roast turkey and chicken, he should have bread and water, for a day or two, with not too much bread in it.

Poor old Hamilton was still in a very sore condition. He, too, was transferred to the *America,* where there was a good hospital in which to lay up and a very excellent doctor to mend his broken head. . . .

Moving to Fort de France Bay, December 21st, repairs were made there till January 5th, 1894, on which date the *Destroyer* again sailed, at early daylight.

Our condition at sea we find is better than it was. The *Destroyer* goes with some degree of safety now, benefited, to be sure, by her late repairs. The trade winds are still blowing very strong, and although towing in the teeth of the wind, the ship is kept free and handled in all respects without the wear and tear on a man's soul that was suffered in the early part of the voyage. But that, now, is neither here nor there. . . .

Jan. 18th the *Destroyer* arrived at Fernando de Noronha where all hands were busied, for the day, taking in coals and water again from the *Santuit.* A very heavy surf on prevented all communication with the shore except by signals and afterwards by dispatches that were brought to us out through the breakers by convicts of the place, in one-man canoes which they skillfully managed. The occupants having no wish, apparently, to end the term of their conviction, which they told us ranged yet ten years ahead of them. Ten years of their lives had already been put in on the windward side of the island. They rejoiced now on the lee side where for the first half of their penal term they might not come, so I was told.

I observed a multitude of people, convicts and guards, on the shore, making efforts to launch a great raft (the governor's "barge" I suppose) which they did not entirely succeed in floating. The heavy breakers on the shore defied all their strength and skill, tossing the cumbersome raft back to land as often as it dipped in the sea. But the nimble canoes—mere cockle shells—came out and went in all right.

Fifty convicts had landed on the island the day before our arrival (President Peixoto's political prisoners). There were, I dare say, senators and congressmen in the busy crowd of workers to-day trying to launch the raft which, like their own thwarted schemes, poor fellows, they could not float. For sinning politicians, even, life on the island met the ends of justice, considering ten years of it on the rugged side, under the constant roar of breakers.

It was about 8 A.M., when the *Destroyer* arrived at Fernando de Noronha. At 7 P.M. of the same day, she sailed with orders for Pernambuco, where she arrived without further incident of note, Jan. 20th 9 A.M. Later in the morning, a pilot with harbor tug brought her into the inner harbor, where she was moored to the Receife, which finishes the worst part of the hardest voyage that I ever made, without any exception at all. . . .

At Pernambuco, we fell in with the loyal fleet of the Brazilian Navy. Passing under the lee of the *Nictheroy*, the crew of that noble ship gave the *Destroyer* three rousing cheers. My old friend, Captain Baker, was on deck, as usual. The *America* and several other small ships were in the inner harbor. And what? my old friend, the *Falcon*, one of New Bedford's most worthy whaleships, which I last saw dismantled and aground at Fairhaven, and out of service: As like as two serving mallets, it is the old *Falcon* or Noah's Ark. Again, how mistaken: It is Admiral Goncalves' flagship, the *Paranahyba*, sure! I see cannon bristling from her sides, and gold-braided officers all about. Yes, it is the Admiral's ship.

My nautical skill is again brought into service at Pernambuco. What a thing it is to be "Navigating Officer in command." Together with the engineers, I am again mending and repairing, for which purpose the ship is grounded on the bank near the Arsenal. A few rivets about the bows having been sheared, consequent upon towing in the heavy seaway, was this time the cause of the leak. One tide sufficed for all the time necessary to repair below the water-line. When about to haul her off the following tide, a boat came from the Arsenal with orders to remain a day longer on the bank, that the work might be regularly inspected. It being a day of *festa,* the ship, even in war time, had to wait over.

On the following day duly appointed officers came, and the work that the engineers and I did in about an hour's time, was in the course of two days "regularly inspected," then, of course, it kept the water out.

I should explain that Sunday is not so much thought of by our Brazilian friends, but all of the fast days are religiously kept, and every thing they can lay their hands upon as well, over there.

The next thing in order was to fire the submarine gun.

A thousand pities it was that the gun itself was not in order. The Count and "specialist" wrote, from his hotel, a polite note to Admiral Duarte, begging the Admiral to witness the coming exploit with the *cannon.* There were several other Admirals about, but for special reasons Duarte had the Count's sympathy, so he invited him to come to the show. The note was written in the politest of French, but the Admiral didn't come—and tell it not to the Marines—the gun didn't go off! Worse than that, the *Destroyer* that was by this time tight and comfortable, had now to be put on the bank again, in order to unload the projectile from the cannon, since it wouldn't discharge by fire. This so strained the ship—a swell setting in that rolled her heavily against the bank, that she became leaky again. Though not a severe leak it was still discouraging. The only trouble about the whole affair with the gun was that the *powder got wet.*

But it was now hurrah for the war, boys, get a cargo of powder in and be off, ship and cargo was supposed to go against the arch rebel, Mello, who would have been "Liberator" of Brazil, but for the other man. Peixoto was bound to be "Liberator" himself. There was no time now to be lost! But wait! I'll tell all about that, too, pretty soon.

The *Destroyer* is carrying powder now for the whole fleet, which burnt all they had saluting the admiral on the way to Bahia in his old ark.

These ships preceded us by a few days; ostensibly, in haste, for Rio, but Mello not being ready to leave just then, the "attack" was postponed. It being untimely, however, to come back for more powder, it was shipped along to them on the *Destroyer*. The dear old craft had in already gun-cotton and dynamite enough to make a noise, but Goncalves wanted more thunder of his own old-fashioned sort, so we filled her chock-a-block with the stuff to make it. The submarine cannon was all stowed over with barrels of powder and was not get-atable at all the rest of the voyage to Bahia. In fact powder was all about. Three barrels of it found stowage in the Captain's room. The fourth one we couldn't get in. It was stowed back of the galley. That it didn't all blow up is how I am here to-day—thinking of my sins.

Well, in due course the stuff was all delivered in good order to the various ships in Bahia, for which the *Destroyer* was heartily maligned by all the Naval Officers, except the Minister of Marine, whom I judged to be with the legal government. Goncalves, the Admiral, was himself so enraged that he "romped" my "trata" at once. It was a portion of this same cargo of powder, which, forwarded on to Rio soon afterwards, was laid in the mine to blow up the *Aquideban*—and was fired after the great battleship got by and comfortably out of the way of it.

When I began the "voyage," I had no thought of writing a history of the whole war. Unconsciously I am drawn a distance beyond my first intent by the facts afloat of great achievements.

Horrors of war! how, when a lad, I shuddered at your name. I was in my ninth year, hired out on a farm when the thrilling news came to our township of a probable religious war. The four little churches bounding our small world, had always been in a light warfare, but *now* the *Catholics* were coming.

My employer, the good farmer, I shall never forget, armed his farm hands and his family with pitchforks, scythes, reaping hooks and the like—to do or die! There was great excitement. My own weapon was a hatchet, but that is no matter. The enemy came upon us, as it were, before we got our courage "screwed up to the sticking point." The rumpus began in the hen house, adjoining the kitchen: a heavy roost fell, and the de-il was to pay among the chickens. "The enemy! the enemy!!"

was the cry; "the Pope's men have come sure enough!!!" Where upon my employer, with laudable discretion, flinging open his doors, made haste to welcome the invaders. "Gentlemen," he cried, "come in, I have always been of opinion with you. Come in, gentlemen, and make yourselves at home in my house." When lo! it appeared there wasn't a man of any kind to come in. An old warrior cock, with bedraggled feathers, strutted in, however, and said "tooka-rio-rooa," or something to that effect, and the dear little chickens were all put back to roost—all except a few which next day went into the soup, and the war was finished.

But that, so far as I know, had nothing to do with this cruel war in Brazil. Nor can I say that history, in this case, repeats itself. The association is with me in the chain of my own thoughts and feelings. In those days, when I followed the peaceful pursuit of the plough, or rather a harrow it was, which towed by the old gray mare, that I navigated over the fields, already ploughed, and followed at three dollars a month. I say I shuddered then at the thoughts of war. But now I find myself deliberately putting my hand to documents which in those days nothing could have induced me to sign. At this time of life, after being towed under and over a large portion of two oceans, I sign articles of war! And notwithstanding my well-known peaceful disposition, I am expected to fight—in gold braid—to say nothing of the halibut-knife as long as my arm to dangle about the heels of my number elevens.

I observed on board of the Admiral's ship several young officers towing their swords well behind on the deck, thus obviating the danger, to the wearer, of being tripped up by the wicked blade. In the face of all the well known dangers I join the navy. . . .

I had by me still the very best of the good crew, which had followed the fortunes of the *Destroyer* all the way from New York. The Yarrow torpedo boat *Moxoto,* perfect in her construction and in perfect order, was added to our expedition. We were ready now to sail against anything afloat; but had yet to meet and pass, if we might, the fleet of the black bean eaters under Goncalves; not open foes, but lukewarm friends of greater danger, which, as I have said, preceded us to Bahia, burning their powder on the way, saluting the Admiral.

February 9th, 1894, the *Destroyer* sailed for Bahia, accompanied by the *Moxoto*, the handy torpedo boat.

On the 13th she arrived at the destination. Everything was funeral quietness at Bahia. The doughty Goncalves I saw often, passing to and fro, always to the music of a band. A captain of my grade, and foreigner at that, don't get any music in Brazil. All else was quiet and serene. The occasional pop of a champagne cork, at the "Paris" on the hill, might have been heard, but that was all, except again the sunset gun. The rising sun had to take care of itself. The average Brazilian Naval man is an amphibious being, spending his time about equally between hotel and harbor, and is never dangerous.

I was astonished at the quietness of Bahia, there was not even target practice. Indeed the further we got away from stirring New York, the less it looked like war in Brazil. There was to be torpedo practice one day. A Howell torpedo was launched, but boomerang-like it returned hitting the ship from which it was hurled. The only thing lacking to have made it a howling success was the dynamite, which these remarkable warriors forgot to put in. On the following day Goncalves, being in a bad humor, seized our ships and then under the pretext of making ready to move the world, nullified the great Ericsson cannon, which alone would have settled the business of the revolt. He rendered it as useless as the "busted" gun at Bunker Hill. Appearances were, now, that Goncalves would do himself all that should be done. And that, to be sure, is not saying much —to which he made a fair beginning.

Goncalves and his officers, I grieve to say, reviled the *Destroyer*, not only, I was told, for bringing the powder so quickly upon their heels, cutting thus into their quiet in port and hastening them on to the front, but for still greater reasons as well. As it proved, however, there was no danger in meeting the enemy, nor any cause of alarm. Goncalves, it is well known, was fitted out with peaceful, harmless people in his ships; Mello's outfit was the same. Both sides as harmless as jay birds! Why should they kill each other? That the *Destroyer*, then, most formidable ship of all, must in some way be disposed of, went without saying. When first she came to Bahia though, and it was reported that this was the long hoped "money ship" to follow the fleet—and pay the bills—the large iron "tank" in which the crew lived fitting in size their expectations of the chest out of which they would all get rich. Many visitors came to see her and called her a very handsome ship, saying many pretty things concerning "her lines," etc. But when to their great disappointment, instead of bank notes teeming forth, they beheld sea-begrimed tars tumbling out of the "tank," and worse still barrels of gunpowder being hoisted out, they said, "*Nao maes,*" we give it up! Their disappointment indeed was considerable, and her fine lines could no longer be seen.

It was proposed by Goncalves and his officers, to dig a hole in the bank, somewhere, and put the *Destroyer* in it under the mean pretext of putting a patch over the old leak spoken of at Pernambuco—a small matter. The meaning of this was practically the condemnation of the ship.

Robinson Crusoe in the fiction was not in a worse fix than this in which Admiral Goncalves would have himself appear. Starting too from this very Bahia, Crusoe in the course of his wonderful adventures, we all know, found himself obliged to dig his ship out to the sea, else let her rot in land. Exactly opposite, was the dilemma of our modern hero. The *Destroyer,* Goncalves said, should be dug into the *land,* else she would sink at sea.

Nothing of the kind! Why not bring the vessel into the small basin already at hand, I suggested, ground her on the smooth bottom and make the repairs. "Oh, no! Oh, no! That couldn't be done," echoed a chorus of voices from officers, all in a plot.

But His Excellency, Mr. Netto, Minister of Marine, friend of the legal Government, seeing my earnestness and good faith, when I told him that I stood only on the order said, "Bring her in." In she came!

The ship was now all the Admiral's. He had romped my contract, made by the Commander of the forces at Pernambuco, with the advice of the Inspector of the Marine; which was to go against the rebel fleet, and sink them all, if we could find them —big and little—for a handsome sum of gold, considering the danger, for each one that we should destroy—I would have commenced on the small ones, to be sure.

I began to think of the little farm, which so many years ago I promised myself. I say now, I could almost hear the potatoes growing—but not quite. As the question of docking in the basin, approved of by the Minister, was a matter of small warfare between he and his officers, who one and all wished to have the hole dug, and to put her in it, I exerted myself to please His Excellency on the Government side. I had great success that day. The leak was found and repaired before I slept that night, and before daylight the *Destroyer* rode at her anchor again in the bay, as tight as a cup. So in the morning, when the officers of the Arsenal came down to the Basin to inspect the work, the vessel wasn't there. Mr. Netto took my hand very warmly whenever after this I chanced to meet him alone. I could readily perceive the Minister's position to be a delicate one indeed.

The *Destroyer* was mended and afloat, and barring some slight repairs needed to her machinery, was in far better condition than she was when leaving New York. Had the voyage extended around the globe, a ship to be proud of would have been the ultimate result. To have sailed her first to the land of boiler-makers wouldn't have been amiss.

Goncalves, however, had one more open chance. He would have made a dozen chances to consummate his plan. It was with great interest that I watched the progress of the whole business, and noted the methods employed to the end that the *Destroyer* herself should be destroyed. The great pneumatic gun on the other ship I heard nothing about. That I believe was fixed and made harmless early in the "preparations." The Ericsson "*cannon*" was the gun to be dreaded now. At New York detectives were put on to keep folk away from the Ericsson gun; but here at Bahia it was impossible to get anybody to go near it. A plan was studied to somehow put it out of the way. "Should that once double on us like the Howell torpedo," they said, "it would be worse than the yellow fever around here," and "we must get it out of the way." So on the 28th Feb., 1894, having discharged the sailors and having filled their places with bean-eaters from the fields and the mountains, and having found a captain unfamiliar with the ways of a ship (a thing by the way not so hard to find), Goncalves sent the ship to sea, he did, with this outfit on board. She was gone only 24 hours, however, and returned with all hands ahoy! flat on deck, seasick and afraid. The Captain—it would be impolite to call sick—lost his appetite and prayed to be thrown overside early in this memorable adventure, which will live in record side by side with the history of the war. The *Destroyer* had proved too much for the greenhorns—they couldn't lose her.

There was, however, one man, a soldier, on board who would have run the engineer through for deserting his post. This man (the soldier) was afterwards thrown in jail, I heard, and, for aught I know, was shot. The Captain, even in his own misery, saved the engineer's life. He said, "Let us each die a natural death. Let us all die friends on deck, since there is no one to help us into the sea, and let us have no more war." Goncalves thought he knew what he was about, when he put that crew on board, but he did not count on the latent strength of the *Destroyer*. On leaving, she at once collided with the stout steamer that towed her from and back into Bahia, and still was not wrecked, in fact, she was but slightly damaged. She was towed with a short steel hawser and no one was at the helm to guide her in the going or in the coming, for there wasn't a soul on board that could steer. She sheered wildly over the ocean. The hawser would have incontinently carried away the bows of a less substantial vessel, but the *Destroyer* of many storms withstood the hard usage.

The day was calm or nearly so, and the sea was smooth; else indeed the ship would have been foundered—with all of those young souls on board! I watched her from the top of the hill going. From the same place the next evening I was rejoiced to see her safely return.

Her best pump was landed before she went out. I saw it at the Arsenal under a tree; her anchors, however, they left on board. She was not pumped from the time she sailed 'til she arrived back into port for reasons already stated. The ballast which would have trimmed the vessel well, was also taken ashore at the same time and same place, with the pump, and was never brought back on board. So the *Destroyer* went by the head, for the want of balance, which caused her to sheer worse than ever. But for all that the other steamship failed to sink her. So the *Destroyer* came back.

And so after triumphantly breasting the winter waves of the North Atlantic Ocean, the *Destroyer* changed her crew, to give up the fight in a summer sea.

I wish I were able to give a better account of the warriors that I met in Brazil, and especially of the sailors (?) who shipped on the *Destroyer*, in lieu of the men who sailed her from New York. But this true account, not always flattering, I know, will be endorsed by every honest Brazilian of whichever side, and will, I am sure, greatly assist the future historian. My own position in the voyage forbids me to say more.

Concerning the last days of my worthy old ship, there is little more to say. The upland navigators at the Arsenal at Bahia, having observed the New York crew put the *Destroyer* in the basin and out again with dispatch, undertook, like some tropical quadrupeds, to do the "trick" themselves. Whether from pure cussedness or not this time, I can't say, but they stove a great hole in her bottom, having grounded her on a rock, "accidentally," they said.

Alas! for all our hardships and perils! The latest account that I heard said that the *Destroyer* lay undone in the basin. The tide ebbing and flowing through her broken hull—a rendezvous for eels and crawfish—and now those high and dry sailors say they had a "narrow escape."

The torpedo boat, *Moxoto*, must not be forgotten. My pen blushes to record it. A crockery-ware clerk was put in command of her, and she was sent on a trial trip among the ships in the bay. Now to the poor clerk and his earthen-ware crew, all this was strange and dangerous, but they cut up high jinks and made things hum in the bay. Everybody was on his guard for awhile, for they had steam up and couldn't stop her—they didn't know how. The Captain hailed a foreign steamer and shouted to the engineer that he would pay 20 mil reis to be stopped. But the engineer couldn't get aboard—he couldn't catch her. She could steam 18 knots and was now at full speed.

The Vice-Admiral's brig, an old craft of many summers at Bahia, came in for the first ram in the collisions that followed. But the *Moxoto*, not hitting her fair, came off second best in the battle. Then away, always at full speed, she made for brig No. 2 not far away, aground on her own beef bones, and gave her a blow in the quarter that brought the crew, officers and all, on deck in a hurry. Being aground, the danger of a collision had not been thought of. The shock, they at first supposed, came from an earthquake, but that's no matter. It wasn't, and as nothing less could move them to action, they all went below again, like good, loyal warriors where they should do the least harm—if they should do anything at all—and be most out of danger. There were no bullets flying about, to be sure, but the sun was dangerously hot at Bahia. It was, in fact, all the fire there was, to speak of, in the whole war.

Early in March, the rebel navy weakened, if I may use the term in their case, and the *Aquideban*, after burning much powder to no effect, proceeded from Rio harbor unmolested to sea; leaving open waters for my old friend Goncalves to take up in turn, which he did, and went on with the business of burning powder in greater salutes than ever. The revolt began in Rio, somewhere in September, 1893, the date don't matter much. The funny war so far as the navy was concerned finished of itself in March, 1894. No historian can ever say more. . . .

JACOB STROYER

(1846–?)

Sketches of My Life in the South. By Jacob Stroyer. Part I.
Printed at the Salem Press, Salem, 1879. 51 pp.

This is the unfinished autobiography of an emancipated
slave; there was no sequel to Part I. Whether the author
stopped writing, or what happened, is not known.

The Emancipation Proclamation, of January 1, 1863, freed
Jacob Stroyer. He was then seventeen. He went north, attended
school, and became a preacher and teacher. As the years passed
he realized that, though chattel slavery had been abolished, the
end of its harmful influence was a long way off. Deprived of
education, his people had a great deal to learn about their history and heritage. Whites, too, needed enlightening. He belonged to the last generation able to speak about slavery first-
hand. He felt the importance of putting his experience on
record.

Memoirs by freedmen followed the genre of earlier accounts
written by slaves who had escaped. Quite a few slave narratives
have been reprinted in recent years, some published for the first
time. There are hundreds in the major collections of Negro history and literature.

The number of narratives written by freedmen is far less.
Jacob Stroyer's little book, only four by six inches in size and
bound in cardboard, had three editions. The last, printed while
he served as minister of the African Methodist Episcopal
Church in Salem, Massachusetts, carried endorsements by two
of the city's mayors. With its title trimmed to *My Life in the
South,* it appeared in 1885, and has not been reprinted since.
Copies of all editions are scarce.

SKETCHES OF MY LIFE
IN THE SOUTH

———•———

CHAPTER I.

MY BIRTH AND PARENTAGE.

I was born in the state of South Carolina, twenty-eight miles northeast of Columbia, in the year 1846; I belonged to a man by the name of Col. M. R. Singleton, and was held in slavery up to the time of the emancipation proclamation issued by President Lincoln.

My father was brought from Africa when but a boy and was sold to the Colonel's father, old Col. Dick Singleton and when his children became of age he divided his plantations among them, and father fell to Col. M. R. Singleton the second son. Father was not a field hand, but used to take care of horses and mules, as the Colonel had a great many for the use of his farm. I did not learn what name father went by before he was brought to this country, I only know that he stated that Col. Dick Singleton gave him the name of William, by which name he was known to the day of his death. He also had a surname Stroyer, but he could not use it in public as the surname would be against the law; he was known only by the name William Singleton because his master's name was Singleton, so the title Stroyer was forbidden him and could be used by his children only after the emancipation of the slaves. There were two reasons given by the slave holders why a slave should not use his own name but the name of his master, one was that if the slave were to run away into a free state he would not be so easily detected by using his own name as if he used that of his master, the second was that in allowing him to use his own name he would be sharing an honor due his master alone, and it would be too much for a negro who was nothing but a servant. So it was held as a crime for the slave to be caught using his own name and it would expose him to severe punishment, but

278

thanks be to God those days have passed and we now live under the sun of liberty.

My mother also belonged to Col. M. R. Singleton, and was a field hand. She never was sold but her parents were once. One Mr. Crough owned the plantation where mother lived and he sold it with mother's parents and the other slaves thereon to Col. Dick Singleton. The family from which mother came had, most of them, trades of some kind; some were carpenters, some blacksmiths, others house servants, and some were made drivers over the other negroes, of course the negro drivers would be under a white man who was called overseer. But mother had to take her chance out in the field with those who had to weather the storms. My readers are not to think that those whom I have spoken of as having trades were free from punishment for they were not, some of them had more troubles than the field hands. . . .

As I have said, my father used to take care of horses and mules, and I was around with him in the barnyard when but a very small boy; of course that gave me an early relish for the occupation of hostler, and I soon made known my preference to Col. Singleton, who was a sportsman and had fine horses, and, although I was too small to work, the Colonel granted my request and I was allowed to be numbered among those who were taking care of the fine horses and to learn to ride. But I soon found that my new occupation demanded a little more than I cared for.

It was not long after I had entered my new work before they put me upon the back of a horse which threw me to the ground almost as soon as I reached his back. It hurt me a little, but that was not the worst of it, when I got up there was a man standing near with a switch in his hand and he immediately began to beat me. Although I was a very bad boy, this was the first time I was whipped by any one except father and mother, so I cried out in a tone of voice as if I would say, this is the first and last whipping you will give me, when father gets you. When I got away from him I ran to father with all my might, but soon found my expectations blasted, as father very coolly said to me, "go back to your work and be a good boy, for I cannot do anything for you." But that did not satisfy me, so on I went to mother with my complaint and she came out to the man who whipped me, he was a groom, a white man who master hired to train his horses, as he was a man of that trade. Mother and he began to talk, then he took a whip and started for mother and she ran from him talking all the time. I ran back and forth between mother and him until he stopped beating her. After the fight between the groom and mother he took me back to the stable-yard and gave me a very severe flogging for a boy of my size. Then the idea first came to me that I, with my dear father and mother, was doomed to cruel treatment through life and was defenceless. Then I saw the chains that were fast forging to bind me as they did my father and mother. But when I found that father and mother could not save me from punishment as they themselves had to submit to the same treatment, I concluded to appeal to the sympathy of the groom, who seemed to have full control over me, but my pitiful cries never touched his sympathy, for things seemed to grow worse rather than better, so I made up my mind to stem the storm the best I could. . . .

CHAPTER II.

MY EXPERIENCE.

I have said, in the above statements, that I was under the groom, and his name was Boney Young. He had a brother by the name of Charles Young, who used to act as groom to John Singleton, brother of Colonel M. R. Singleton. But Boney Young was the better groom and the meaner fellow. One day, about two weeks after he and mother had the conflict, he called me to him, he was singing as though in a very pleasant mood, and I ran to him as if to say by my actions, I am willing to do anything you bid me, willingly. When I got to him, he said, "go and bring me a switch, sir," I answered, "yes, sir," and off I went and brought him one, then he said, "come in here, sir;" I answered, "yes, sir" and went into a horse stall, but while I was going in a thousand thoughts passed through my mind as to what he wanted me to go into that stall for. But when I got in he gave me a severe flogging.

A day or two after that, he called me in the same way, and I went again and he sent me for a switch, but I brought him a short stubble that was worn out, he took it, beat me on the head with it, then said to me, "go and bring me a switch, sir;" I answered, "yes, sir," and off I went the second time, and brought one a very little better than the first, he broke that over my head, saying, "go and bring me a switch, sir;" I answered, "yes, sir," and off I went for the third time, and then he said to me, "come here, sir," I answered, "yes, sir." When I went into the stall he told me to lie down, and I stooped down, when he kicked me around for awhile and then making me lie on my face he whipped me to his satisfaction. That evening when I went home to father and mother, I said to them, "Mr. Young is whipping me too much now, I shall not stand it, I shall fight him," father said to me, "you must not do that, because if you do he will say that your mother and I had advised you to do it, and it will make it hard for your mother and me, as well as for yourself, you must do as I told you my son, do your work the best you can and do not say anything." I said to father, "but I don't know what I have done that he should whip me, he does not tell me what wrong I have done, he simply calls me to him and whips me when he gets ready." Father said, "I can do nothing more than to pray to the Lord to hasten the time when these things shall be done away, that is all I can do."

Then mother stripped me and looked at the wounds that were upon me and she burst into tears and said, "If he were not so small I would not mind it so much, but this will break his constitution, I am going to master about it because I know he will not allow Mr. Young to treat this child so," but father told her that she had better not, because while master might stop him from treating the boy badly, he might revenge himself through the overseer, for he and Mr. Young were very good friends, so she would gain nothing in the end, the best thing he thought was to pray much over it, for he believed the time would come when we all should be free. When father spoke of liberty, his words seemed a great comfort to me, and my heart swelled with the hope of the future and we sat up very late that night talking about it. When the time came for us to go to bed we all knelt down in family prayer, as was our custom. When morning came father went to his work in the barn-yard and mother to hers on the farm, and I to my work but father was careful to charge me to keep his advice, as he said that would be the easiest way for me to get along.

But in spite of father's advice I had made up my mind not to be submissive as I was before, seeing that it did not help me any; things went smoothly for a few days until one day the groom called me to him and told me to bring him a switch, I told him that I would bring no more switches for him to whip me with, but that he must get them himself. After repeating the command very impatiently and I refusing, he called to another boy named Hardy, he brought the switch, and taking me into a stall, he whipped me unmercifully. After that he made me run back and forth every morning from a half to three quarters of an hour, about two hundred and fifty yards and every now and then he would run after me and whip me to make me run faster. Besides that, when I was put upon a horse if he threw me he would whip me if it were five times a day. So I did not gain anything by refusing to bring switches for him to whip me with. . . .

One day as I was riding along the road the horse that I was upon darted at sight of a bird, which flew across the way, throwing me upon a pile of brush. The horse stepped on my cheek and the head of a nail in his shoe went through my cheek and broke a tooth, but it was done so quickly that I hardly felt it, it happening that he did not step on me with his whole weight, if he had my jaw would have been broken. When I got up, the colored groom was standing by me, but he could not whip me when he saw the blood flowing from my mouth, so he took me down to the creek, which was but a short distance from the place, and washed me, then taking me home sent for the doctor who dressed the wound. When the white groom saw my condition, he asked how it was done and upon being told, said it ought to have killed me. After the doctor had dressed my face, of course I went home, thinking they would allow me to stay until I got well, but I did not more than get there before the groom sent for me, I did not answer as my jaw pained me very much. When he found that I did not come, he came after me himself, and said if I did not come to the stable right away he would whip me, so I came out with him. He did not whip me while I was in that condition, but he would not let me lie down, so I suffered very much from exposure.

When mother came home that night from the farm and saw my condition, she was overcome with grief, she said to father, "this wound is enough to kill the child and that merciless man will not let him lie down until he gets well, this is too hard." Father said to her, "I know it is very hard, but what can we do? For if we try to keep this boy in the house it will cause us trouble." Mother said, "I wish the Lord would take him out of the world, then he would be out of pain and we should not have to fret about him, for he would be in heaven." Then she would take hold of me and say, "does it hurt you, son," I answered, "yes, mama," and she would take hold of me and shed tears, but she had no little toys to give me to comfort me, she could only promise such as she had, eggs and chickens. Father did not show his grief for me as mother did, but he tried to comfort mother all he could and at times would say to me, "never mind my son, you will be a man by and by," but he did not know what was passing through my mind at that time.

Though I was very small I thought that, if while a boy my treatment was so severe, how heavy it would be when I became a man, and having had a chance to see how men were being punished it was a very poor consolation to me. Finally, the time came for us to go to bed, and we all knelt down in family prayer, father thanked God for having saved me from a worse injury and then he prayed for mother's comfort, and also for the time which he predicted would come, that is the time of freedom, when I and the rest of the children should be our own masters and mistresses, then he commended us to God and we all went to bed.

The next morning I went to my work with a great deal of pain. They did not send me up the road with the horses in that condition, but I had to ride the old horses to water them, and work around the stable until I was well enough to go with the other boys. But I am happy to say, that from the time I got hurt by that horse I was never thrown except through carelessness, neither was I afraid of a horse after that. Notwithstanding mother and father fretted very much about me, they were proud of my success as a rider, but my hardships did not end here. . . .

Master went away that spring for the last time, he never returned alive. When they brought his remains home all of the slaves were allowed to stop at home that day, to see the last of

him and to lament with mistress. After all the slaves who cared
to do so had seen his face, they gathered in groups around mistress to comfort her, they shed false tears saying, "never mind
misses, massa gone home to heaven," while some were saying
this, others said, "thank God, massa gone home to hell, massa
gone home to hell." Of course they all were to comfort mistress,
but after his death mistress was a great deal harder than master.

The creditors came in for settlement so all of the fine horses,
some others such as carriage horses and a few of the mules, had
to be sold; the slaves could not be sold, because they were given
to him by his father, until the grandchildren(that is master's
children) were of age. What master bought himself could be
sold after his death, and it was.

After all the fine horses were sold, mistress ordered that the
men and boys who were taking care of the horses should be put
into the field, and I was among them, though small; but I had
become so attached to the horses that they could get no work
out of me, so they began to whip me but every time they
whipped me I would leave the field and run home to the barn
yard. Finally mistress engaged a very bad man as overseer
whose name was William Turner, two or three days after he
came he took me into the field and whipped me until I was sick,
so I went home. I went to mistress and told her that the overseer
whipped me, she asked me if I did the work in the field that he
gave me, I told her that master promised me that when I got too
heavy to ride race horses he would send me to learn the carpenter's trade, she asked me if she were to put me to trade if I
would work, I told her I would, so she did. But the overseer did
not like the idea of having me work at the trade which was my
choice. He said to mistress, "that is the worst thing you can do,
madam, to allow a negro to have his choice about what he shall
do, I have had some experience as an overseer for many years,
and I am able to give a correct statement about the nature of
negroes in general, I know a gentleman who allowed his negroes to have their own way about things on his plantation and
the result was that they got as high as their master. Beside that,
madam, their influence rapidly spread among the neighbors
and if such should be allowed South Carolina would have all

masters and mistresses, and no servants, and as I have said, I
know somewhat about the nature of negroes, I notice madam,
that this boy will put you to a great deal of trouble unless you
begin to subdue him now while he is young. A very few years'
delay will enable him to have a great influence among his fellow negroes, for that boy can read very well now, and you
know madam, it is against the law for a negro to get an education and if you allow him to work at the carpenter's trade it will
thus afford him the opportunity of acquiring a better education, because he will not be directly under the eye of one who
will see that he makes no further advancement." Then mistress
asked me, "can you read, Jacob?" I did not want her to know
that I had taken notice of what they were saying, so I answered,
"I don't know, ma'am." The overseer said, "he does not know
what is meant, madam, I can make him understand me," then
he took a newspaper from his pocket and said to me, "can you
say these words," I took the paper and began to read, then he
took it from me. Mistress asked when I learned to read and who
taught me, the overseer did not know, but said he would find
out from me. Turning to me he took the paper from his pocket
again, and said, "Jacob who told you to say words in the
book," I answered "nobody sir, I said them myself." He repeated the question three or four times and I gave the same
answer every time, then the mistress said, "I think it would be
better to put him to the trade than to have him in the field,
because he will be away from his fellow negroes and will be less
liable to influence them, we can manage to keep him away."
The overseer said "that might be true, madam, but if we can
manage to keep him from gaining any more education he will
eventually lose what little he has, and now, madam, if you will
allow me to take him in hand, I will bring him out all right
without injuring him." Just at this juncture a carriage drove up
to the gate and I ran as usual to open it, the overseer went
about his business and mistress went to speak to the persons in
the carriage. I never had a chance to hear their conclusion.

A few days after the conversation between the overseer and
mistress, I was informed by one of the slaves who was a carpenter, that she had ordered that I should go to work at the trade
with him; this gave me great joy, as I was very anxious to know

what they had decided to do with me. I went to my new trade with great delight, and soon began to imagine what a famous carpenter I should make and what I should say and do when I had learned the trade. Everything seemed to run smoothly with me for about two months, when suddenly I was told one morning that I must go into the field to drop cotton seed, but I did not heed the call as mistress was not at home, and I knew she had just put me to the trade, also, that the overseer was trying to get mistress' consent to have me work out in the field. The next morning the overseer came into the carpenter's shop, and said, "did I not order ye into the fields, sir," I answered "yes, sir," "well, why did ye not go," I answered, "mistress has put me here to learn the trade," he said, "I will give ye trade." So he stripped me and gave me a severe whipping and told me that was the kind of trade I needed, and said he would give me many of them. The next day, I went into the field and he put me to drop cotton seed, as I was too small to do anything else, and mistress was very far away from home.

When I got through with the cotton seed, which was in three weeks, I went back to the carpenter's shop to work; so he came there and gave me another severe whipping and said to me, "ye want to learn the carpenter's trade but I will have ye to the trade in the field." This was in the time of the war, in the year 1863, when a man was going around to the different plantations, gathering slaves from their masters to carry off to work on fortifications and to wait on officers; there were ten slaves sent from Mrs. Singleton's plantation and I was among them. They carried us to Sullivan's Island at Charleston, S. C., and I was there all of that year; I thanked God that it afforded me a better chance for an education than I had at home and so was glad to be on the Island.

The next year after I went home I was sent back to Fort Sumter (in the year 1864); I carried my spelling book with me, and although the Northerners were firing upon us I tried to keep up my study. In July of the same year I was wounded by the Union soldiers, on a Wednesday evening; I was taken to the city of Charleston, to Dr. Ragg's hospital, and there I stayed until I got well and was sent to Columbia where I was, when the horn of liberty was proclaimed to me in 1865; this was the year of jubilee, the year which my father spoke of in the dark days of slavery when he and mother sat up late talking of it. He said to mother, "the time will come when this boy and the rest of the children will be their own masters and mistresses." He did not live to see it, but mother enjoyed a portion of it with her children.

I have said that I fell from a horse and he stepped on my face cutting it and breaking a tooth, the scar of which is still visible. And no doubt my readers would like to know how I was wounded in the war. We were obliged to do our work in the night as they were firing on us in the day, and on this Wednesday night just as we went out we heard the cry of the watchman "look out," there was a little lime house near the southwest corner of the fort, and some twelve or thirteen of us ran into that and all were killed but two, a shell came down on the lime house and burst and a piece cut my face open. But as it was not my time to die I lived to enjoy freedom.

When the yoke was taken from my neck I went to school in Columbia, S. C., awhile, then to Charleston, afterward I came to Worcester, Mass., in February, 1870. I studied quite awhile in the evening schools at Worcester, and after that I got a little money and went to the Worcester Academy and studied nearly two years. During this time I was licensed a local preacher of the African Methodist Episcopal Church, sometime after this was ordained Deacon at Newport, R. I.

Shortly after I was sent to the city of Salem, Mass., where I have remained for the last fifteen months, trying in my feeble way to preach that gospel which our blessed Savior intended for the redemption of all mankind when he proclaimed; "Go ye into all the world and preach the gospel."

I must say I have been surrounded during my stay in Salem by many good friends, including many of the clergy, who have always been willing to aid me in the great and good work. My intention at this time is to pursue a course of study in order that I may be better prepared to do the labor required of me in the Master's great vineyard.

CHAPTER III.—SKETCHES.

THE SALE OF MY TWO SISTERS.

I have stated that my father had fifteen children: four boys and three girls by his first wife, and six boys and two girls by his second. Their names are as follows: Toney, Aszerine, Duke, and Dezine, of the girls, Violet, Priscilla, and Lydia; those of the second wife as follows: Footy, Embers, Caleb, Mitchell, Cuffee, and Jacob who is the author, and the girls Catherine and Retta.

As I have said old Col. Dick Singleton had two sons and two daughters and each had a plantation. Their names were John, Matt, Maryanna, and Angelico, they were very agreeable together so that if one wanted negro help from another's plantation he or she could have it, especially in cotton picking time.

John Singleton had a place about twenty miles from master's who used to send him slaves to pick cotton, at one time my master Col. M. R. Singleton sent my two sisters Violet and Priscilla to his brother John, and while they were there they married two of the men on his place; by mutual consent master allowed them to remain on his brother's place. But sometime after this John Singleton had some of his property destroyed by water as is often the case in the South at the time of May freshets, what is known in the North as high tides.

One of these freshets swept away John Singleton's slave houses, his barns with horses, mules and cows; these caused his death by a broken heart, and owing a great deal of money his slaves had to be sold. A Mr. Manning bought a portion of them and Charles Login the rest, these two men were known as the greatest slave traders in the South, my sisters were among the number that Mr. Manning bought.

He was to take them into the state of Louisiana for sale, but some of the men did not want to go with him, and he put those in prison until he was ready to start. My sisters' husbands were among the prisoners in the Sumterville Jail which was about twenty-five or thirty miles across the river from master's place. Those who did not show any unwillingness to go were allowed to visit their relatives and friends for the last time. So my sisters with the rest of their unfortunate companions came to master's place to visit us; when the day came for them to leave, some, who seemed to have been willing to go at first, refused, and were handcuffed together and guarded on their way to the cars by white men. The women and children were driven to the depot in crowds, like so many cattle, and the sight of them caused great excitement among master's negroes. Imagine a mass of uneducated people shedding tears and yelling at the tops of their voices in anguish and grief.

The victims were to take the cars from a station called Clarkson turnout, which was about four miles from master's place. The excitement was so great that the overseer and driver could not control the relatives and friends of those that were going away, as a large crowd of both old and young went down to the depot to see them off. Louisiana was considered by the slaves as a place of slaughter, so those who were going did not expect to see their friends again. While passing along, many of the negroes left their master's fields and joined us as we marched to the cars; some were yelling and wringing their hands, while others were singing little hymns that they were accustomed to for the consolation of those that were going away, such as,

> "When we all meet in heaven,
> There is no parting there;
> When we all meet in heaven,
> There is parting no more."

We arrived at the depot and had to wait for the cars to bring the others from the Sumterville Jail, but they soon came in sight, and when the noise of the cars died away we heard wailing and shrieks from those in the cars. While some were weeping, others were fiddling, picking banjo, and dancing as they used to do in their cabins on the plantations. Those who were so merry had very bad masters, and even though they stood a chance of being sold to one as bad or even worse yet they were glad to be rid of the one they knew.

While the cars were at the depot, a large crowd of white people gathered, and were laughing and talking about the prospect of negro traffic; but when the cars began to start and the conductor cried out, "all who are going on this train must get aboard without delay," the colored people cried out with one voice as though the heavens and earth were coming together, and it was so pitiful, that those hard hearted white men who had been accustomed to driving slaves all their lives, shed tears like children. As the cars moved away we heard the weeping and wailing from the slaves, as far as human voice could be heard; and from that time to the present I have neither seen nor heard from my two sisters, nor any of those who left Clarkson depot on that memorable day.

THE WAY THE SLAVES LIVED.

Most of the cabins in the time of slavery were built so as to contain two families; some had partitions, while others had none. When there were no partitions each family would fit up his own part as he could, sometimes they got old boards and nailed them up, stuffing the cracks with old rags; when they could not get boards they hung up old clothes. When the family increased, the children all slept together, both boys and girls, until either got married, then a part of another cabin was assigned to the one that was married, but the rest would have to remain with their mother and father as they did when children unless they could get with some of their relatives or friends who had small families, or when they were sold; but of course the rules of modesty were held in some degree by the slaves, while it could not be expected that they could entertain the highest degree of it on account of their condition. A portion of the time the young men slept in the apartment known as the kitchen and the young women slept in the room with their mother and father. The two families had to use one fireplace. One, who was accustomed to the way in which the slaves lived in their cabins, could tell as soon as they entered whether they were friendly or not, for when they did not agree the fires of the two families did not meet on the hearth, but there was a vacancy between them, that was a sign of disagreement. In a case of this kind when either of the families stole a hog, cow, or sheep from the master, he had to carry it to some of his friends for fear of being betrayed by the other family. On one occasion a man who lived with one unfriendly, stole a hog, killed it, and carried some of the meat home. He was seen by some one of the other family, who reported him to the overseer and he gave the man a severe whipping. Sometime after, this man who was betrayed thought he would get even with his enemy; so about two months after he killed another hog, and after eating a part of it stole into the apartment of the other and hid a portion of the meat among the old clothes. Then he told the overseer that he saw the man go out late that night and he did not come home until the next morning, when he came he called his wife to the window and she took something in, but he did not know what it was, but if the overseer would go there right away he would find it. The overseer went and searched and found the meat, so the man was whipped. He told the overseer that the other man put it in his apartment while the family were away, but the overseer told him that every man must be responsible for his own apartment.

No doubt you would like to know how the slaves could sleep in their cabins in summer when it was so very warm. When it was too warm for them to sleep comfortably they all slept under trees until it grew too cool, which would be along in the month of October. Then they took up their beds and walked.

CUSTOM OF WITCHES AMONG SLAVES.

The witches among slaves were supposed to have been persons who worked with them every day, and were called old hags or jack lanterns. Those, both men and women, who, when they grew old looked odd, were supposed to be witches. Sometimes after eating supper the negroes would gather in each other's cabins which looked over the large openings on the plantation, and when they would see a light at a great distance and saw it open and shut they would say "there is an old hag," and if it came from a certain direction where those lived whom they called witches, one would say "dat looks like old Aunt Susan," another said "no, dat look like man hag," still another "I tink dat look like ole Uncle Renty."

When the light disappeared they said that the witch had got into the plantation and changed itself into a person, and went around on the place talking with the people like others until those whom it wanted to bewitch went to bed, then it would change itself to a witch again. They claimed that they rode human beings like horses, and the spittle that run on the side of the cheek when one slept was the bridle that the witch rode with. Sometimes a baby would be smothered by its mother and they would charge it to a witch. If they went out hunting at night and were lost it was believed that a witch led them off, especially if they fell into a pond or creek. I was very much troubled with witches when a little boy and am now sometimes, but it is only when I eat a hearty supper and then go to bed. It was said by some of the slaves that the witches would sometimes go into the rooms of the cabins and hide themselves until the family went to bed, and when any one claimed that they went into the apartment before bed time and thought he saw a witch, if they had an old bible in the cabin that would be taken into the room and the person who carried the bible would say as he went in "In de name of de Fader and of de Son and de Hole Gos wat you want?" then the bible would be put in the corner where the person thought he saw the witch as it was generally believed that if this were done the witch could not stay. When they could not get the bible they used red pepper and salt pounded together and scattered in the room, but in this case they generally felt the effects of it more than the witch, for when they went to bed it made them cough all night. When I was a little boy my mother sent me into the cabin room for something, and as I got in I saw something black and white, but did not stop to see what it was, and running out said there was a witch in the room, but father having been born in Africa did not believe in such things, so he called me a fool and whipped me and the witch got scared and ran out of the door; it turned out to be our own black and white cat that we children played with every day. Although it proved to be the cat, and father did not believe in witches, still I held the idea that there were such things, for I thought as the majority of the people believed it that they ought to know more than one man. Sometime after I was free, in traveling from Columbia to Camden, a distance of about thirty-two miles; night overtook me when about half way there, it was very dark and rainy, and as I approached a creek I saw a great number of lights of those witches opening and shutting, I did not know what to do and thought of turning back, but when I looked behind I saw some witches in the distance, so I said if I turn back those will meet me and I will be in as much danger as if I go on, and I thought of what some of my fellow negroes had said about their leading men into ponds and creeks; there was a creek just ahead, so I concluded that I should be drowned that night, however I went on, as I saw no chance of turning back. When I came near the creek one of the witches flew into my face; I jumped back and grasped it, but it proved to be one of those little lightning bugs, and I thought if all the witches were like that one I should not be in any great danger from them.

THE WAY THE SLAVES DETECTED THIEVES AMONG THEMSELVES.

The slaves had three ways of detecting thieves, one with a bible, one with a sieve, and another with graveyard dust. The first way was this:—four men were selected, one of which had a bible with a string attached to it, and each man had his own part to perform. Of course this was done in the night, as it was the only time they could attend to such matters which concerned themselves. These four would commence at the first cabin with every man of the family, and one who held the string attached to the bible would say John or Tom, whatever the person's name was, you are accused of stealing a chicken or a dress from Sam at such a time, then one of the other two would say, "John stole the chicken," and another would say, "John did not steal the chicken." They would continue their assertions for at least five minutes, then the men would put a stick in the loop of the string that was attached to the bible, and hold it as still as they could, one would say, "Bible, in the name of the Father and of the Son and of the Holy Ghost, if John stole that chicken, turn," that is if the man had stolen what he was accused of, the bible was to turn around on the string, and that would be a proof that he did steal it. This was repeated three times before they left that cabin, and it would take those men a month sometimes when the plantation was very large, that is, if they did not find the right person before they got through the whole place.

The second way they had of detecting thieves was very much like the first, only they used a sieve instead of a bible, they stuck a pair of scissors in the sieve with a string hitched to it and a stick put through the loop of the string and the same words were used as for the bible. Sometimes the bible and the sieve would turn upon names of persons whose characters were beyond suspicion; when this was the case they would either charge the mistake to the men who fixed the bible and the sieve, or else the man who was accused by the turning of the bible and the sieve, would say that he passed near the coop from which the fowl was stolen, then they would say, "Bro John we see dis how dat ting work, you pass by de chicken coop de same night de hen went away."

But when the bible or the sieve turned on the name of one whom they knew often stole, and he did not acknowledge that he stole the chicken of which he was accused, he would have to acknowledge his previously stolen goods or that he thought of stealing at the time when the chicken or dress was stolen. Then this examining committee would justify the turning of the bible or sieve on the above statement of the accused person.

The third way of detecting thieves was taught by the fathers and mothers of the slaves. They said no matter how untrue a man might have been during his life, when he came to die he had to tell the truth and had to own everything that he ever did and whatever dealing those alive had with anything pertaining to the dead, must be true, or they would immediately die and go to hell to burn in fire and brimstone, so in consequence of this the graveyard dust was the truest of the three ways in detecting thieves. The dust would be taken from the grave of a person who died last and put into a bottle and water was put into it, then two of the men who were among the examining committee would use the same words as in the case of the bible and the sieve, that is, one would say, "John stole that chicken," another would say, "John did not steal that chicken," after this had gone on for about five minutes, then one of the other two who attended to the bible and the sieve would say, "John, you are accused of stealing that chicken that was taken from Sam's chicken coop at such a time, and he would say, "In the name of the Father and the Son and the Holy Ghost, if you have taken Sam's chicken don't drink this water, for if you do you will die and go to hell and be burned in fire and brimstone, but if you have not you may take it and it will not hurt you." So if John had taken the chicken he would own it rather than take the water.

Sometimes those whose characters were beyond suspicion would be proven thieves when they tried the graveyard dust and water. When the right person was detected if he had any chickens he had to give four for one, and if he had none he made it good by promising him that he would do so no more; if all the men on the plantation passed through the examination and no one was found guilty, the stolen goods would be charged to strangers. Of course these customs were among the negroes for their own benefit, for they did not consider it stealing when they took anything from their master.

ALBERT PINKHAM RYDER

(1847–1917)

Paragraphs from the Studio of a Recluse. By Albert P. Ryder. *Broadway Magazine,* New York, vol. 14, no. 6, September 1905, pp. 10–11.

In ten paragraphs, Albert Pinkham Ryder revealed more about his inner life and philosophy than many are able to express in any number of pages. The distillation of what he discovered for himself in a lifetime of painting he put into *Paragraphs from the Studio of a Recluse.*

The youngest of four brothers, he was born in New Bedford, Massachusetts, when it was the greatest of whaling ports. The sea entered into his earliest recollections, and its presence stayed with him. While two of his brothers were practical seafearing men, Ryder became the poet-painter of the sea. He had a rare ability to capture and compress on little canvases his feeling for the depths and its moods. His concepts of small boats tossed on great waters, romanticized darkly on the journey of life and the vastness of the unknown.

Ryder's third brother, William, went to New York and prospered in the hotel restaurant business. About 1870 Ryder, with his father and mother, followed. For a short time he attended the National Academy of Design, where the instruction was mainly drawing from casts. Academic conformity, however, did not interest him. He soon left and went his own way. The disadvantage of little schooling was that he never learned to handle paint properly. His self-taught techniques and highly individual experiments with pigments resulted in serious cracking and deterioration of his canvases. Virtually all his paintings have required restoring.

Ryder's material wants were extremely few; money did not concern him. He remained single, and lived with his parents until he was past thirty. From time to time his brother William

296

helped him; he could always go to William's restaurant for a meal.

During the 1880's, Ryder lived and worked in a studio on Washington Square. In the 1890's, he moved to a house on West 15th Street, where, two flights up, he had his studio—two rooms without a north light. As the years passed, he grew eccentric and increasingly indifferent to housekeeping. His rooms became choked with all manner of litter, dirty dishes and clothes, milk bottles, newspapers, boxes, trunks, and furniture, as well as old canvas and paint. Persons who visited him described the place as piled waist-high with trash through which paths led to the door, easel, and fireplace. Ryder slept on a rug on the floor and cooked on an open grate. He did not allow his rooms to be painted or papered. Nevertheless, he enjoyed friends, admirers, and a growing number of buyers of his paintings.

Ryder was a big man, and even when young wore a full red-brown beard. A fellow artist said Ryder had a gentle voice and a sweet smile. A friend, Captain John Robinson, of the Atlantic Transport Line, wrote, "I have read of Ryder being a recluse. I can hardly think that, for the small luncheon and dinner parties, where a few friends met, were never complete without him. He never talked much; he was an excellent listener, and his laugh was very infectious."

In time, Ryder's beard became grizzled, and he put on weight. Dressed in an old sweater, long coat, and knitted fisherman's skullcap such as he had seen in his boyhood in New Bedford, he was sometimes taken for a tramp or an old sailor hard up. A carpenter, Charles Fitzpatrick, and his wife, an amateur painter, took care of him during the last two years of his life. The Fitzpatricks had lived on the floor below him and become his friends. Mrs. Fitzpatrick had even tried to clean his rooms. Ryder died at their home in Elmhurst, Long Island.

A poet with words as well as paint, Ryder now and again composed verse to go with a picture, examples of which I include here. Some of his poems appeared in the catalog of the Loan Exhibition of his paintings, The Metropolitan Museum of Art, 1918. Poems and paintings augmented one another; both verged on the primitive and showed the same turn of mind.

Ryder's interest in literature influenced his paintings; old legends and fables appealed to him. He lived in the world of his imagination. Woman was idolized, stylized, and unreal.

I have no idea how many poems Ryder wrote or how many may be extant; they have not yet been collected. Those I have found I have placed in what seems to be chronological order.

In his unworldliness and lack of everyday professional sophistication, Ryder seldom signed his pictures and never dated them. He gave no thought to preserving his poems; some were not even written down. *Paragraphs from the Studio of a Recluse* enjoyed only fleeting publication. *Broadway Magazine,* where it appeared, vanished long ago. The issue that included Ryder's *Paragraphs* is scarce. I have seen copies in The Free Library of Philadelphia and the library of the Metropolitan Museum of Art, New York.

PARAGRAPHS FROM THE STUDIO
OF A RECLUSE

———•———

The artist should not sacrifice his ideals to a landlord and a costly studio. A rain-tight roof, frugal living, a box of colors and God's sunlight through clear windows keep the soul attuned and the body vigorous for one's daily work. The artist should once and forever emancipate himself from the bondage of appearances and the unpardonable sin of expending on ignoble aims the precious ointment that should serve only to nourish the lamp burning before the tabernacle of his muse.

I have two windows in my workshop that look out upon an old garden whose great trees thrust their green-laden branches over the casement sills, filtering a network of light and shadow on the bare boards of my floor. Beyond the low roof tops of neighboring houses sweeps the eternal firmament with its ever-changing panorama of mystery and beauty. I would not exchange these two windows for a palace with less a vision than this old garden with its whispering leafage—nature's tender gift to the least of her little ones.

Imitation is not inspiration, and inspiration only can give birth to a work of art. The least of a man's original emanation is better than the best of a borrowed thought. In pure perfection of technique, coloring and compositon, the art that has already been achieved may be imitated but never surpassed. Modern art must strike out from the old and assert its individual right to live through Twentieth Century impressionism and interpretation. The new is not revealed to those whose eyes are fastened in worship upon the old. The artist of today must work with his face turned toward the dawn, steadfastly believing that his dream will come true before the setting of the sun.

When my father placed a box of colors and brushes in my hands, and I stood before my easel with its square of stretched canvas, I realized that I had in my possession the wherewith to create a masterpiece that would live through the coming ages. The great masters had no more. I at once proceeded to study the works of the great to discover how best to achieve immortality with a square of canvas and a box of colors.

Nature is a teacher who never deceives. When I grew weary with the futile struggle to imitate the canvases of the past, I went out into the fields, determined to serve nature as faithfully as I had served art. In my desire to be accurate I became lost in a maze of detail. Try as I would, my colors were not those of nature. My leaves were infinitely below the standard of a leaf, my finest strokes were coarse and crude. The old scene presented itself one day before my eyes framed in an opening between two trees. It stood out like a painted canvas—the deep blue of a midday sky—a solitary tree, brilliant with the green of early summer, a foundation of brown earth and gnarled roots. There was no detail to vex the eye. Three solid masses of form and color—sky, foliage and earth—the whole bathed in an atmosphere of golden luminosity. I threw my brushes aside; they were too small for the work in hand. I squeezed out big chunks of pure, moist color and taking my palette knife, I laid on blue, green, white and brown in great sweeping strokes. As I worked I saw that it was good and clean and strong. I saw nature springing into life upon my dead canvas. It was better than nature, for it was vibrating with the thrill of a new creation. Exultantly I painted until the sun sank below the horizon, then I raced around the fields like a colt let loose, and literally bellowed for joy.

It is the first vision that counts. The artist has only to remain true to his dream and it will possess his work in such a manner that it will resemble the work of no other man—for no two visions are alike, and those who reach the heights have all toiled up the steep mountains by a different route. To each has been revealed a different panorama.

The artist should fear to become the slave of detail. He should strive to express his thought and not the surface of it. What avails a storm cloud accurate in form and color if the storm is not therein? A daub of white will serve as a robe to Miranda if one feels the shrinking timidity of the young maiden as the heavens pour down upon her their vials of wrath.

Art is long. The artist must buckle himself with infinite patience. His ears must be deaf to the clamors of insistent friends who would quicken his pace. His eyes must see naught but the vision beyond. He must await the season of fruitage without haste, without worldly ambitions, without vexation of spirit. An inspiration is no more than a seed that must be planted and nourished. It gives growth as it grows to the artist, only as he watches and waits with his highest effort.

The canvas I began ten years ago I shall perhaps complete today or tomorrow. It has been ripening under the sunlight of the years that come and go. It is not that a canvas should be worked at. It is a wise artist who knows when to cry "halt" in his composition, but it should be pondered over in his heart and worked out with prayer and fasting.

The artist needs but a roof, a crust of bread and his easel, and all the rest God gives him in abundance. He must live to paint and not paint to live. He cannot be a good fellow; he is rarely a wealthy man, and upon the potboiler is inscribed the epitaph of his art.

SOME VERSES ABOUT HIS PICTURES

In "Dancing Dryads," only nine by seven inches, even the trees seem to be in motion.

> In the morning ashen-hued
> Came nymphs dancing from the wood.

For "The Sylvan Dance," Ryder wrote a Delphian couplet.

> Oh, no, I have no voice or hand
> For such a song in such a land.

"The Lovers' Boat, or Moonlight on the Waters" mingles the realism of the countryside with the unreality of a phantom sailboat.

> In splendor rare, the moon,
> In full-orbed splendor,
> On sea and darkness making light,
> While windy spaces and night,
> In all vastness, did make,
> With cattled hill and lake,
> A scene grand and lovely.
>
> Then, gliding above the
> Dark water, a lover's boat,
> In quiet beauty, did float
> Upon the scene, mingling shadows
> Into the deeper shadows
> Of sky and land reflected.

"Toilers of the Sea," done in brooding colors, shows tremendous strength and energy in the drive of a little boat homeward through heavy seas.

> With the shifting skies,
>   Over the billowing foam,
> The hardy fisher flies
>   To his island home.

Never-ending turbulence and chaos epitomizes the fate of the subject of "The Flying Dutchman."

> Who hath seen the Phantom Ship,
> Her lordly rise and lowly dip,
> Careering o'er the lonesome main
> No port shall know her keel again.
>
> But how about that hopeless soul
> Doomed forever on that ship to roll,

Doth grief claim her despairing own
And reason hath it ever flown
Or in the loneliness around
Is a sort of joy found
And one wild ecstasy into another flow
As onward that fateful ship doth go.

But no, Hark! Help! Help! Vanderdecken cries,
Help! Help! on the ship it flies;
Ah, woe is in that awful sight,
The sailor finds there eternal night,
'Neath the waters he shall ever sleep,
And ocean will the secret keep.

"Joan of Arc" shows a peasant girl watching her flock. With her buck teeth and eyes rolled upward, she looks strange and supernatural in an otherwise natural setting.

On a rude, mossy throne
Made by Nature in the stone
Joan sits; and her eyes far away
Rest upon the mountains gray.

And far beyond the moving clouds
That wrap the sky in vap'rous shrouds,
Visions, she sees—
And voices come to her on the breeze.

With a Nation's trouble she's opprest
And noble thoughts inspire her breast.
Ah, gentle maid, and can it be
Thou willst do more than chivalrie?
That thy weak arm shall strike the blow
That hurls the invading conqueror low?
Who knows what God knows?
His hand he never shows,
Yet miracles with less are wrought,
Even with a thought.

On a tiny wood panel (four by eight inches), Ryder painted, in "Passing Song," a dreamlike figure of a woman in the foreground and a little boat in the background. Without the poem it would be hard to know what this painting is about.

By a deep, flowing river,
    There is a maiden pale,
And her ruby lips quiver
    A song on the gale.

Adown the same river,
    A youth floats along;
And the lifting waves shiver
    As he echoes her song.

Nearer, still nearer,
    His frail bark doth glide.
Will he shape his course to her
    And remain by her side?

Alas! there's no rudder,
    To the ship that he sails.
The maiden doth shudder—
    Blows sea-ward the gales.

Sweeter and fainter
    The song cometh back;
And her mind it will darken
    And her heart it will rack.

And then she'll grow paler
    With this fond memory;
Paler and paler—
    And then she will die.

"The Wind" is a poem with, apparently, no painting to go
with it. It appeared in the *Century Illustrated Monthly Magazine,* June 1890.

The wind, the wind, the wind,
The breath of balmy, balmy evening,
That am I, that am I!
My unseen wanderings
Who can pursue, who comprehend?
Soft as a panther treads
When moving on its prey,
I fly o'er beds of roses sweet

And violets pale,
Till, disturbed within their slumbers,
They bend from my gay caress—
Only to lift their heads again
And send the aroma of sweet perfumes
To call me yet once more
Ere that I pass away.

I am the wind, the wind, the wind,
As fickle as lightning, swift as light.
I seize on the giants of the forest
And shake them to their roots!
I make them tremble to their sap!

I am the wind, the wind, the wind!
I'll away, I'll away to where maidens
Are sighing for fond lovers,
And softly coo and woo and whisper in their ears,
With sigh answering sighs,
Making their hearts to throb,
Their bosoms rise
Till I seem hardly from without—
Almost within the voice
Of their soul's illusion!
What lover would not give his all for this:
To kiss that rosy cheek,
Those dewy lids, that luscious mouth;
So wantonly to lift those woven tresses,
And breathe upon those rounded bosoms?

But I'm the wind, the wind, the wind!
I'll away, I'll away to gloomy pools profound,
Stirring the silence of their reflective depths
With rippling laughter
At my wanton freaks—
For I'm the wind, the wind, the wind,
And my fantastic wanderings
Who can pursue, who comprehend?

ACKNOWLEDGMENTS

———————•———————

First, my thanks to Betty Vas Nunes Burroughs, who worked with me and shared my enthusiasm for the people in this book, their prose, and their poems.

I also thank Mrs. Edward Hicks Carle, owner of the portrait of Edward Hicks, for permission to reproduce a photograph of it; City Art Museum of Saint Louis, for the photograph of *Self Portrait* by Chester Harding and permission to publish it; Aaron Siskind, for the photograph he took of the Nancy Luce tombstones; Dr. Geraldine W. Wilmot, for the photograph of Andrew Taylor Still; the Houghton Library, Harvard University, and Houghton Mifflin Company, for permission to quote from their records of Ticknor and Fields; the Nicholson Whaling Collection, Providence Public Library, F. Charles Taylor, Librarian, for permission to excerpt from the journal written by Lucy P. Vincent Smith; Susan R. Waddington, Head, Art and Music Department, for help in choosing and reproducing a page of the journal; the Dukes County Historical Society, Edgartown, Massachusetts, Margaret R. Chatterton, Curator, for permission to use their photograph of Lucy P. Vincent Smith; the Phillips Collection, Washington, D. C., for the photograph of *Albert Ryder* by Kenneth Hayes Miller.

I am indebted to libraries noted in the preceding pages, and to the Frick Art Reference Library, New York City; the Arthur and Elizabeth Schlesinger Library on the History of Women in America, Radcliffe College; the libraries of Princeton University, and Rutgers, the State University of New Jersey.